THANK YOU FOR
YOUR SERVICE!
I PRAY THAT GOD
ALWAYS WATCHES
OVER YOU AND
YOUR FAMILY IN
WHATEVER ARENA
YOU STEP INTO!
3-1 HOUSE OF
    PAYNE!
GO NAVY!
    BEAT ARMY!

P.S: p.250
"DIEGO MANALO"
DIEGO - HONORING
YOUR HOME TOWN
MANALO - MEANS
"TO WIN" IN
FILIPINO.

PRAISE FOR
IN THE ARENA

The journey through plebe year, as all of us who have taken that journey are aware, is one of self-awareness. The combination of physical and mental stress requires you to go deep down to find the reserves to keep on going. This book takes you through that experience through the eyes and emotions of a young woman looking back on her own voyage. It is a story of discovery as well as a navigation through the Yard of USNA.

ROBERT DIAISO, CLASS OF 1962

Five stars! It was superb! It relates to both military and civilians with honor and commitment, but most of all faith. This book is absorbing and hard to put down—full of captivating personal anecdotes from the inside of the first year at the Naval Academy.

SENIOR CHIEF EDNA MCKENNA, USN, RET.

IN THE ARENA
A Plebe's Life at the United States Naval Academy

Published by Hellgate Press (An imprint of L&R Publishing, LLC)

Hellgate Press
PO Box 3531
Ashland, OR 97520
www.hellgatepress.com

Book design: Michael Campbell
Cover design: George Deyo

ISBN: 978-1-954163-23-2

Printed and bound in the United States
10 9 8 7 6 5 4 3 2 1

IN THE ARENA

A Plebe's Life at the
United States Naval Academy

CATHY MAZIARZ

CONTENTS

To Tully, who inspired me to write this and
who held my hand along the journey.

PREFACE

I NEVER INTENDED TO BE A WRITER. To this day, it is still a mystery to me as to how this was written. What I do know is that I always had a story, but it had been locked inside of my heart. Locked until a small child entered my life, and with him was the key.

My nephew Tully entered my life in 1998. By that time, I had earned a teaching degree, lived in New Zealand, and had taught on a Navajo Indian Reservation. By the year 2000, I had climbed to the Base Camp of Everest and backpacked solo through Europe. By 2002, I turned my attention to my hometown of Maryland and began an outdoor adventure business. Tully was four at the time and joined me on my various adventures. Besides kayaking and fossil hunting, Tully began to show an interest in the military. Luckily, I knew of a place that would expose him to his newfound interest and so much more: the United States Naval Academy. It did not take long before Tully and I were making weekly visits to the Academy.

Little did I know that these simple visits would change my life forever. The sights, the sounds, the questions of a child, forced me to relive the memories, to understand them more clearly, and to ultimately share them with others.

This is a true story, a memoir of a plebe at the United States Naval Academy. It is written as a series of flashbacks that occurred as Tully and I visited the Academy. Real names have been changed, except for publicly recognized individuals. Conversations among the characters are based on my journals, memories, and interviews. The visit occurred in the spring of 2002, and the flashbacks occurred during my Plebe Year from July 1994 to May 1995. All other dates are approximated.

I want to apologize now for any mistakes I may have made regarding my work. I ask you to keep in mind that Plebe Year at the Naval Academy is a year is hard to remember and easy to forget. It is a year of emotional stress, physical pain, and demanding academics. It can cause the mind to lock the memories away or keep them in a blur.

Actually, what am I saying?

I take that all back! If there are any mistakes…

"NO EXCUSE, SIR!"

Like I said before, I did not intend for this to happen. But since it did, then I am hoping that the purpose for writing this will be revealed.

Maybe it is intended to focus on the positive, to present an encouraging and uplifting view of the Academy. For it is too often, that the focus is on the few negative incidents that overshadow what the Academy is all about.

Or maybe, it simply is intended as a story to thank those who have gone before and to inspire those who may soon follow…

All that I can hope for is that it will inspire you to live your life *"In the Arena."*

THE MAN IN THE ARENA

It is not the critic who counts,
not the one who points out
how the strong man stumbled
or how the doer of deeds might
have done them better.
The credit belongs to the man
who is actually in the arena,
whose face is marred with
sweat and dust and blood;
who strives valiantly, who errs
and comes short again and again,
who knows the great enthusiasms,
the great devotions, and spends
himself in a worthy cause;
who if he wins, knows the triumph
of high achievement;
and who, if fails, at least fails
while daring greatly,
so that his place shall never be
with those cold and timid souls
who know neither victory nor defeat.

THEODORE ROOSEVELT

CHAPTER 1:
WE'RE NOT IN KANSAS ANYMORE

Annapolis, Maryland; U.S.N.A., May 2004

"Do you think they will see me?" The voice of a scared four-year-old squeaked out from the bushes beside me.

"What? Where are you? Tully! Where did you go?" I spun around, pretending to panic as I looked for my MIA nephew.

"I'm here, Aunt Cathy!" A tiny hand poked out from the top of the jungle of shrubbery.

"Oh, there you are! You are camouflaged so well, that I had lost you for a minute!"

Tully was dressed from head to toe in a collage of green, brown, and black. His square-top camouflage hat was pulled down low upon his head. His brown hair was shaved short on the sides and longer on top, a miniature High and Tight[1] worn by his emulated heroes. His small jungle camouflage t-shirt was tucked neatly into a pair of matching cargo shorts that hung down to his ankles. Tully looked up at me from beneath the shadow of his hat, his eyes wide with excitement. His fair skin, and sky-blue eyes softened the tough look he was dressed in. Tiny freckles kissed his white cheeks.

"Don't worry, they won't see you!" I said reassuringly. "Just be brave and don't make a sound, okay?"

Tully nodded as a smile stretched across his delicate face. I reached down and took his hand in mine as we walked quietly through a large, opened gate. The iron gate was flanked on both sides by a grey stone

....

1 *High and Tight:* A standard hair cut in the Marine Corps, in which the hair is cut to a stubble at the back and sides and short on top. The top contrasts with the back and sides, in which the hair on top looks like a lid on a jar, hence a Marines nickname: "jarhead."

wall. We passed the iron and stone sentry and continued along a side-walk lined with flowering bushes and small trees.

It was a beautiful Maryland day. The sky was a pure blue, marbleized with swirls of white clouds. The sun was shining, and the cool seaside air was blowing through the new spring blossoms, which fell like snow upon the ground. Tiny birds sat at attention in the treetops, each singing their own cadence. I glanced up ahead at an enclosed guard post in the middle of the road. There were two Marines, dressed in fatigues[2], standing at attention inside the small-windowed box. A black car passed us and immediately stopped at the post. One of the Marines stepped out from his post and approached the car. With a slight bend in his perfectly poised body, he glanced into the driver's side of the car. He then quickly took a step back to the position of attention, while his arm sprung to the brim of his hat for a perfect salute. He slowly pulled his arm back down to his side, as if resetting his spring-loaded limb. The car moved forward after its rite of passage.

"Tully," I whispered, slowing down.

"Yes, Aunt Cathy?"

"There are the Marines. Are you ready?"

"Yes," he whispered quickly. Tully immediately left my side and ducked behind a row of bushes to the right of the sidewalk. One of the Marines stepped out of his post as he saw me approaching. With his rifle held in both hands, he maneuvered stiffly around the bunker of sandbags that were placed in front of the post. He crossed the street and moved toward me with a sense of poise and control.

I glanced over at Tully and gave him the hand signal to start moving.

Tully laid on his stomach, and with his head and butt low to the ground, he began moving underneath and around the bushes. I had taught him how to "low crawl," a form of movement that a soldier uses, in which you stay low to the ground by pulling yourself forward with your elbows and knees. As the Marine was approaching me, Tully was slowly making his way past the guard post.

"Good afternoon ma'am, may I please see a form of ID?" The statuesque figure stood with a firm grip on his rifle as I fumbled through

....

2 *Fatigues:* The military clothing worn for field duty; camouflage.

my straw purse. The sleeves of his camouflage top were rolled up into a three-inch cuff above the bicep. The tightness of the cuff made his muscles bulge with hardly any room to breathe. His black toe-shined combat boots were laced up with his pant legs tucked over the rim. He was an image of dress parade perfection and at the same time, combat readiness. His cloth nametag had black lettering that read "Michaels."

"Here you are," I said handing the Marine my driver's license.

As he took my license, I noticed the bushes to the right of us, one right after the other, shaking with movement.

The Marine tilted his head down to where his hat and chiseled jaw were perfectly aligned. As he looked at my license from beneath his square brimmed hat, I noticed him glance over towards Tully, and suddenly a smile appeared, softening his hardened face. As he handed my license back, I quickly said, "You don't see anyone else, *do you?*"

The Marine's dusty-brown eyes appeared out of the shadow of his hat, as he lifted his head into a position of attention. I smiled and gave him a wink, hoping he would play along with me.

"Ahhh, No ma'am. *I sure don't!*" The Marine turned to his buddy who was standing back at the post.

"Rodriquez, do you see anyone besides this lady here?"

"That's a negative, Michaels, I only see one visitor."

Michaels began to circle me. He began to come to life; it was as if air had been breathed into a statue of stone.

Tully let out a small giggle of excitement as he peered through a clump of tall grass.

"Wait," said the Marine, "I think I just heard something! What was that noise?" His command voice deepened with urgency.

"Uuuhhh, nothing!" I replied acting along. The Marine carefully walked over to the bushes where Tully was hiding.

"I heard something, but I just don't see anything!" He shook his head as if completely confused. "Whatever it is, it sure must a good soldier."

"Why is that?" I asked smiling back at the Marine.

"Well, a good soldier is one who can stay hidden; one who knows how to camouflage."

"Oh, and a really good soldier would be one who could even sneak by the United States Marines, right?"

"Yes ma'am. If that was the case, they should probably join the Marine Corps; we could use a good a soldier like that!"

"Well, if I know of anyone, I will pass that along. Also, thank you for the great job *you* are doing; for protecting this special place."

"Your welcome ma'am, and you have a nice visit today."

"Thank you." I nodded my head towards Tully indicating to the Marine how appreciative I was of his kindness. He had made my nephew's day.

The Marine took one more walk back and forth along the edge of the bushes, pretending to look for Tully. With a shake of his head and a shrug of his shoulders, he turned around and returned to his post. The two Marines watched as I left, with smiles that would soon harden over. After I cleared the post and was at a safe distance from the Marines, I stopped and glanced over at the bushes.

Among the green, was a small face peering out. Tully's blue eyes were filled with excitement. I gave him a thumbs up and signaled for him to pull out. He slowly emerged out of his pretend jungle.

"You did it, buddy," I said as I hugged him. "You were such a good soldier, you snuck by the United States Marine Corps guards! I think they could use a good soldier like you. You were so brave and disciplined."

Tully turned around smiling with delight as he looked at the guard post.

"They couldn't see me, I was so camouflaged. I snuck in!"

"You sure did. You completed your mission!"

Tully loved the military, so whenever I had the opportunity, I played along with his passion, heightening the excitement and glamour of it all. I had turned a simple ID check at the guard post into a top-secret mission with the objective to sneak past the U.S. Marines.

I turned around and looked down the road. The Marines had gone back to their post, and back to the position of attention; their eyes fixed on the gate, and their smiles hardened over. I looked past the post to the iron gate that we had just passed through. The blue-painted gate was connected to the fifteen-foot-high gray stone wall that branched off to the left and the right. The wall enclosed the United States Naval Academy. The wall separated two different worlds, the midshipmen's "Annapolis" and the city of Annapolis. Visitors were granted permission to enter the Academy at certain times through one of the three gates. Two enlisted Marines were always posted at each of the gates. Their duty as keeper of the gates began back in the year 1865 when the first permanent Marine detachment was stationed at the Academy. They had been brought to lend their "martial presence to ceremonial occasions." [3] In keeping with the old traditions, the Marines symbolized the Academy's prestige and pageantry, however today their duties go well beyond that. They filter the passage of visitors, greet, and salute officers, and provide protection. Their main duty of defense, which is often overlooked, has become more evident as of "9/11." The sandbag bunkers in front of the posts are a sign of this important duty; the safeguarding of our future officers.

Tully sneaking past the Marines at the main gate of the Academy

I looked down at Tully who was filled with the excitement of the world he had snuck into. I desperately wanted to share this world with him. His eyes sparkled with the glimmer of Academy gold; the glimmer that had blinded so many outsiders. Visitors blinded with prestige,

3   Sweetman, Jack. *The US Naval Academy: An Illustrated History.* (Maryland: Naval Institute Press, 1979), 94.

parents blinded with pride, and small boys blinded with wonder. They would all catch a small glimpse of a world that would fascinate and intrigue them; a world filled with fine-looking officers, marching bands, sailboats, and ornate stone buildings cradling the waters of the famous Chesapeake. The glimmer was blinding, and I wanted Tully to be able to *see*. I wanted him to see this world as if he had worn the Navy "Blue and Gold."[4] I wanted him to see beyond the glimmer to what the Academy was all about.

I took Tully's hand as we looked back at the gate. "Welcome to the Naval Academy, Tully! You are very brave to come here today."

I promise that we will have fun today and that you will learn all about this special place!"

"Can I sneak past the guards again?" Tully asked as he tugged at my hand.

"Sure, but how about on our way back out?"

Tully nodded his head in agreement, as a mischievous smile stretched across his face.

As I continued to stare at the gate and the large gold emblem of the Academy at its center, I began to think about the day when I had first passed through that gate—my first day in this shiny new world.

Annapolis, Maryland; U.S.N.A., June 30, 1994

I was 19, salted from a year in the Navy, and I had just landed on the shores of a new world. The journey had seemed long and tedious, but my ship had finally docked. I did not happen upon the shores by chance, but I had earned passage by hard work and determination. It had been a dream of mine ever since I was a young child, and now as I stood upon the legendary banks, the new world was within my reach.

The land that spread before me was carpeted with green grass and flowerbeds. Grand oak trees lined brick walkways and ornate stone buildings stood tall and majestic. A river cradled the land and ran its waters into a nearby bay. The air was hot and the breeze, salty. The summer haze blurred the horizon, creating a watercolor of sailboats

....

4 *Blue and Gold:* Navy's team colors.

painted upon a sapphire blue. I closed my eyes. It was quiet, except for a lone seagull's cry and the toll of a buoy's bell. When I heard the familiar voice blow by, I pictured the restless buoy, rocking obediently upon the sparkling blue waves. I pictured the waves crashing up against the jagged barrier of rocks, leaving behind pillows of white foam nestled among the cracks. I could smell the salty air and feel its stickiness upon my face. I rested in the sun's warmth and the buoy's toll for a moment longer and then slowly opened my eyes.

This world that spread before me had been founded in 1845. It was a world weathered and aged by tradition, but one that had never lost its reputation as a world built on America's greatest values. Men and women of great character had founded it, and it continued to pass these values on, giving birth to presidents, great leaders, and heroes.

My ship had docked on the banks of the Severn River, and I stepped onto the shores of the United States Naval Academy.

"Let's go!" I said glancing at the two girls standing beside me. I had arrived with two of my closest friends, Abby and Kala, classmates of mine from the Naval Academy Prep School. We had just finished a year there together, where the strongest of friendships had been forged.

We began walking towards the main entrance of Bancroft Hall, the dormitory of the Naval Academy. We had been instructed to report to the Main Office one day before the rest of the new arrivals. We were dressed in our enlisted white uniforms with olive green duffle bags heaved over our shoulders. As the three of us quickened our pace under the shadows of the towering stone building, we suddenly heard yelling from up above.

"Welcome to *hell*, ladies!"

We stopped and looked up to see a midshipman leaning out of a 3rd story window. The three of us looked at each other and began to laugh.

"This isn't Kansas anymore," Abby said with a smile. Abby was repeating what Major Parrino, our Executive Officer, had once said to us during our first day at NAPS. The Major had quoted the "Wizard of Oz" to get across the point that we were now part of something new. He did not care if we were from Kansas, California, or Maryland; we were now in our new home, the United States Navy.

Kala, Abby, and I ignored the welcoming midshipmen as we walked across the open courtyard and up a set of large marble steps into the main entrance of Bancroft Hall. We stepped into the middle of a marbleized grand foyer, the Rotunda. Pillars of marble circled the foyer as winding staircases wrapped around from both sides. The floor was laid with tiles of rose, green, and beige marble. Doorways were rounded and elaborate light fixtures adorned the Hall as chandeliers or as wall-mounted candles. The ceiling rose high creating hollowness to any sounds floating throughout. The Rotunda echoed the grandeur of what Dorothy must have found when stepping into the Emerald City.

To the left of the entrance was the main watch station for all of Bancroft. It was manned and operated twenty-four hours a day by the midshipmen. To the right was a long corridor closed off by a set of double doors, the curtain that hid the inner workings of Oz. These were the offices of the Superintendent, the Commandant, and other high-ranking officers, the great wizards of the Academy.

The girls and I soaked up the magic that we found ourselves standing in. We were so proud to be at the Academy; it was a dream that had come true. We had our picture taken to commemorate the moment, standing arm and arm beneath the dome of the Rotunda. After we received our assigned company numbers and locations of our rooms, the three of us split up to find our rooms and unload our gear. I was assigned to 34th Company, and my room was located on the 3rd Deck of the 8th Wing.

I had to go to the southeastern most point in Bancroft Hall, one of the furthest points from the Rotunda. The 7th and 8th Wings of Bancroft were the newest additions and had been built on to Bancroft in 1961. Their proximity to the water was a picturesque advantage, but their distance from the rest of Bancroft was a disadvantage.

With no Yellow Brick Road to follow, I soon found myself in a maze of corridors and passageways. Little did I know that I was in the largest college dormitory in the world;[5] one with 4.8 miles of corridors and 33 acres of floor space. I passed through various companies, evident

....

5 *Bancroft Hall:* The Academy's dormitory, designed by Beaux-Arts architect Ernest Flagg and built in 1901–06. Bancroft has eight wings, arranged, as on a ship, with evens on the port side and odds on the starboard. There are five floors (decks) numbered 0–4.

by manned watch posts and decorated bulletin boards. The halls were quiet, and the tiled floors shined with the reflection of overhead flores-cent lights. It was an eerie silence and reminded me of the stillness out at sea with a looming storm off in the distance. After I made the hike out to the 8th Wing and the climb up to the 3rd Deck (4th Floor), I found my room and immediately dropped my duffle bag of personal items.

I walked over to a full-length mirror that was bouncing a ray of sunlight onto the polished floor. As I looked into the mirror, I saw that stranger staring back at me; her eyes were filled with blue and with innocence and youth. There was an expressionless look upon her face, as if not knowing what to feel or being too afraid to feel. She was dressed in a stiff white uniform. She stood straight and rigid. Her thick blond hair was braided back tightly against her head. A navy-blue neckerchief was draped around her neck and tied with a sailor's knot. Her bibbed white blouse was lined up perfectly with her straight white skirt. The sunlight glistened off a shiny silver eagle that was pinned to the front of her hat, which she held in her hands. Her polished white heeled shoes poked out beneath a pair of panty-hosed legs. A black lacquered nametag was pinned above her left shirt-pocket. It was engraved with yellow lettering that read, "ERVIN 98."

Who are you? I thought to myself as I stared at the reflection. I turned away from the mirror, away from the stranger, that even after a year, I was still not comfortable with. As I walked away from the mirror, I heard footsteps behind me.

"Hey, Ervin."

I turned around to see a large, 6-foot-tall man leaning against my doorframe. I assumed he was an upperclassman, so I immediately stood at attention. I noticed blue eyes peering out from underneath the shadow of blond hair. He seemed friendly and relaxed; the complete opposite of what I knew an upperclassman[6] to be.

"How's it going?"

....

6 *Upperclassmen:* The name given to all 2nd, 3rd, and 4th year students at the Naval Academy, which would be equivalent to a sophomore, junior, and senior in College. A senior is called a "Firstie" or "1st Class", a junior is called a "2nd Class," and a sophomore is called a "Youngster" or a "3rd Class." Another name for the upperclassmen that oversaw training during Plebe Summer, were called "Detailers" or "Cadre."

"Fine, Sir," I replied, my voice escaping with confidence.

"You're a Napster,[7] huh?"

"Yes, Sir."

"Cool, well I wanted to come to say *Hi* and welcome you to 34th Company: *The Club*."

"Thank you, Sir,"

He smiled and turned to leave the room. "Oh, and I wanted to give you a heads-up: it would be a good idea for you to memorize 'Man in the Arena.'"

"Yes Sir," I replied with a quizzical look on my face.

"It's on the last page of your *Reef Points*,"[8] he said cocking back his baseball cap. I stared at his cap, trying to make out the logo on the front. At first glance, it looked like the Navy "N", but as I moved closer, I realized that it was a picture of beer cans.

"It's a passage by Teddy Roosevelt. *An important passage*."

"'Man in the Arena,' yes sir," I replied with all seriousness. However, I knew that there was no way I would be taking him seriously. *This guy is a joke*, I thought as I looked at the beer cans on his hat. I couldn't even picture him in a uniform. It was easier to imagine him in shorts and flip-flops, sitting under the shade of a palm tree with a Corona in one hand and a guitar in the other.

"By the way, my name is Mr. Montgomery, and I will be your Platoon Commander for the first set of Plebe Summer."

I nodded and smiled as Mr. Montgomery left my room. I felt a sense of relief, for if Mr. Montgomery represented 34th Company, then I was in for some smooth sailing. I reached into my pocket and pulled out a

---

7 *Napster:* Slang for someone that attended NAPS (Naval Academy Preparatory School)

8 *Reef Points:* A palm-sized book, 235-pages long, given to all plebes. It is a guide that is referred to throughout all of Plebe Year. It contains information such as: Academy history, officer insignia, famous quotes, military conduct, and even "Naval Academy Slang." As a plebe, we were asked questions from *Reef Points* every hour of every single day. According to *Reef Points*, "Reef points are pieces of small stuff used to reduce the area of a sail in strong winds, making for smoother sailing, just as this *Reef Points* is intended to make your transition into the Navy a smooth one. In it, you will find information that you will use throughout your military career—take heed! A good mariner knows his instruments well; likewise, you should know this handbook from cover to cover. So, remember its words and live by them." *Reef Points*, 9–10.

small palm-sized blue book. I flipped to the last page and found "Man in the Arena."

There is no way I will be memorizing this anytime soon, I thought as I looked at the 119-word passage. *Like that guy, Montgomery was serious anyhow."* I walked out of my room with a sense of relief and confidence. I had come from NAPS and I knew what to expect. I was ready. I had stepped into a new world; a world that glittered with Academy gold.

> *The Emerald City was at my feet and I could have*
> *cared less that I wasn't in Kansas anymore.*

CHAPTER 2:

SWEPT AWAY

I FELT A TUG at my hand, pulling me away from my memory and back to the gold emblem on the gate and the little man beside me.

"Let's go, Aunt Cathy," Tully said as he darted off in front of me.

We turned away from the gate and continued down the sidewalk. An electronic sign waved at us with the major sporting events of the day scrolling across in gold letters. The sign was in front of Halsey Field House, a sporting complex named after Fleet Admiral William "Bull" Halsey, Commander of the Third Fleet in the Pacific during World War II. We turned left, crossed a street, and walked toward a large bronze statue.

"Look Aunt Cathy," Like a loaded gun, Tully sprang from my side, making a straight shot toward a target: a large goat.

"That is Bill,"[9] I replied walking towards the memorialized mascot. Tully stopped and looked up in awe at the large bronze goat. The head and horns were lowered as if in a position of charging. It appeared strong and ready to fight.

"Bill?" Tully questioned as he tried to climb the immovable beast.

"Yes," I replied as I lifted Tully towards the head of the goat. "Bill is the Academy's official mascot; he represents the Navy. A goat is tough, dependable, and very brave."

....

9   *Bill the Goat:* Long before midshipmen began tossing the pigskin around the site of old Fort Severn, goats were an integral part of Navy life. Over 200 years ago, livestock was kept aboard some sea-going naval vessels to provide sailors with food, milk, eggs and, in some cases, pets. There are differing stories about the first "Bill the Goat." One story goes that in 1893, a live goat made his debut as a mascot at the fourth Army-Navy game. It was young naval officers who supplied the mids with their sea-faring pet. The USS New York dropped anchor off Annapolis and the ship's mascot, a goat bearing the name El Cid (The Chief), was brought ashore for the service clash. The West Pointers were defeated for the third time, and the midshipmen feted El Cid along with the team. "Bill the Goat," *USNA.edu*, https://www.usna.edu/PAO/faq_pages/BilltheGoat.php

"Oh," Tully replied hugging the goat around its neck, instantly transforming the molded metal into a living animal.

"Bill the Goat likes to come to all of Navy's football games and basketball games. He likes to cheer on the midshipmen," I patted the smooth metal, "He is proud to be the Academy's official mascot."

"I like Bill," Tully said as he kissed Bill on the horn.

"So do I Tully. One day you may get to see the *real* Bill the Goat!"

"The reeeeal one?"

"Yes, at one of the football games."

"I want to meet him," Tully said smiling up at his newfound friend. Tully continued to hold on to Bill.

"Aunt Cathy, was Bill ever a plebe?"

I smiled at Tully's innocence and imagination. I was impressed that he remembered the unusual name given to a first-year midshipman."[10] The word was comparable to "freshman" used at universities but unique in the sense that it was derived from the word "plebian," which had been the title given to the lower class in Ancient Rome.

"No, Bill was never a plebe. Come to think of it Tully, he has it pretty easy here. I mean, he never had to go through a *Plebe Year* and yet he gets to live here like a midshipman. He has people who care for him and feed him, he gets to go to all the Navy games for free, and he has millions of fans that love him.

I began to laugh as images of Bill the Goat, "The Plebe," pranced into my head.

"What Aunt Cathy?"

"Oh, I was just imagining Bill as a plebe, with his head shaved, wearing a uniform, with a little Dixie-cup hat on his head!"

"Yeah," Tully laughed "And doing push-ups!"

"That would be funny, wouldn't it?"

"What other things would he have to do Aunt Cathy?"

"Well, he would have to learn how to salute, which would probably be tricky to do with a hoof!"

....

10 *Plebe:* The name given to a first-year student at the Naval Academy, equivalent to "Freshmen" in a civilian college. Another name for a plebe is a "4th Classman." According to upperclassmen, a plebe is "that insignificant thing that gets all the sympathy and chow from home." *Reef Points,* 8.

Tully and I continued to laugh as we entertained the idea of "Bill the plebe." As memories of being a plebe began to resurface, and as images of shaved heads, uniforms, and Dixie-cups clouded my eyes, I was immediately back again to that first day, the first day of being a lower-class citizen in a different kind of Rome.

June 30, 1994, 1800 Hours

I had left my room in 34th Company and was on my way to find Abby and Kala when the words of Mr. Montgomery entered my thoughts. I began to wonder why he had mentioned wanting me to memorize "Man in the Arena." *Reef Points* was filled with other information that I had already begun memorizing, information that was useful and that I knew we would be questioned on. There was information such as military rank and insignia, the "Laws of the Navy," and the "Honor Concept." *Why was Montgomery worried about some motivational quote on the very last page of the book?*

After finding Abby and Kala, the three of us began to compare notes. Who had the biggest room? Who was closest to the ground floor? Who had the best upperclassmen? I ended up having the room with the best view since I could see the water, but the one with the worst location. And after describing my meeting with Mr. Montgomery, it was determined that so far, I had the best upperclassmen. Abby had the biggest room; the size of two of mine put together, and Kala had the best location, being closest to the Rotunda.

It was getting late in the day, and we decided that it was time to head to my home in Crofton. I lived about twenty miles from the Academy, and I had already designated my home as our "Base Camp." We were hungry, and we were looking forward to the bon voyage dinner that my mom had been planning; our last real meal before we embarked to climb the mountain of all mountains.

However, we never made it to Base Camp. Our guides rounded us up and sent us back to our companies. We had misunderstood the procedures, and to our disappointment, we would not have one last night of freedom, rest, and refueling. We had checked in, and the Navy now had us in its hold.

I don't remember my first night in Bancroft, or what happened that next morning. All I remember is that Abby, Kala, and I were joined by 1,000 other Napsters, high school graduates, and enlisted men and women that following day.

I do remember suddenly finding myself standing in a line inside Alumni Hall, a large arena where Navy Basketball was played. Strangers surrounded me. Some were tall; others were short. Some of them had accents; some did not talk at all. Some of them walked with a strut, while others just stood still. We all had one thing in common though, the look of fear upon our faces. Even though I was surrounded, I felt alone without the comfort of Abby's familiar smile or Kala's Chicago-laugh. It would probably be six weeks before I would get to see them again, yet I knew that the Napster bond would keep us together even when separated.

Kala came from a town south of Chicago. She had a tough outer edge where she grew up playing basketball in a city of Michael Jordan worshipers. Her straight brown hair was often pulled up into a ponytail and her mesh basketball shorts hung past her knees. She would talk in her windy-city accent of the famous beer battered pizza, the city life, her tight-knit family, and how she grew up playing "hoops." Her smile would light up a room, and the softness of a simple Midwestern girl would shine through.

She was the oldest in a family of four and was a role model to her younger siblings. The Academy presented itself as a challenge, the promise to play on a Division I basketball team, and a financial opportunity to help out her hard-working parents. Kala was excited to play ball at Navy and for the challenge of a lifetime.

It was through basketball, as well as volleyball, that I came to know Kala. We both played for NAPS where we developed a friendship both on and off the court. Kala was someone you would want on your side. She was tough and smart. She not only knew her plays, but she knew how to be a good friend. She was caring and thoughtful, and someone you could open your heart to. She had surprised me at my 19th birthday party by inviting the one guy I had had a crush on. From then on, our weekends were filled with double dates, wild rides in the back of a red beat-up Jeep, midnight strolls along the ocean cliffs, and gourmet campfire breakfasts.

Kala and I were good friends at the Prep School; however, it was through our Academy weekends in which our bond grew even stronger and to this day remains the strongest of my friends.

Abby came from the green rolling hills of Vermont's backcountry, where summers were warm and smelled of sweet orchards, where autumns were colorful and crisp as a ripe apple, and where winters were filled with soft snow.

Abby had a child's face, innocent and still full of wonder. She grew up running barefoot through the hills, tending the family's small farm, and working the summers in the apple orchard across the dirt road. She grew up in a home that was never locked, that was heated by a wood-burning stove, and that had a backdoor leading to untouched wilderness, sleigh rides, cross-country skiing, meals of freshly laid eggs, and pulled vegetables.

From the time Abby was a little girl she had decided on her future. She had watched the movie *Top Gun*, and her life was mapped out in front of her. She would go to the Academy, graduate, and become a Naval Flight Officer. She was determined to do something different with her life, different from the tree-huggers, snowboarders, and the carefree environment that she had grown up in. She got *A's* in school, scored well on the SAT's, skied on the cross-country team, and spent her summers in the orchards, picking fruit while listening to "Top Gun" on her Walkman.[11]

Abby and I had become close at the Prep school. Inseparable. Our Math teacher at NAPS had nicknamed us "Frick and Frack." Wherever Frick was, there was always Frack. Whether it was exploring the town of Newport together, or sunbathing in between classes, Abby was that child in me. Her youth and energy; her innocence and pure enjoyment in the little things; stopping to pick a wildflower or to play on a swing. I had never had a friend like Abby. I had close friends in high school, but this was a friendship in which not only did we connect, but we were connected by the military bond.

I had been born and raised on the outskirts of Annapolis in a small town called Crofton. I was born with a full head of blonde hair, or as

....

11   Even to this day, if you ask Abby about a scene from the movie, she will be able to quote it line for line, word for word.

my parents described it, "platinum" hair. I was instantly adorned with bows from the black nurses of the city hospital, who made frequent visits to my mother's bedside to see the baby with "white hair."

I grew up with my two brothers, Lindsay being two and a half years older than me, and Paul being two and a half years younger. I was the only girl in the neighborhood, so whatever the boys were doing, I was doing. By the age of 5, I had given up dresses and Barbie dolls, opting for sweats and GI-Joe men. My long hair was always up in a ponytail, never in bows, and my fair white skin was painted with the day's mud and dirt. Tea parties and playing house were replaced by war parties and Cops and Robbers. Also, at this time, I had developed a love for the outdoors; I felt at home in Mother Nature's arms. Most of my summers were spent in the small patch of forest behind my home building teepee forts and swinging from the tips of trees. My adventures often came home with me, keeping my parents quite busy. Muddy sneaker tracks across the floors, grass-stained t-shirts, and bouquets of the neighbor's flowers were the least of my mother's worries. It was the bathtub full of hopping toads, or the carton of eggs that had gone MIA[12] during a neighborhood war, that kept things exciting.

I was one of the boys and filled my early days with street hockey games in the parking lot, touch football with dad at the school field, and dirt bike races on my purple-tasseled, banana-seat bike. On warm firefly nights, I would sneak out in camouflage with my band of brothers to practice our SEAL team missions on innocent sleeping homes.

In school, I was shy and quiet. I was an excellent student, never allowing myself anything less than a *B* on a report card. I was never in trouble and was only criticized for my extreme shyness. I had never felt comfortable in school, I felt trapped. I was like one of the toads I had caught, who was not suited for life in a bathtub, who needed to be hopping free.

In 6th grade, I remember getting my first pair of blue and gold Navy sweats for Christmas. In the summer of my 8th-grade year, I went to my first of three Navy volleyball camps.

....

12 *MIA:* Missing In Action

By my sophomore year in high school, the Navy's head volleyball coach recruited me to play for her. By my junior year, I applied to the Academy and by my senior year, I filled out the paperwork, completed the medical and physical fitness test, went to an interview with our state congresswomen, and spent a weekend at the Academy as a "drag."[13]

Due to my low SAT and ACT scores, I failed to receive an appointment, but with the help of the volleyball coach, I received an appointment to the Naval Academy Preparatory School in Newport, Rhode Island. A boat had pulled into the harbor and the wild blonde-haired child jumped on board and set sail for the winds of change.

Kala, Abby, and I were now feeling those winds of change. Our lives had changed dramatically after our year at the Prep School, and now as we stood in line inside Alumni Hall, the wind was blowing even stronger.

We were lined up according to our last names. The line moved rapidly, and before I knew it, I was standing in front of a table with a midshipman seated behind it. He had a sharp flat crew cut, a crisp white uniform, and tired eyes. I noticed that pinned to his immaculate uniform was a red nametag, indicating that he was a "Plebe Summer Detailer." He was part of the handpicked midshipmen that were here to take on the demanding job of training the Class of '98 plebes. The detailer glanced up without moving his head.

"Your name?"

"Catherine Ervin, *Sir*," I replied proudly, hoping to impress him. The midshipman handed me a brown folder and then looked up at me unimpressed. He glanced back down at his stack of papers and made a checkmark.

"Ervin, huh?" he said. "You're a *lucky one*. You get the privilege of being in *my* company." His slow southern drawl slid into my ear as the words, "lucky one" began to repeat in my head. I left the table holding on to my folder and wondering if I wanted to find out what he meant by *lucky*.

....

13   *Drag:* A term given to a prospective candidate who has hopes of attending the Academy. They are assigned to a plebe who has the job of "dragging" them around for the day. Every aspect of a plebe's life is made known to them, which either will make or break the candidate's decision to attend.

Plebes and cadre during Plebe Summer

As I made my way to the second floor, I was almost trampled by a stampede of plebes. They were coming from every direction, and within a few seconds, it was like I became part of a very confused and startled herd of sheep. Everyone was bunched together, the heads of the taller ones peering out over the top. We were pushed so tightly together that we moved as one large mass. We were rounded up in groups and then pushed along without any idea of where we were going or what was happening.

The first thing we did was hand over our bags of personal items. The bags were searched for contraband or for other items that did not meet the regulations. We were told that our belongings were now the property of the US Navy and that soon we would be property as well.

Next, we trampled through a maze of tables, chairs, and enlisted personnel, who were armed with needles and other devices. Wide-eyed and nervous we moved from one gate to another, taking turns being poked and prodded. We were measured, weighed, and punctured for blood. Our ears, eyes, and teeth were looked at, our skin was examined, and we were checked for piercings or tattoos. For the next half hour, we were handed back and forth from one rubber glove to another, hoping that no new flaws or discrepancies had appeared since our last medical exam.

We were learning that if the Navy didn't like what they saw; that if we were considered "bad stock" they had the right to not take us. They had "strict medical standards" [14] that each candidate had to meet. For example, the vision had to be 20/20 (a waiver was allowed if eyeglasses corrected vision to 20/20), your weight had to meet certain criteria based on your height, your height had to be in the range of 60–78 inches, your heart had to be free of abnormalities, ears had to hear a specific number of decibels at various frequencies, and everything down to your toes had to be in working order. Disqualifications ranged from colorblindness, obesity, and asthma to severe acne, inflammatory bowel disease, and any history of hyperactivity.

Once our brown folders were shut, we could breathe a little easier, for DODMERB [15] had qualified us. We could continue, still questioning if we even wanted to.

We had been stripped of our personal belongings, of our modesty and personal medical history, and now we were on our way for further reduction of the person we had walked in as.

We were each given a different number. I was no longer Midshipman Cathy Ervin, but rather "981938." (Everyone's number began with 98. Our class year being 1998.)

I was ordered to memorize my number, and to write my number on everything that would be given to me. I was handed an empty canvas laundry bag and a black marker. Within the course of the next half hour, I had branded over one hundred items with "981938." These items included anything and everything, from underwear to sneakers to shampoo. They were referred to as "navy issue." I walked around with my bag open as different items were tossed in.

By simply filling my bag, the Navy was teaching me one of my earliest lessons: *you do not have a choice. We have taken that away from you. You will use this shampoo when we tell you to take a shower; you will use these running shoes when we tell you to run.* By giving me a number, I

....

14   *Naval Academy Medical PDF,* 157.

15   *DODMERB:* Department of Defense Medical Examination Review Board

was learning another lesson; I was no longer an individual but rather just a number in a long list of numbers.

I heaved my bulging bag over my shoulder and proceeded along with the rest of the herd. Things began to slow down as we made our way to the fitting room. Suddenly there was a backup, so as I waited in line, I decided to pull out the small hand size book, *Reef Points*, which I had made sure to keep with me. As I flipped to the last page of the book, I heard the words of Mr. Montgomery, the upperclassman I had met the day before, *"Ervin it would be a good idea to memorize 'Man in the Arena'. It's on the last page in your Reef Points."*

As I looked at the passage written by Teddy Roosevelt, the passage of 119 words, I decided it just wasn't going to happen. I was not going to waste my time on a long, meaningless passage that an insignificant upperclassman wants me to memorize. I flipped to the front of the book and looked at the colored pictures of Bill the Goat, the Blue Angels, and sailboats.

Within a matter of minutes, I had to put my *Reef Points* away as the mass of chaos began to move again. I soon noticed that our herd was being separated by gender. I noticed little old ladies, with yellow measuring tapes draped around their necks, scurrying back and forth like beavers. Soon they were scampering around me, frantically taking my measurements. The measurements were inaccurate, either they were taken too quickly, or it was all done on purpose.

I looked down at myself and realized that I was now covered in a heavy white uniform that was almost five sizes too big for me. It felt like I was drowning in a sea of starched polyester. I rolled up my sleeves and the cuffs on my pants as best I could, while different sized hats were placed on and taken off my head. Our civilian clothes had been replaced by our first Academy uniform, "White works."[16] I looked around at the

16 *White Works:* A uniform prescribed for plebes during Plebe Summer. There are different variations of the uniform (ie: with or without neckerchief or white bayonet belt), but basically it is a uniform made of thick, white polyester. Not only does the material trap in heat, but also it smells when it contacts sweat. The uniform top is long sleeved with a stylish rectangular bib that is folded against the back. The uniform pants have a drawstring and a small pocket sewn inside near the left hip. (It's ironic how *Reef Points* fits perfectly in this pocket!) The hat (aka cover) is called a "Dixie Cup" and is made of white canvas with a flipped-up brim that is trimmed with navy blue. The uniform is purposely issued a few sizes too large as to make a plebe's life more difficult.

rest of the herd and realized that we now had more in common than just a bag full of "Navy issue." We all looked alike too.

I continued plodding along at a much slower pace due to the trapped heat in my white uniform and the weight of my canvas bag. I left a trail of clean floor behind me, as my pant cuffs swept up the dirt. I noticed that our flock was now being funneled towards the most dreaded experiences of all; an experience that has over the years symbolized "being a plebe."

I approached an area in which the floor looked like the canvas of a child's painting. Random piles of color spotted the floor. Black, brown, red, and blond locks of hair were scattered about. I looked up to see a poor victim approaching the chair. The buzzing of numerous hair clippers created the overall sound of a chainsaw. A victim sat in the chair with his head down as if he was being sheered of his dignity. Within a matter of seconds, another new heap of hair was added to the collage upon the floor. The victim, now looking naked, got up from the barber chair, rubbed his shiny head in disbelief, and walked away while tears welled up in his eyes. After witnessing this, I walked by with no fear. I had known the hair regulations for female midshipmen and therefore I had already gotten my hair cut and styled to my likings. My hair was cut above the top edge of my collared shirt, right where it should be for a plebe. I was not about to be a victim of the merciless barbers.

I had almost made it past the chairs when one of the barbers caught sight of my hair and said it was too thick and that it would have to be cut.

"But it's regulation," I told her nervously. Just then, a detailer overheard our conversation and walked over to where I was.

"Cut it shorter," he said. "It is too blond anyhow, and we don't want it to stand out in the black uniforms." I glared at the upperclassman as I took a seat upon the chopping block. The barber pulled back my hair to the back of my neck, and in one quick hack, it was cut.[17] I hopped down from the chair, afraid to even look in the mirror. The barber was shaking her head.

....

17 *Plebe Chop:* Previously, females had to cut their hair to chin length, in what was known as "the Plebe Chop." This was last done to the Class of 2022; the Class of 2023 and forward no longer have to cut their hair. This move was resented by some of the female upperclassmen in the Brigade. https://en.wikipedia.org/wiki/Plebe_Summer

"What a shame," the woman said as she swept away my platinum blond locks.

I walked over and joined a group of plebes who were lined up in rows. Like me, they had all been pricked, stripped, and sheared; I am sure that they felt as bare, exposed, and vulnerable as I did. We were stripped of our name, our clothes, our individuality, and replaced with a number, a uniform, and similarity.

They all had their right arms frozen in the position of a salute. A detailer was slowly weaving in and out of the rows correcting each one of the arms. I joined the ranks, wondering if my friends were in this group. As I stood among the flock, I watched the woman continue to sweep away the hair on the floor, and I realized that within those first few hours at the Academy, everyone had some part of them "swept" away. We were losing our individuality, whether it was our hair, our personal belongings, or the shoes on our feet. We were being swept away to the bare minimum.

More red-tagged detailers appeared out of nowhere and quickly took charge, shepherding us into ranks. They ruled with an iron staff, as they walked among us teaching and correcting us on how to stand at attention, how to hold our arm for a proper salute, and how to stand in a straight line. They kept us together, never losing sight of any one of us among the flock, never wanting anyone of us to get lost. They guided us toward a bus where we were loaded up and pinned in. As the upperclassmen saw it, they would be leading us to greener pastures. As us plebes saw it, they were leading us to the Valley of the Shadow of Death.[18]

I looked around the bus for Kala or Abby but soon realized that even if they were here, I probably would not be able to recognize them.

I would no longer see Kala's long brown hair or hear Abby's playful laugh. They had been swept away, as I had been.

....

18   Valley of the Shadow of Death: Reference to Bible verse, "The Lord is my shepherd; I shall not want. He maketh me to lie down in green pastures: he leadeth me beside the still waters. He restoreth my soul: he leadeth me in the paths of righteousness for his name's sake. Yea, though I walk through the valley of the shadow of death, I will fear no evil: for thou art with me; thy rod and thy staff they comfort me." "Psalm 23, *Bible*

CHAPTER 3:

THE OATH

TULLY AND I LEFT BEHIND Bill the Goat as we continued our journey into the Academy. I pushed back my long blond hair that had now grown to the middle of my back, free now from the sheers of the Academy. Thoughts of being a plebe were still stirring in the mind of both my nephew and me. As we walked along, I could still see rows of newly transformed plebes, lined up in the parking lots.

"Aunt Cathy is it hard to be a plebe?"

"Yes, Tully. It is very hard."

"Why?"

"Well, as a plebe you are being trained to do many things. A lot is expected out of you. Your day starts very early in the morning and it doesn't end until very late at night. Your day is filled with schoolwork, marching, room inspections, uniform inspections, physical challenges, and many other things. You barely have time to eat or even to sit down!"

"Do you have to be a plebe?"

"Well, if you want to come to the Academy to be a midshipman, then you first have to be a plebe for a whole year. The Academy wants to teach you all about the Navy and about being a midshipman. If you make it through Plebe Year, it's kind of like passing a test."

"You were a plebe, right Aunt Cathy?"

"That's right! I liked being a plebe. It was hard, but there were many things I liked. I liked running and doing push-ups. I even liked waking up early! I didn't like the white works uniforms we had to wear; it was so hot in the summertime!"

"I want to be a plebe!"

"The Academy would love to have you, Tully, but you must remember that it's very serious business being a plebe."

"Why?"

"Because you are joining the military. Unlike other jobs, in the military, you make a serious promise. You promise our country, the United States, that you are going to defend it—even if that means dying."

"Oh," Tully whispered.

"I think it is one of the greatest jobs in the world and being a plebe prepares you for a job in either the Navy or the Marine Corps! We had to learn about all kinds of ships, airplanes, and weapons. We had to learn how to follow orders and how to give orders. We learned that our job was very special!"

Tully was quiet as we continued to walk down the sidewalk.

The fresh morning sunlight bounced off the white concrete path. The Academy glimmered like a polished gold anchor on a midshipman's shoulder boards. It smelled of springtime, as sweet moist soil and budding flowers drifted in the air. New green leaves had unfolded upon the branches and the squirrels were dashing along from limb to limb.

The sound of a jet airplane filled the air, and we looked up to see a white trail of smoke drawing a line across the sky. My stomach twisted with nervousness as the rumble in the jet passed over. The jet was stirring a memory inside of me and as it disappeared into the horizon, I disappeared with it—into my thoughts and instantly back to that first day...

July 1 "I-DAY" Indoctrination Day
Plebe Summer, Training, Day 1

I was surrounded by a sea of endless white; an entire flock of freshly made plebes. It was hazy out and the summer heat hung lazily in the air. There was a feeling of excitement. My stomach rumbled with butterflies echoing a rumble from the heavens. Suddenly, an F-14 Tomcat broke through the haze and through the tension we were all feeling. I was nervous and scared, yet proud and excited. I looked around, trying to recognize any of the faces upon the motionless wave of white.

I was sitting with my back straight against a metal foldout chair. We were seated in rows placed in the middle of Tecumseh Court, an open T-shaped area that was bordered by an immense gray building, Bancroft

Hall, "a mammoth complex, the heart of the Naval Academy."[19] The heart of the Academy *was* found behind these stone walls, for it was the home to all 4,000 midshipmen. Soon it would be home to Kala, Abby, and I as we too would come to know it as "Mother B," the affectionate name used by the midshipmen.

I had become familiar with Bancroft during a few privileged sleepovers throughout the years. I rested in its empty rooms during tiring days at Navy Volleyball Camp. I ran through its hallways alongside a plebe that I dragged with during my senior year of high school. I toured its inner workings as a Napster on a Prep School visit during homecoming weekend. With each visit, the complexity of Bancroft became more apparent. I was nervous, knowing that I would soon find myself lost in its maze.

This heart of the Academy was named after George Bancroft, the founder of the Naval Academy. It made sense that a place, which held the foundation of our future, was named after the founder himself.

Since the beginning of the 1800s, the foundation of an Academy had been advocated by seven other secretaries, supported by a President, and had the subject of over twenty bills but had never once materialized. Bancroft used his intellect and political pull to succeed where others had failed, and in 1845, when Bancroft was appointed as Secretary of the Navy, the dream of a "Naval Academy" became a reality. An old Army Fort on the banks of the Severn River was acquired for free, and a veteran of thirty years of service, Commander Franklin Buchanan, was selected as the first Superintendent. On October 10, 1845, the school was officially opened. Bancroft had composed a letter of instruction to Commander Buchanan, which in a sense was the Academy's first charter:

> *The officers of the American Navy, if they gain but*
> *opportunity for scientific instruction, may make themselves*
> *as distinguished for culture as they have been for*
> *gallant conduct. To this end it is proposed to collect the*
> *midshipmen who from time to time are on shore and give*

....

19 *Reef Points*, 159.

*them occupation, in the study of mathematics, nautical
astronomy, theory of morals, international law, gunnery,
use of steam, the Spanish and French languages, and other
branches essential, to the accomplishment of a naval officer.
The effect of such employment cannot but be favorable to
them and to the service. In collecting them at Annapolis for
the purposes of instruction, you will begin with the principle
that a warrant in the Navy, far from being an excuse for
licentious freedom, is to be held a pledge for subordination,
industry, and regularity, for sobriety and assiduous devotion
to duty. Far from consenting that the tone of discipline a
morality should be less than at universities or colleges of
our country, the President expects such supervision and
arrangement as shall make of the man exemplary body of
which the country may be proud.[20]*

I sat there in awe, captivated by Bancroft's size and architectural beauty. Composed of gray granite and gray stone bricks, it was largely ornate and accented with detailed stone carvings. It stood five stories high and was capped with a green metal roof, shaped like a trapezoid. The main entrance had two rectangular doors flanking a larger middle one, which led into the rotunda. From the rotunda, Bancroft branched out to the left and the right.

To the right (the south side), it connected with the 2nd, 4th, 6th, and 8th Wings. From these wings, a long colonnade connected to Dahlgren Hall. To the left (the north side), Bancroft connected with the 1st, 3rd, 5th, and 7th Wings. From these wings, there was another long colonnade connecting to McDonough Hall.

Bancroft wrapped around me like an iron clamp. I could feel it closing in on me, suffocating me, as my eyes drifted upwards. The rectangular stones of Bancroft were cold and hard, like the faces of the upperclassmen that would soon be training us. They were worn from years of experience, yet they were strong from years of endured hardships. I

20   Jack Sweetman, *The US Naval Academy: An Illustrated History.* (Maryland: Naval Institute Press, 1979), 16–17.

looked into the face of Bancroft. I felt its power. I now knew that I was under its control.

I pulled my eyes away from Bancroft's hold and looked in front of me towards a small wooden podium. The podium was on the verge of drowning in all the grandeur that surrounded it. It was kept afloat, however, by one commanding voice. A dignified man with a white Navy Uniform was standing behind the podium. The gold from his Admiral bars matched the crest on the podium in both color and prestige. He was the Superintendent; he was the captain of this huge ship docked on the banks of the Severn. I could see him speaking as he looked out towards all of us, the new members of his crew. He spoke of honor, tradition, and a worthy cause. His words floated through the thick air like a gentle breeze.

The sun was shining brightly in the cloudless sky. My eyes were tearing from the glare of the 1,000 white uniforms surrounding me. I felt like a little child, wrapped in a blanket of white, in fear of the unknown under my bed. I began to tell myself not to be afraid, that nothing could scare me—not even the stone monster that was trying to grab hold of me.

It was hot and thick. I could feel the Maryland humidity like a weight upon my body. Sweat, unable to escape into the saturated air, was sticking to my face. I was wearing the stiff white uniform. The starched polyester clung to my skin and smelled of sweat, dirt, and dry-cleaning chemicals. Not only was I uncomfortable, but my pants were too long, my top was too big, and my hair was too short. I stared at the shiny baldhead in front of me; a head that once had hair but was now just sweaty skin with a white hat placed upon it. The hat, nicknamed a "Dixie Cup," was circular with a wide rim folded back and one navy blue stripe around its perimeter. I felt the hat upon my head, like a solar oven trapping the heat. Sweat continued to run down my face at a steady pace, but I dared not wipe it—not even just once.

The ceremony continued and I was now standing with my right hand raised. I was repeating, "I do solemnly swear that I will support and defend the Constitution of the United States against all enemies, foreign and domestic; that I will bear true faith and allegiance to the same; that I take this obligation freely, without any mental reservation or purpose of evasion; and that I will well and faithfully discharge the duties of the office on which I am about to enter; so help me God."

I lowered my hand back down to my side. The "Oath of Office" was over, and it was now time for a new chapter in my life to begin. It was the day I had been waiting for and at the same time, the day I had been dreading. It would be a day that I would never forget and a day that I would never want to return to. I now had officially been sworn in with the Class of '98 at the United States Naval Academy.

After the ceremony was over, we were given fifteen minutes to visit with our family members and friends who had come to wish us well and say their final goodbyes. I swam through the chaotic sea of frantic classmates who were moving about in all directions. Within a few minutes, I had found my parents. They glowed with happiness and wrapped me in their arms. I looked into their eyes, knowing that I would find the reassurance and strength, which I needed at the moment.

"You look cute in your uniform," my dad said, gently brushing a piece of hair away from my face.

"We love you, Cathy," my mom said reaching out to hug me. As I gave them one last hug good-bye, my mom's eyes began to glaze over. I tightened my fist as I fought to hold back my tears. My throat tightened as I whispered, "I love you."

I abruptly turned around and walked away from Tecumseh court. I left behind my parents who were security, reassurance, love, and acceptance. I left behind my freedom as a civilian, as an individual, as "Cathy." I left behind a world that was swept away like the hair on the floor of Alumni Hall. Little did I know that everything I had left behind would later be replaced, by items that could not be thrown into a bag or placed upon my head.

It was July 1, 1994: I-day. Indoctrination Day. George Bancroft's dream of a "Naval Academy" had become a reality, and now it was official: so had mine. I had taken an Oath and I had made a promise.

> *Little did I know that a promise had been made*
> *to me—the promise to change my life.*

CHAPTER 4:

BEHIND DOUBLE DOORS

THE AIRPLANE HAD PASSED, and its trail of smoke had faded, unlike the memory of I-day, which for me, would never fade. Tully and I continued down the sidewalk past a white rectangular building called LeJeune Hall. It was a modern building in design, but home to the long-standing swimming team. The building was the first to be named after a member of the Marine Corps, Major General John LeJeune,[21] who was Commandant of the Marine Corps from 1920 to 1929.

We walked under a small overpass, which connected a walkway to the 2nd floor of the building. I remember as a plebe, lining up with my company underneath the overpass, waiting to be marched back to Bancroft Hall. On certain days during Plebe Summer, our schedule included an hour of swimming lessons. Not only did a block of swimming time free you from the grips of your detailers, but also the scorching summer heat. I remember standing underneath the overpass, with water from my hair dripping down my back, my body loose and relaxed, and the clean smell of chlorine sticking to my skin. I would enjoy those few moments, for I knew that it would only take minutes until my body would overheat until every muscle would tense up, and the smell of sweat and dirt would once more seep out of my pores.

"Where are we going, Aunt Cathy?" Tully asked as we continued under the overpass.

....

21 *Lieutenant General John A. Lejeune, USMC:* Often called the "greatest of all Leathernecks," Lejeune led the famed Second Division (Army) in World War I and from 1920 to 1929 he was Commandant of the Marine Corps. He is most remembered for being the first Marine officer to hold an Army divisional command but is also credited for saving the Marine Corps from budget cuts during the period of isolationism and disarmament after WWI. He also promoted the Marine Corps's uniqueness as an expeditionary force and steered the Corps toward amphibious warfare. "Lt. Gen. John A Lejeune," *Marines.mil,* https://www.lejeune. marines.mil/About/About-LtGen-Lejeune/

"There," I replied pointing up at the enormous structure in front of us. Together we looked up at the ornate, stone building with the roof capped in copper. The copper was coated in a blue-green patina,[22] and the rectangular blocks of gray stone had aged from the sun.

"I am *sneaking* you up on deck," I said as I grabbed Tully's hand. His eyes widened as we stepped into the shadow of the towering wing.

"Now, this building is called Bancroft Hall, it is where the midshipmen live. I lived in this part of the building; it is called 8th Wing."

8th Wing was shaped like the capital letter *H*. It faced the sea wall to the east and the rest of Bancroft to the west. There were five floors in each wing of Bancroft Hall, starting with the 0 Deck and ending with the Fourth deck.

"I get to sneak up on deck—up there," Tully said pointing to the building.

"Yes," I replied noticing a bit of hesitation from my small soldier.

"Don't worry, Tul, I think you will like it. And guess what? Only midshipmen are allowed up there, not visitors, but one of my friends, Lt. Wyatt, is the Company Officer of 29th Company and he lives on the same deck that I lived on when I was a plebe. He said that we could sneak up on deck so that I could show you where I once lived."

Within minutes, Tully and I were at one of the side entrances into the 8th Wing of Bancroft Hall. I opened the heavy wooden door and Tully and I tiptoed inside. I looked around and turned to Tully, "Okay, the coast is clear. Let's go." I opened a set of doors to our right and walked into a small ladderwell. I took Tully's hand and said, "We have to climb up to the 4th floor which is called the 3rd Deck."

I bent down and hugged Tully. "Tully, I can't believe you get to go up on deck! Do you realize how special this is? No one in my family or any of my friends have ever gotten to see where I lived; you will be the only one." Tully looked into my eyes and smiled.

"This is so special," I said as I squeezed him close to my chest. Deep down, I knew that he had no idea why this was important to me, but I hoped that one day he would.

....

22 *Patina:* A term that refers to the blue-green layer of corrosion that develops on the surface of copper when it is exposed to sulfur and oxide compounds. "What is Patina?" ThoughtCo., https://www.thoughtco.com/what-is-patina-2339699

As I approached the first step of the staircase, I felt a wave of anxiety rush through my body. I felt a familiar feeling of nervousness and fear.

This is crazy, I thought to myself, *I am no longer a plebe—what is my problem? I can now walk up on deck in peace. I should be enjoying this. Why am I afraid?*

I was now hesitating, and Tully sensed it.

"What's wrong, Aunt Cathy?"

"Uhhhh… I was just remembering how scared I was as a plebe going up this ladderwell."

"Why?" Tully asked, backing away from the steps.

"Well, I was afraid of what was on 3rd Deck—my upperclassman and all the tough training that we would go through. I spent long hot summer days up there on deck; each day was a challenge; each day you were afraid of something."

"Well, I am scared also, Aunt Cathy—but we can go up together!"

I squeezed his hand, and said, "You are so brave Tully, and bravery is *not* about not being afraid *but* having the courage to do something even when you are afraid!"

I looked up into the ladderwell, and then down at Tully, "Let's do it, soldier!"

Tully stepped on to the first step and pulled my hand to initiate our ascent.

As we began our climb, I thought of how all these feelings had been buried inside of me until now; until I stepped into the ladderwell, until I felt the cold hardness of the steps beneath my feet, until I smelled the old and musty smell of the 8th Wing. If only I had had Tully with me to hold my hand as I ran up to 3rd Deck as Midshipman 4th Class Ervin.

Plebe Summer, Training, Day 1, 1600 hours

It was only minutes after leaving the side of my parents that I was now standing alone on the bottom step of the 8th Wing ladderwell. Besides a small amount of light coming in through the window on my left, the ladderwell was empty and quiet. I took a deep breath of the hot, musty air, and then with a quick burst of energy, I began to sprint up the steps.

I reached the first floor, tripping over the cuffs of my long, white pants and wondering if I would get a chance to change into shorts. I had been in this "white works" outfit all day. It was heavy from my sweat and from Maryland's humidity, which it had been soaking up all day. I turned a corner, then another, and then continued up another flight of steps.

I reached the 2nd floor sweating from the 90-degree heat and wondering if this whole "Plebe Summer" thing was going to be as hard as they had told us, or was it going to be like a summer camp. I turned a corner, then another wiped the sweat from my face, and continued up another flight of steps.

I reached the third floor shaking with nervousness and anticipation. I could hear a thunder of sounds pounding from above and below me. The whole building seemed to be shaking; it sounded as if I was approaching the front lines in a war. I slowly turned a corner, then another, and then continued up my last flight of steps.

I reached the 4th floor breathing heavily and wondering how many more steps I would have to climb. I noticed the black lettering above the double doors in front of me, it read "3rd Deck." I stopped in front of the closed double doors. *This is it*, I thought to myself. As I stood in front of the closed doors, I became scared and nervous and even thought of turning around and running back down. I stood paralyzed with fear, my hands unwilling to reach out for the doors. I did not know if I was ready. I thought I had been prepared for this, but now I found myself doubting. I thought I had wanted this, but now I found myself questioning. My fears were behind those double doors, and at that moment, I prayed for the courage to face whatever was behind them.

I took a deep breath and then pulled the doors open. Immediately, it was as if I had stepped onto a battlefield. I was bombarded with gruesome images of our enemy: the detailers. Voices were exploding off around me; cries of pain and surrender; shouts of control and victory. Bodies were everywhere; some were paralyzed with fear, others were running with nervousness.

I saw white flashing around me as I ran with the others back and forth through the center of the hallway. The angry voices of our enemy matched their angry faces that blazed before me. I smelled white works drenched with sweat. I felt one hot breath after another brushing across my face. I soon joined the front lines as I stood with my back against a pale-green cinderblock wall. I was lined up with the others and felt comfort knowing that I had someone to my left and my right; the comfort of not being alone. I looked across from me at another row standing at attention lined up shoulder-to-shoulder with their backs against the wall. Each one of them looked frightened, with eyes widened and bodies trembling. Each one was dressed as I was, in an outfit of white with a hat held in the right hand. Each one had a new haircut, some with shaved heads, others with chin-length hair. Each one was sweating and shaking. Each one was called a "plebe."

The middle of the hallway swarmed with the angry enemy, who moved around us like lions on the prowl. I noticed that they hunted in small packs. If you attracted the attention of one, then in no time at all you would be surrounded by three, four, maybe five; they would circle in on you and then close in for the kill. Each one of them looked angry. Each one was dressed in a white officer's uniform with a red nametag. Each one was in control as they moved through the hallway with poise and confidence. Each one was called a "detailer."

I was tempted to look around me, to turn my head whenever I heard a voice or a cry of pain. I knew, though, that I needed to stay focused, with my "eyes in the boat"[23] while standing at attention. I decided to fix my eyes on a plebe across from me. The plebe looked scared. He looked like a deer caught in a car's headlights; his eyes were opened wide with fear. His bald head shined from the reflection of the overhead lights, and beads of sweat clung to his skin. His body was trembling, and his eyes were shifting nervously back and forth. From the looks of him, he was a prime target; he was scared and lacking confidence. In no time at all, the detailers had spotted him. I watched as the attack unfolded. Gunfire erupted from the mouths of the enemy.

"*Brace up!*" one upperclassman yelled.

"*Eyes in the boat!*" another one screamed.

I watched as the plebe focused his eyes straight ahead of him pressing his chin down against his chest.

....

23 *Eyes in the Boat:* Refers to keeping your eyes fixed on a certain spot in front of you. Any movement away from this fixed position shows a lack of discipline, or "lack of baring." Oh, and upperclassmen are not required to keep their eyes in the boat, only plebes.

"Is that the best you can do?" both of the upperclassmen roared.

"Sir, Yes Sir!" the plebe said turning his head towards the upperclassmen.

"Eyes in the boat, you moron, don't look at me!" replied an upperclassman with a Southern accent. He was now practically standing on top of the plebe.

"My name is Mr. Trevor," continued the upperclassman. "You will come to fear me." I took a glance at the plebe's face. It was not only more distorted with fear, but it had changed color and was as white as his uniform.

"Are you weak?" yelled Mr. Trevor pausing to glance down at the plebe's black nametag, *"Edwards!* Are you going to pass out on me?" The upperclassman was almost standing on top of the plebe.

"Maybe, Sir," Edwards quivered.

"Maybe! What the hell is maybe? Is that one of your 'Plebe's Five Basic Responses?'"

"No, Sir."

"Well then what are they?"

Edwards froze, unable to answer. The upperclassman turned to the plebe to the right of Edwards. The plebe was shorter but seemed to stand taller. His chest was pushed forward, and he had a confident look upon his Asian face. Mr. Trevor glanced down at the nametag and said, "Tao, what are the plebe's five basic responses?"

Tao spoke up quickly, "Sir, the Plebe's Five Basic Responses are 'Yes Sir, No Sir, Aye-Aye Sir, I'll find out Sir, and No Excuse Sir.'"

"That is correct Tao," Mr. Trevor replied calmly, "but why don't you pull that knife out of your classmate's back?" His voice now rising with anger. Tao looked confused as Mr. Trevor jumped in front of him, shifting his focus away from Edwards.

"Go ahead pull it out. Pull out the freak'n knife you just stabbed your classmate with."

Tao reached over and pulled the imaginary knife from Edward's back. Mr. Trevor's voice became louder. "You are not better than him, I don't ever want to see you bilge[24] another classmate again. The next

....

24 *Bilge:* In Navy lingo, to bilge is to damage the hull (bottom) of a ship so that water comes in. At the Academy it takes on the added meaning of undercutting or stabbing someone in the back to make them look bad.

time, Tao, you will say 'Sir, permission to help my classmate out.'" Mr. Trevor stepped forward so that his face touched the face of Tao, "Is that understood you worthless piece of trash?"

"Sir, Yes, Sir" Tao replied softly; his body shrinking as air slowly deflated from his chest.

As I watched, I took note of what I had witnessed, so that I could learn from my classmate's mistakes. As I stared at Edward's pale face across from me, I suddenly heard my name being called by a voice that I recognized.

It was the voice of a person who I had met the day before, one of my Firsties: Mr. Montgomery.

Now as I stood at attention listening to my name being called, I felt a bit more relaxed, not only because Montgomery was a familiar face, but also because I knew he would just pass by me with no attempt to join in on the attacks. I smiled at him, as he came into peripheral view. As he moved in front of me, I noticed that he was not smiling back. He had ice in his no-longer-friendly blue eyes, and there was anger in his voice. "*Ervin!* Recite the 'Man in The Arena.' GO!"

I began to panic. Not only did I not have it memorized, but I did not think that I would ever have to. I was shocked that Mr. Montgomery was acting like this. A blank look came across my face as I stood at attention with no reply. I soon realized that not only was I upsetting Mr. Montgomery, but the rest of the pack as well. The next thing I knew, more of the enemy were circling in for an attack. Within seconds, I had two of them, one on each side of me, yelling with their noses pressed up against my ears. They were the two that had taken part in the earlier attack. They began chewing me apart, as more questions were fired at me, more questions that I could not answer. I became dizzy with the sudden rush of adrenaline and the instant anxiety attack.

"You have got to be kidding me, Ervin," continued Montgomery, "didn't I specifically ask you to memorize 'Man in the Arena?'"

"Yes, Sir," I replied.

"Well, then why in the hell didn't you?"

"I don't know, Sir," I said hesitantly.

"How about, '*NO EXCUSE, SIR*,'" yelled Mr. Trevor.

"No excuse sir," I said looking at Montgomery.

"You just decided to blow me off, didn't you?" Montgomery said stepping closer to me. I could feel the sweat dripping down my face, and the heat rising around my neck. I was so warm that I felt as if I was going to pass out.

"So, what do you think, Mr. Williams," Mr. Trevor said looking over at the light-haired upperclassman to the right of me.

"I think that this is going to be one hell of a plebe summer," Williams said breathing the words slowly into my ear.

"I think this sorry excuse for a plebe better memorize 'Man in the Arena," Montgomery said as he took a step forward.

"Yes, Sir," I said with a smirk on my face, wanting to show them that I was not afraid.

Suddenly in a rage of fury, all three of them yelled with such intensity that I felt as if I was being pounded into the floor.

"This is not funny!"

"Wipe that smile off your face!"

"Show some discipline, Ervin!"

I stopped smiling and stood still as they devoured me, unable to move, unable to speak, unable to escape. I was having trouble processing all that was going on around me. I stood still but every part of me was trembling. The questions, the yelling, and the angry faces all became a blur as I stood in shock trying to figure out where I was and what exactly was going on. I also began to question my initial perceptions of Mr. Montgomery, and it was now obvious that I had been completely wrong. In fact, from that point on, I began to hate the man. Mr. Montgomery would become a large part of the fear that was behind those closed double doors.

In no time at all, the enemy left and moved on to another victim. I stood against the cinderblock wall feeling bare; I had been torn apart. I was panicked and confused. I felt as if I had stepped into a battle, and I was quickly realizing that not only was I outnumbered, but I was unprepared as well—even if I was a Napster.

I had stepped through the double doors and now I wondered if that had been the right thing to do.

CHAPTER 5:

HELL WEEK

"THERE ARE a lot of steps," Tully said with a sigh. I glanced down to see him tiring a bit, but with a look of determination on his face. As we walked up the first flight, I noticed how nice it felt to walk *normally* up a Naval Academy staircase.

"We just passed the 0 deck. We have to go all way up to the 3rd Deck," I said enthusiastically hoping to motivate him.

As we continued up the second flight, I realized that the ladderwell was a mix of gray and pale green colors, a detail one would miss when only looking at the steps beneath your feet.

"Guess what Tully," I said concentrating on the steps beneath me, "Do you know how a plebe has to walk up these steps?"

"How?" Tully asked as we passed the 1st Deck.

"Well, first, a plebe is not allowed to walk up these steps. Oh, no way! They have to *run*, and they have to run as fast as they can. It is called "chopping."[25] Not only do they have to run, but they have to run along the outside of the staircase, *and* whenever a plebe comes to a corner they have to yell 'Go Navy, Beat Army!'"

"Why?" Tully replied with his favorite question.

"Well, Tul... you see... being a plebe is meant to be hard. You are being trained to be the best of the best, so everything we did had to be a challenge. Now don't you think running up the stairs would be harder than walking up?"

"Yes!"

"Would you like me to show you how it's done? How to run up the steps like a plebe?"

....

25 *Chop:* "To double-time; outdated plebe mass transit system." *Reef Points* (p.228). It is a form of running with exaggerated high knees that cannot really be explained—it must be seen in action. Plebes are required to chop whenever in Bancroft Hall.

"Yes, and can I try it too Aunt Cathy?" Tully asked letting go of my hand.

"Of course, you can. Now, why don't you follow right behind me." I moved over to the right side of the ladderwell. I looked behind me at the Academy's youngest plebe and took a deep breath.

"Let's go, plebe!" I said as I sprinted up the set of steps in front of me. Soon we came to a turn in the ladderwell where the last step leveled out to a set of double doors with "2nd Deck" painted above. I ran to the first corner, and with an abrupt turn to the left, I shouted, *"Go Navy!"*

I ran to the corner across from me, and with another abrupt turn to the left, I shouted, *"Beat Army!"*

Before I began the sprint up the next set of steps, I glanced behind me to see Tully right on my heels.

"Nice job pleber.[26] Keep it up, we have more steps to go!"

We continued up another flight of stairs, another turn with "Go Navy" and a "Beat Army", another flight, and then finally the entrance to 3rd Deck. I stopped in front of the double doors and turned around to my little plebe. I bent down and hugged him. He looked a little tired but not bad, I thought, for a 4-year-old.

"Tully," I said with excitement, "I am so proud of you; you ran those steps like a *real plebe!*" Overlooking the fact that he didn't square corners, he actually ran the steps better than many of my classmates had!

"That was lots of steps," Tully raised his chin in pride.

"Yes, and Tully," I said peeking back down the staircase, "you snuck up without anyone knowing! You are now officially on 3rd Deck!" I pointed at the black lettering above the double doors. "Are you ready to go on deck?"

"Yes," Tully said walking toward the large wooden doors. As I stood in front of the doors, I felt fear hooking its claws into my back. Was it just the familiar sights and sounds that stirred memories of being afraid? Or was there something I was still afraid of? What would I be afraid of this time around?"

I opened the doors and together we walked through. The doors led us into the center of the front hallway. Each deck had three different

....

26 *Pleber:* A nickname for a plebe

hallways. The midshipmen, when referring to them, called them "P-ways," and when referring to their location, called them "shafts." The "back shaft" and "front shaft" were parallel, connected by the perpendicular "middle shaft."

In front of Tully and me was a small wooden podium, the only thing afloat in an ocean of green tiled linoleum. A group of midshipmen crowded around it, sailors at the helm. This was the "watch station." One of the midshipmen, who was standing directly behind the podium, had his uniform hat on and wore a gold arm patch; he was on "watch duty." I had to tug at Tully to come with me, suddenly he had become shy and immovable. Five strange people in uniform were all staring at us.

"Hey," a friendly voice floated from the podium. "Y'all took the ladderwell?"

I recognized the slow southern draw; it was Mr. Wyatt, or rather, *Lieutenant* Jake Wyatt. He was a former upperclassman of mine. We had reconnected last year when he had been transferred to a position at the Academy as 29th Company Officer. I came to know Jake in a new way, on a friendship level rather than on a professional level. It was awkward at first calling him by his first name and not having to say "Sir" to him. It was a strange transition from an upperclassman to a friend. He had turned into a human, a human with even a personality, a wife, and a son.

"You could have taken the elevator," Mr. Wyatt continued with a welcoming smile.

"Yes, we could have," I said pulling Tully along with me, "but Tully and I wanted more of a challenge. In fact, we *chopped*—just like a *real plebe*, right Tul?" I said patting Tully on the back.

The other midshipmen smiled as they saw the small boy, dressed from head to toe in camouflage, shyly approaching them.

"Tully, this is Mr. Wyatt. Mr. Wyatt, this is my nephew Tully."

Mr. Wyatt reached his hand down, and Tully shook his hand softly saying, "Hello, Sir."

"I have heard so much about you; your Aunt tells me that you are a great soldier and that one day you may want to be in the military."

Tully smiled and slowly stepped out from behind me.

"Oh, he would make such a fine officer," I said as I looked at Mr. Wyatt and the other midshipmen who were enjoying this small interruption on their deck.

"He does pushups, runs stairs, he can low crawl,[27] he is honest and courageous, and he *even* knows the 'Plebe's Five Basic Responses.'"

"Ya don't say?" replied Mr. Wyatt.

Tully continued to smile now fully enjoying the spotlight that he was standing in.

"He does," I continued. "He's amazing. Go ahead Tul, what are the 'Plebe's Five Basic Responses?'"

Tully hesitated.

"Go ahead Tully," I said reassuringly. It became silent, and in a whisper, Tully began to speak.

"Yes, Sir... No, Sir... Aye-Aye, Sir... I'll find out Sir... and..." Tully paused as he always did on the last one.

"*And No Ex...,*" I whispered leading him on.

"No Excuse, Sir!" Tully said finishing with a proud smile. The other midshipmen were astonished at what they had just witnessed.

"Wow," replied a wide-eyed Mr. Wyatt, "I don't even think half of my plebes know them as well as you do Tully!" As I glanced down at my little man, I was overwhelmed with pride; pride in my Naval Academy, and pride in my nephew who had adopted it as *his* own.

"Tully, did you know that your Aunt was one of my best and favorite plebes?"

Tully looked up at Mr. Wyatt from beneath the shadow of his brimmed hat and shook his head *no*.

"Well, she was, and she learned a lot!"

"I sure did, Mr. Wyatt, but thanks to you and 34th Company," I said as I glanced down the familiar hallway. The hallway was quiet except for a sudden ringing coming from a nearby room.

"Excuse me for a minute, I believe my phone is ringing." Mr. Wyatt said as he disappeared into a room next to the watch station.

"Take your time," I called after him, "Tully and I will just go and explore the deck!"

....

27 *Low Crawl:* A form of movement in which "the Soldier is in the prone position. Pulling with both arms and pushing with one leg, accomplish forward movement. The other leg is dragged behind. The legs are alternated frequently to avoid fatigue." FM 7-22, *Crawling*, ArmyPrt.com, http://www.armyprt.com/obstacle_negotiation/crawling.shtml

We left the watch station and walked down the center of the hallway across polished linoleum tiles, bulletin boards, and closed wooden doors. We went through a set of double doors at the end of the hallway that led into a smaller ladderwell. It was called the "First Class Ladderwell" and was only used by Firsties.

We walked up three steps, and I crouched down as I pointed through a rectangular window on the wall to the left of us. The tiny pane of glass framed a bright blue sky, a football field of green grass, and a bay of blue with small waves crashing against jagged rocks.

"Do you see the sailboats, Tully?" I pointed to the small triangles of white skimming along the horizon.

"Yes," Tully replied quickly. "Aunt Cathy, can we go up there?" Tully pointed towards the next flight of stairs.

"Okay, but it just leads to the 4th Deck where another company lives, and it looks the same as this one."

"But I want to see it."

"Alright, let's go check it out."

As Tully and I climbed up to the 4th Deck, I thought of the many times I had climbed up this, not as a Firstie but as a plebe.

"Hey Tul, guess what this ladderwell is called?"

"What?"

"The *Ladder of Death*!" I replied, deepening my voice. "Part of our training involved running up and down this ladderwell over and over again. Mr. Montgomery gave it this name. He didn't want us to *die*, but he wanted us to feel pain, that's for sure!"

Tully listened as I explained to him a watered-down, G-rated version of a Plebe Summer story. A story that involved characters such as the "Ladder of Death," "The Grinder," and "Mr. Ball." A story that took place during a time called "Hell Week," where Plebe Summer presented itself in its most real and most grueling form.

Plebe Summer, Training, Day 21

The battle I had stepped into continued to rage on. Sides had been chosen and battle lines had been drawn. The plebes had manpower on their side, usually outnumbering the detailers forty to five, however, the detailers had experience on their side. The first three weeks of Plebe Summer hit hard, fast, and with no mercy. Our detailers of this "First Set" reigned with fear and physical torment. To this day, the memories of the first twenty-one days are a blur. The days I do remember, however, always seemed to involve Mr. Montgomery.

"Welcome to Hell Week!" Montgomery thundered as he walked commandingly through the P-way. I had heard a similar phrase when I had first arrived. Before I had thought it was funny, but now I was no longer laughing. My stomach ached with nervousness as I stood with my back to the wall and my 10-pound rifle at my side. I had also laughed before at the thought of taking Montgomery seriously. Now twenty-one days had passed, and I was taking him more than seriously, I was taking him to be my worst living nightmare.

For the first set of Plebe Summer, a period of twenty-eight days, Montgomery reigned as king. He was not only in a position of leadership, as Platoon Commander, but he had power over the minds of every single plebe.

Mr. Montgomery was a large, tall man with dirty blond hair. Due to his friendly smile and relaxed demeanor, he had first appeared nonthreatening. Within a matter of a day, however, his smile and his relaxed walk was just the calm before a storm. Now at the sight of him or the sound of his voice, instant fear and anxiety would overtake any plebe stranded in his ocean. He could paralyze your thoughts and actions. His laugh would mock you, and his yell would break through your defenses. His intelligence would outsmart you, and his command presence would control you. He patrolled the hallways and our lives with a sense of purpose and determination. He never let a day go by without deviating from his objective; an objective, which he had personally taken upon himself to accomplish. *He was going to break us down in order to build us back up.* Mr. Montgomery was a man who, I believe, epitomized what Plebe Summer was and should be.

Every day was a battle, whether it was with our bodies, minds, or spirits. The past twenty-one days had been hell, and we all began to wonder how it could get worst.

What could be worse than going from 5:15 am to 10:00 pm every day as a plebe? Having to run everywhere while wearing a heavy canvas uniform in the middle of a summer heatwave. Having to stand for hours at an awkward form of attention with your chin pressed against your chest and your eyes straight forward.

What could be worse than having to stop and greet every single upperclassman by their name and thus constantly exposing yourself to instant hazing?

What could be worse than having to memorize an unrealistic number of items to be spouted off to anyone at any time? Items such as thee articles from the newspaper, breakfast, lunch, and dinner menus, professional military knowledge, and all 235 pages of *Reef Points* (in my case 236, "Man in The Arena" is the last page of *Reef Points*—an unnumbered page.)

What could be worse than being given only minutes to accomplish a task? Five minutes to take a shower, four minutes to make a bed, three minutes to change a uniform, two minutes to make it out of the building, one minute to make it back into the building.

What could be worse than room and uniform inspections that are only designed for failure, and when just being a plebe is a discrepancy in itself?

What could be worse than sitting down at a table of food with a hungry stomach and no time to eat?

What could be worse than only being able to answer in Five Basic Responses? What could be worse than being tired, hot, in pain, hungry, and treated like the lowest scum of the earth every single day?

As Montgomery continued to storm through the hallway, the one thought that raced through each plebe's mind was, *How could this be worse? What is Hell Week when you are already in hell?*

"I only have seven more days as your Platoon Commander before the second set of detailers come and take over where I've left off. I am determined to make these seven days *hell* for you *pitiful maggots*. I want to finish this job right and leave all of you with a lasting impression of your first couple of weeks of Plebe Summer. Named after the Navy Seal's seven-day training period, I am calling this week "Hell Week."[28] This is a chance for all of you to prove yourselves, to make 34th Company proud, and maybe even to advance from 'maggots' to 'roadkill.'"[29]

I kept my eyes in the boat and my body completely still as I froze in fear at the sound of Montgomery's voice. As he walked by, I thought about how it would be a relief to have a new Platoon Commander; I was looking forward to a break from him. Little did I know that "a break" would never happen; Montgomery would continue to play an integral role in my life as a plebe.

"So, my little Maggots, welcome to Hell Week," Montgomery said, his storm brewing in the middle of the P-way.

"Mr. Stevens, when was the attack on Pearl Harbor?" Montgomery turned towards the large, solid football player braced up against the wall.

"Sir, it was June 6, 1941," replied Stevens as sweat rolled down his face.

"June 6th!" yelled Montgomery, "You've got to be kidding me, Stevens!"

My stomach began to twist as Montgomery's voice became louder.

"How hard," thundered Montgomery, "is it for you maggots to remember a date! Not only that but a date that will *live in infamy*." The waves and wind began to rise as we all braced for the impact.

"December 7, 1941, Stevens," Montgomery yelled, "a simple date, but *obviously* means nothing to you because you can't remember it! So why don't you tell that to all those people who risked their lives defending our country that day; I'm sure they would appreciate the fact that what they did had no importance to you."

....

28   *Hell Week:* The third week of the First Phase of BUD's (Basic Underwater Demolition School-Navy Seal Training). "Hell Week consists of 5 1/2 days of cold, wet, brutally difficult operational training on fewer than four hours of sleep. Hell Week tests physical endurance, mental toughness, pain and cold tolerance, teamwork, attitude, and your ability to perform work under high physical and mental stress, and sleep deprivation. Above all, it tests determination and desire. On average, only 25% of SEAL candidates make it through Hell Week, the toughest training in the U.S. Military. "Hell Week," *Navyseals.com*, U.S. Navy Seals, https://navyseals.com/nsw/hell-week-0/

29   *Maggots:* Mr. Richardson had given us the nickname symbolizing our lowest position within the company. As a maggot we were basically worthless and a disgusting sight for our upperclassmen. However, we had the potential of one day reaching the level of "Roadkill" which was a step above a maggot and thus less degrading.

I could feel Stevens's pain as Montgomery's words cut through him like a knife. I had trouble remembering the historical dates that Montgomery had taught us. It was not that I didn't care; I just was not good under pressure or maybe it was a lack of confidence. Whatever the case was, it was frustrating and demoralizing to make a mistake, especially in the presence of Montgomery.

"Extend *arms!*" Montgomery commanded abruptly. Immediately I grabbed a hold of the barrel of my rifle that had been by my side. I then lifted the ten-pound riffle off the floor and extended my arm straight out in front of me. I could feel my bicep and shoulders burn as we all held our guns silently.

"Okay, let's try this again, *shall we?*" Montgomery said lowering his voice. He proceeded down the hallway towards a woman across from me.

"Summers, who was the American President during the bombing of Hiroshima and Nagasaki?"

"Sir, I'll find out sir!" replied Summers.

"You have got to be kidding me, Summers," Montgomery thundered, "This is absolutely unbelievable!"

Muffled sighs of pain were heard throughout the hallway as the extended arms were slowly lowering from the tired muscles giving out.

"Get those rifles up," yelled Montgomery, "Your freak'n arms should be completely extended. They won't be resting until one of you maggots can answer a question correctly!"

In one quick thunderclap, Montgomery was now over on my side of the P-way, moving in on a tall, skinny guy to the left of me.

"Langley, what happened in Panama?"

"Sir, I'll find out sir!"

"This is unbelievable! Do you guys even care? Do you even stop to think that while your little sorry butts were kicking back in the Podunks, one of your Firsties here was risking his life over in Panama? Mr. LaPointe and his SEAL team went to war; he risked his life for his Platoon Commander and *received the Silver Star!* You better find out what Panama was all about, each one of you maggots, and you better pray that you live through today!"

As Montgomery continued to yell, I could see Mr. LaPointe carrying his commander over his shoulders, (who would end up dying), dodging enemy gunfire, and racing towards black inflatable boats on a sandy beach. We had heard the heroic story and had met the mythological man. Mr. LaPointe was a tall man, with dark piercing eyes. He was slightly balding and looked more like a computer nerd rather than a Navy SEAL. His face was like a blank slate as if all types of emotion had been erased. He kept his distance from us and was rarely involved in our daily lives. We would on occasion see him slowly walking down the hallway or feel him sneaking up behind us during a chow call. His mysterious absence in our lives and the whisperings of his heroic stories created an almost fictitious aura around him.

The other upperclassmen instilled fear, respect, and daily lessons by yelling, belittling, and physically and mentally challenging us. They demonstrated leadership by being in our faces twenty-four hours a day and involving themselves in every block of our planned time. Mr. LaPointe instilled fear, respect, and training without ever speaking a word; he demonstrated leadership without ever being around. He didn't need our time, he didn't need plebe training manuals, he didn't need to waste his breath. All he needed was a Silver Star.

I watched as my arm was slowly lowering, as if out of my control. I tried to hold it in position, but it was shaking, as my muscles quivered from exhaustion. *Do not let it drop*, I thought to myself as the burn in my arm consumed my entire body. I looked across the hallway and saw the strain on the faces of my classmates; rifles were slowly lowering, as sweat glistened in puddles on the waxed floor. Sighs and groans echoed to the right and the left of me as my arm continued to lower.

"Ervin!" Montgomery turned and faced me, "Just for shits and giggles, 'Man in the Arena'—*go!*"

I took a deep breath and focused my thoughts away from the pain in my arm. "Sir, it's not the critic who counts, not the one who points out how the strong man stumbled or how the doer of deeds might have done them better. The credit belongs to the man who is actually in the arena, whose face is marred with sweat, dust, blood; who strives valiantly, who errs and comes short again and again…"

"Stop!" yelled Montgomery.

I froze as he rode a wave of anger, heading closer towards me. I could feel the wind and thunder. I became queasy as the room seemed to rock back and forth.

"You left out 'and'. 'Whose face is marred with sweat AND dust and blood.' Begin again, Ervin. NOW!"

I was flustered; my focus was gone. The rocking became stronger. I just kept thinking how upset my other classmates were; we were still holding our rifles at "extend arms." The sweat poured down my face and I began again.

"Sir, it's not the critic who counts, not the one who points out how the strong man stumbled or how the doer of deeds might have done them better. The credit belongs to the man who is actually in the arena, whose face is marred with sweat, *and* dust and blood; who strives valiantly, who... " I took a short pause. "Who..." I was having a mental block with a panic attack mixed in. Within a matter of seconds, my mind was completely blank.

"Holy crap Ervin, you mean to tell me that you still do not know this passage?" Montgomery's voice became deeper and slower. "You have had all this time—what the hell is going on here?" Montgomery turned and faced the rest of the company, "Get those rifles up! I am so disappointed that I can't even look at all of you! Get your butts down to the *grinder* now!"

As if we had been held back with bungee cords, all thirty-one of us immediately sprang from the walls and into the middle of the P-way. With our riffles now held with both hands, corners were squared while a jumbled mix of "Go Navy, Beat Army" shouts blasted through the air. We funneled into the stairwell like nervous ants disappearing into an anthill.

My knees began to ache as I pounded down the four flights of stairs and out onto the tennis courts (aka Grinder). As I stood at attention, I could feel the heat rising off the court. I shook with fear, waiting for the worst, yet hoping for the best.

Out of the corner of my eye, I could see Montgomery walking out of the entrance of the stairwell; it seemed that he was carrying something. As he moved into closer peripheral vision, I realized that he was carrying a large, round object.

"I would like to introduce you all to Mr. Ball," Mr. Montgomery shouted. "He will become a close personal friend of yours over the next week." As Montgomery passed, I took a glance at what he had been cradling in his arms. It was a tattered leather ball about a foot and a half in diameter.

"Here Mr. Stevens," Montgomery tossed the ball to the large linebacker, "Why don't you be the first to meet Mr. Ball." As Stevens grabbed the ball, his arms lowered from the impact, lowering almost to the point of dropping the ball.

We all witnessed his struggle with the new friend and realized that we would be dealing with a medicine ball; a ten-pound medicine ball.

"Why don't you put Mr. Ball down for now Stevens," Montgomery said as he passed in between the rows of sweating bodies.

"Down!" Montgomery yelled. We immediately lowered our bodies into a pushup position.

"Down... 1, down... 2, down... 3," Montgomery continued as bodies began to sweat and burn. After the count of 30, Montgomery yelled, *"Recover!"*

We all quickly stood up, recovering from the pushups and waiting for another wave of torture. I decided to keep my mouth shut; I was known for yelling "We want more Sir!" while doing push-ups. It was a way for me to try to motivate everyone. Unfortunately, it had been having an opposite effect on my classmates, and it did not go over well with the upperclassmen as it had with my Gunnery Sergeant back at NAPS.

"Now I will introduce you to 'LOD': the 'Ladder of Death.' You are to use the First Class ladderwell and sprint to the top deck and back down on to the Grinder," continued Montgomery, "We will do this until your legs become rubber! Mr. Stevens, why don't you go ahead and grab Mr. Ball."

As Stevens grabbed Mr. Ball, Montgomery yelled, *"move it,* you pitiful maggots!"

We all sprinted to the ladderwell with Stevens cradling Mr. Ball in the middle of the pack. *Here we go*, I thought as I entered the ladderwell. I flew up the steps, "Go Navy" I yelled squaring the first corner.

"Beat Army" I yelled at the next corner.

I bolted up another set of steps. "Go Navy" I yelled.

"Beat Army," I yelled as I cornered my way around the 1st Deck.

Soon I was rounding 2nd Deck and onto the 3rd in a tightly squashed line of frantic plebes. On my way up to the 3rd Deck, it was a relief to see familiar faces coming down in the opposite direction. I was closing in on the top.

Once to the top, I followed as the plebe in front of me did, and pounded the 4th Deck door with my fist, yelling "Go Navy", and as I turned around to head back down, I noticed Mr. Trevor (one of our 2nd Class detailers) quietly lurking behind the door. He was obviously on patrol for any slackers, making sure that we all made it to the top without cheating.

We all took turns carrying Mr. Ball as we ran the LOD relentlessly.

Hell Week raged on for a week as the spirit of it continued to rage inside Mr. Montgomery. The halls of 34th Company were filled with sweat, shouts, and sounds of pain. Not a day went by that wasn't filled with trips to the Grinder or the Ladder of Death, and each mistake we made fueled Mr. Montgomery's means of torture.

The types of torture varied from physically demanding to mentally demanding to just plain aggravating. At times, our rooms were "vaporized", a creative way of making us empty every item from our room into the hallway, and then returning it all in proper order. Vaporizations were timed, and if we took too long, our rooms were vaporized repeatedly until we made the cut off time.

Along with vaporizations, we had "Uniform Races." Mr. Montgomery would yell out a particular uniform in which we had to change into. We had only a matter of minutes to strip out of what we were wearing and properly put on the desired uniform. It always seemed to work out that the uniform races took place on the hottest and most humid of days, when every article of clothing would stick like glue to your body.

During our seven intense days of hell, our bodies, minds, and spirits were pushed to the edge. It was a test to not only see what we had learned over the past twenty-one days but more so, a test of our inner strength. Montgomery wanted to instill more than just an understanding of the history of the US Navy, or the development of teamwork, or proving that we were worthy to be a member of 34th Company. He wanted each one of us to take the strain, and to overcome a personal struggle within ourselves.

We each took turns running with Mr. Ball. Mr. Ball was more than just an extra 10 pounds of weight; it represented an extra burden that each one of us would end up having to carry. I had been handed the extra burden of memorizing "Man in the Arena." I had overlooked the fact that my inability to memorize "Man in the Arena" was the same as my inability to take the strain. I had failed with the extra burden that had been handed to me; I let down the rest of my company and had ultimately dropped "Mr. Ball."

As with the rest of my classmates, I never once stopped from picking the ball back up. My hands were "marred with sweat and dust and blood" from the continuous strain of my burden, and my spirit was weak, though "striving valiantly."

Our "Hell Week" could not hold a flame to the real Navy SEAL's Hell Week, where hell is Coronado, California, where the training is the toughest in all of the military and where the instructors would make Mr. Montgomery look like an angel.

But the one thing that we did have in common, was that through the strain of the week, we became stronger, individually and as a team.

> *Through the depths of hell we had to reach down into*
> *the depths of ourselves and persevere. As Hell Week*
> *raged on, we continued to struggle, but never once did*
> *we quit. Never once did the brass bell ring.*[30]

---

30 During SEAL training, a recruit will ring a brass bell to indicate that they want to drop out and quit.

CHAPTER 6:

ROOM 8315

TULLY AND I opened the door to the 4th Deck, took a quick look, and finding nothing interesting decided to go back down the ladderwell. As we quietly descended, I was able to find peace with the "Ladder of Death", even though I could somehow hear the voice of Montgomery echoing among the walls. Tully, on the other hand, was trying to figure out what exactly this Academy was all about.

"Why was Mr. Gumry so mean?" Tully asked as I smiled at his mispronunciation.

"Well, he was training us, and some upperclassmen were mean, and some were nice to you."

I had asked that same question to myself many times, *why was Montgomery so mean to me? Why was I the one he always picked on? Why did he hate me so much?"* It was a question I would ask throughout the entire course of my whole Plebe Year.

"Did you get tired?" Tully asked as his little legs began to slow.

"Oh, yes, we sure did. At times I even wanted to stop. Whether it was running up and down the ladderwells, or right in the middle of a uniform race, but I never did. I was being taught how to not give up—to always keep going—even when you think you can't go on."

"Can I see Mr. Ball?" Tully asked as we stepped out of the L.O.D and back onto 3rd Deck.

"I am not sure if Mr. Ball is still around. But there is something that I want to show you—something very special—but let's go ask Mr. Wyatt first."

"What Aunt Cathy?"

"It's a surprise," I said leading Tully back down the P-way. I poked my head into Mr. Wyatt's room, as Tully waited quietly in my shadow.

"Hey, Sir, I was wondering if I could show Tully my old room?"

Mr. Wyatt smirked, knowing that I did not need to address him in that way, "Sure! Mr. Peters will go with you in case it is locked."

I smiled and mouthed thank you as I turned to exit.

"Oh, and Ervin," Mr. Wyatt paused as a grin stretched across his face. "Attention to Detail…"

"Sir, yes, Sir." I rolled my eyes playfully but with all seriousness, knowing the importance of those three words. Three words that Mr. Wyatt had ingrained into my uneducated plebe brain.

As Tully and I stepped back into the P-way, the midshipman on watch duty, Mr. Peters, walked over to us holding a ring of keys.

"Your old room may be occupied, Ma'am, most midshipmen are gone because of Spring Break holiday, but some are finishing off exams and may still be around."

"Oh, no worries Peters, thank you. We will just take a quick peek," I said as I walked over towards one of the many closed wooden doors.

I slowed down and looked down at my side, "Tully you are going to get to see my room, where I lived for a year."

Tully's eyes were wide with anticipation as we stood in front of the 2nd door down from the end of the hallway, on the right-hand side: Room 8315. It was in the front shaft, which was a bad location to be if you were a plebe. It was like being in a prison cell that was located right next to the office of the Warden. The "watch station," the announcement board, the Company Officer's office, and the "wardroom" (upper-class lounge) were all located in the front shaft. Most of the action of the company always seemed to take place in the front shaft, and therefore a majority of the upperclassmen were always found swarming throughout.

Running through the front shaft and sounding off at the corners was like shouting to the enemy, "Hey! Here I am, come out and kill me!" The hallway was infested with them, and as soon as they heard you, they were on you. Even if they didn't hear you, they were there. It was like setting off land mines as soon as you stepped in the front shaft. The simple task of going to and from your room was not only an added stress but also it often left you injured.

To make matters even worse, my room was right next door to Mr. Montgomery. I had always wondered if it had been planned that way or if it had been a manifestation of God's sense of humor.

Polishing shoes and reading the newspaper in Room 8315

Despite the few problems I had with my room, there were some definite advantages to living in Room 8315. The first advantage was 4th Class Lily Sinclair, my roommate and newfound friend. Lily was from Orlando, Florida; home of Mickey Mouse and sun-ripened oranges. As if a reflection of her hometown, Lily had child-like energy and a personality that overflowed with sweetness and kindness. This brown-haired, half-Asian girl was of small stature, yet had an inner strength that went beyond her size. She was soft-spoken, however, when it came to sounding off, she could belt it out better than most guys (let alone most Marines). It was a mystery to us all, how such a small girl could make such a loud noise. It was like watching a mouse roar like a lion.

Lily had book smarts and common-sense smarts. She worked hard both as a plebe and as a student. She was disciplined, well organized, and a team player. She was one you would not only want fighting beside you, but she was one you would want as a friend. She was honest, kind, and genuinely cared for others. We shared the same Christian faith and shared many nights in prayer at our bedside. She was a great roommate but an even better friend. There was only a 10% population of females at the Academy, so your chances of getting a roommate you could get along with, and maybe even become friends with, was quite slim. From the moment I had met Lily, I knew how lucky I was. Lily was there for me, and I for her, and together we knew we could make it through anything. She also shared my love for adventure and had a wild side like my own. There was never a dull moment as we fed off each other's energy, leading us often into mischief and trouble. We could turn a simple boating lesson into a battle, an Army-Navy week into hours of relentless retaliations on our upperclassman, and a quiet night into an off-base Recon mission. There had never been a better match in all of Bancroft Hall, as far as we were concerned.

The other advantage to living in Room 8315 was the view. From our window, you could see the churning bay and the large wall of jagged grey rocks, that held the waters in check. The seawall bordered the easternmost part of the Yard[31] and was located across from Turf Field, the Navy football team's practice field. The sunrises that filled our room in the early mornings were moments of peace that Lily I would cling to. I remember the sun as a red ball of fire sitting on top of the water and painting everything surrounding it in deep colors of yellows, oranges, and reds. The colors lessened in intensity as they moved away from the sun. The rest of 8th Wing was transformed from an ominous grey to a mixture of pinks and purples. Not only was it beautiful to look at, but also for a moment, a simple sunrise could erase the grey inside.

Not only did I appreciate our room in the mornings, but in the evenings as well. At night, I would often sit on the ledge of the window and stare out into the darkness. The yellow lights from the sailboats out on the water were like diamonds scattered throughout a blanket of black velvet. The stars would blend in with all the shimmering, adding an elegant mysteriousness to the Yard. The wind would blow through our room, clinging to my face and carrying the smell and dampness of the sea. Buoys could be heard off in the distance, playing solos in an orchestra of crashing waves and clanging sailboat masts.

My room was a beautiful and safe harbor in the mornings and evenings, however at different times during the day, one could find dangerous sharks lurking throughout the waters.

....

31   *Yard:* Another name for the Naval Academy grounds.

As midshipmen Peters unlocked and opened the door I had been standing in front of, Tully and I stepped into Room 8315 and I stepped back in time to an attack that I would never forget...

Plebe Summer, Training, Day 28

Hell Week may have passed, but being a plebe had not. I was a plebe every week and that in itself was hell. It was now August, and as the trees stood waiting for autumn and dreading the inevitable loss of their leaves, I stood waiting for our room inspection, dreading the inevitable loss of my morale, for we had not passed a room inspection yet.

Fear and anticipation increased with each footstep I heard out in the P-way. A slow drumbeat of fear echoed down the hallway, pounding its way closer and closer to me. On the inside I felt like the canvas sails on a sailboat; the fear was like the wind, bashing me from all directions. On the outside, though, I dare not show the storms that were raging inside of me. I had learned to be like the mast, always still, steady, and never bending. I was standing straight with my legs shoulder-width apart and my hands resting behind me upon my lower back. I looked down at my black shoes. The toes reflected hours of tedious shining as I noticed my reflection through the black glass. I straightened my back and tightened every muscle in my body, as I looked back out into the P-way. I picked a spot on the cinderblock wall across from me where the paint had chipped off. I stared at it until my eyes went out of focus; I drifted out of my body, which had now been in the position of "parade rest" for over an *unrestful* half hour. I decided to practice reciting "Man in the Arena" in my head while I waited. I whispered to myself,

> *It is not the critic who counts... not the one who points*
> *out how the strong man stumbled or how the doer of deeds*
> *might have done them better...*

"*Attention on deck!*" yelled Lily, her voice a fire alarm yanking me out of my trance. My body snapped to attention as Mr. Wyatt stepped into our room.

"Room 8315 ready for inspection, Sir!" Lily continued to ring. My arms were now pressed at my side, straight and as hard as boards. My hands became tight fists with my thumbs pointed down along the seam of my pants. My heels were pressed together with my toes spread apart at a 45-degree angle. It was as if I had looked into the eyes of Medusa and had been instantly turned to stone. I became stiff and lifeless except for the slow rhythm of my controlled breathing.

The footsteps were getting closer and closer. I could feel Mr. Wyatt's sleepy brown eyes locked on me. I did not dare look into his eyes. Soon, I could feel his breath as he began to circle me as a shark does its prey. It was as if he was waiting to devour me but seemed to find delight in prolonging the inevitable. I knew that he was waiting to find something wrong with me, a discrepancy, whether it was with my uniform, or with the room in which I was standing in. With every slow and deliberate circle he made around me, he continued to torture me, and with every deep disapproving sigh, he caused me to doubt my abilities and myself.

He was now in front of me looking at me as if I were a specimen under his microscope. My uniform was always briefly inspected whenever I was in the presence of an upperclassman. Today, however, he would not be using high power magnification for his viewing, that was only used during an official "personnel inspection." Instead, *my room* would be under his intense scrutiny. Today was Friday: "Room Inspection Day."

"Did you tape off, Ervin?" Wyatt asked as he continued to circle.

"Yes, Sir," I replied as I thought of the amount of masking tape I used daily to constantly keep my black uniform lint-free.

"Well, what the hell is this then?" Wyatt said pulling a piece of my blond hair off my sleeve.

Mr. Wyatt reached over and took the small white piece of paper, called a "Room Inspection Chit", and the black pen that we had carefully placed at the corner of our desk. He began filling in the blanks: "Ervin… Sinclair… August 10… 0900 hours… 8315."

I took a deep breath trying to relax my body.

"Let's get started," Wyatt said as he picked up the clean white glove that we had meticulously placed on the desk. He slowly placed his right hand into the stretchy material. Immediately he reached under the desk with his hand and ran his fingers underneath the ledge. I held my breath as the suspense began to build. He lifted his hand up and held it out in front of his face, checking for dirt. The fingertips were still white. I let out a sigh of relief.

Next, he ran his hand along the top of the door to our room. The glove was still white—no dirt. He brushed his hand across the top ledge of the mirror, then above our sink. Still no dirt. Lily and I had made sure to dust every single object imaginable. I smiled on the inside, knowing that to his disappointment that glove would stay white in our immaculate and dust-free room.

Mr. Wyatt continued to patiently swim about the room with his white hand brushing across anything and everything, from underneath our chairs, to every single rung on our Venetian blinds, to the small corners in our desk drawers. With each swipe, he would inspect his hand, and with each swipe, the glove remained white.

I had thought he was finished when he moved back to the front of our room. Unfortunately, he was not. His eyes glared with determination. He approached our door again and rubbed his finger across the top edge of our nameplate; an edge that was no bigger than the width of a toothpick. He turned his finger over, smiled, and then held up the tip of his glove that was now grey with the tiniest speck of dust.

"Let me see here", Mr. Wyatt said as he looked down at the paper, "Door dirty," he said snickering as he made a checkmark.

He peeled the glove off his hand and threw it down upon the desk in disgust. Lily glanced over at me, communicating her shock; the shock that Wyatt had found a microscopic surface to check. It reminded me of a time back at the Prep School (NAPS), when I was using the end of a paper clip to scrape dirt out of the corners in my room. Our XO (Executive Officer) at the time, Major Parrino, would find the smallest surfaces to check, places that you never thought even existed. He expected perfection and hours were spent trying to meet his expectations.

I looked back over at Mr. Wyatt and noticed that he was now picking up the black sock that had also been carefully left on our desk.

Mr. Wyatt spun around and glided over to the right side of the room towards the shower. He pushed aside the plastic shower curtain and stepped into the sea-green tiled shower. I knew another check was coming for sure. No matter how hard Lily and I had scrubbed, or how much mildew remover we used, we just could not manage to get the tiles clean. The tiles were so old and had a build-up of soap scum that probably dated back to the 1800s.

Mr. Wyatt took the black sock and rubbed it in the corners of the shower. I looked over not surprised to see the black sock soiled with white streaks of soap scum.

"Shower dirty," Wyatt sneered placing another check upon the paper. "Did you guys even attempt to clean your room?" Wyatt asked. His question struck a blow to my pride and fueled frustration for the relentless hours of effort that we had put forth.

Lily and I continued to watch Wyatt out of the corners of our eyes. I tried not to look worried but with each step he made, I would question myself. I would question whether I had missed a spot, or whether I did a good enough job. This was all very typical of Plebe Year. It seemed that no matter how hard you tried, it was never good enough. It seemed that no matter how complete you did your job, there was always a spot you missed. It was like the upperclassmen had special sonar, sonar that could detect imperfection.

I glanced over to see Mr. Wyatt bobbing around in front of our mirror. Lily and I had used Windex and newspaper to clean the mirror. Newspaper, I had learned at NAPS, was the trick to producing a streakless mirror. Thus, to Mr. Wyatt's disgust, he was unable to detect any streaks. He was only able to see himself in the mirror, which Lily and I would have considered a discrepancy.

Next, the medicine cabinet was flipped open and inspected for proper cleanliness. Also, the items on the shelves had to be lined up properly, left to right, large to small. Lily was great at organizing, and our cabinets below and above the sink were truly organized with perfection. We had also used a type of liquid cleaner called "Brasso" to polish all of the "bright-works" in our room; this included anything metal, such as the faucets, drains, and the pipes underneath the sink. Everything was shining and in order. Mr. Wyatt couldn't even find anything wrong with the towels, which were folded in precise thirds upon the untarnished towel rack. Without a checkmark, Mr. Wyatt moved on over towards our lockers. I began to breathe easier for the first time, and a small ounce of hope drifted in. *Maybe Lily and I would survive the attack.*

As Mr. Wyatt looked over our clothing, I thought in my head, "*Left to right, black to white.*" He checked to make sure that our uniforms were lined up in this manner, black uniforms on the left, white uniforms on the right. Everything also had a certain way to be folded. T-shirts, sweatshirts, underwear, and socks had their unique look. Socks were rolled up into a ball with a half-circle crease on the outside. If placed a certain way, the creases looked like a smile, and thus your socks not only had to be lined up in precise rows of black to white, but they all had to be "smiling" because "they were so happy to be at the United States Naval Academy."

After pulling out our clothing from the shelves and disarranging everything we had spent hours arranging, Mr. Wyatt finned his way in and out of our closets. Suddenly, one of my black shoes came flying out of the closet, like a piece of shrapnel, and soared across the room nearly missing my roommate's head.

"One of your shoestrings, Ervin, was not tucked inside. I guess I can check that off for 'Closet Stowage Improper.'"

As Wyatt said this, I felt the pain of another blow and watched as the small ounce of hope drifted away.

After leaving the lockers in shambles, Mr. Wyatt made his way over to our racks[32]. On his way over to mine, he suddenly stopped and looked down at the deck[33]. I figured that he was admiring our "Mop and Glow" job. He dove down and picked up something from underneath one of the legs of the metal desk. He held up his prize in front of my face with pure joy, as if he had just found a buried treasure.

"You seemed to have missed a dust-bunny," he announced. A *dust-bunny* was a midshipman's term for any bit of dust found on the floor. Wyatt quickly scribbled another check as he snarled with delight. "'Deck... dusty or dirty... check!'"

With each check he marked upon the paper, he tore away a part of our self-esteem. I finally realized that this "immaculate" room was far

32 *Rack:* Naval Academy jargon for "a bed," which is the ultimate goal of most midshipmen, especially a Plebe where sleep is a precious commodity.

33 *Deck:* Naval Academy jargon for "the floor." In keeping with nautical terminology, a wall is referred to as a "bulkhead."

from being immaculate, and that Lily and I had a long way to go before it would ever meet Wyatt's expectations. At this point, I was beginning to not care anymore.

Suddenly I heard the screech of my metal drawer on my desk open. Mr. Wyatt pulled out my plastic ruler and approached my rack. He began to measure the folds. The sheet and blanket had to be folded down 12 inches from the top of the bed. The white sheet had to be folded down on top of the blue blanket (aka blue magnet[34]) with a 3-inch fold. Every inch of the blanket and sheet had to be tucked tightly underneath the mattress and the edges had to have hospital corners with exact 45-degree angles. The surface of the bed had to be tight and free of wrinkles or creases. Mr. Wyatt checked and rechecked the measurements, and to his satisfaction found no discrepancies.

As Mr. Wyatt made his way over to Lily's rack, I looked at mine thinking about how I had never once slept underneath the sheets. Making my bed in the morning took up an extra seven minutes of my time. As plebes, we had perfected the art of saving time and one way of saving time was sleeping on top of your precision-made rack without breaking the sheets. In the morning, all your rack needed was a few quick tucks and smoothing with a wire hanger to get any wrinkles out.

While I was looking at my rack, wishing I could lie down for a quick nap, I suddenly heard, "Three and 1/4 inches, is that the correct measurement Miss Sinclair?"

"No Sir," Lily quietly replied.

"What is the correct measurement then?"

"Three inches, Sir."

"Why is it not three inches?"

"No excuse, Sir."

"And the hits keep on coming, don't they!" Mr. Wyatt laughed loudly. "Let's see, that would be another check for you guys: 'Rack Untidy.'"

He continued to circle about the room checking our bookshelves, our computers, our windows, the blinds, the light fixture, the radiator, and even the trashcan (which was a discrepancy if any trash was in it).

....

34 *Blue Magnet:* Bedspreads at USNA are Navy Blue; Sleep can be big draw for many MIDs, thus Racks become Blue Magnets. "USNA Jargon," *Sppausnaparents.com,* https://sppausna-parents.files.wordpress.com/2014/10/usna-jargon.pdf

By the end of his inspection, more checks had been added to the list. Not only did this add to Mr. Wyatt's pleasure but our destruction. Death was now certain for us. He had come into a room we were proud of, picked it apart, defaced it, rejected it, and now he was circling in for the kill. He scratched one last mark upon the paper and placed it back on our desk. I quickly looked down to see that he checked off the "General Condition of the Room" to be "Untidy and Unsatisfactory." He had also written a number, "1.4," which was our total score out of a possible 4.0.

I looked up to see Mr. Wyatt standing in our doorway.

"Ladies, I have been disappointed today, not only by you but by the rest of your classmates. These rooms are unacceptable, and it is obvious that you do not yet understand what is meant by 'Attention to Detail.'"

As he turned to head out of the room, I began to think to myself, *I really don't care. This is a complete joke. The upperclassmen are just finding more ways to mess with our heads. Who cares if one little piece of dust is left on the floor, who cares if a fold is a 1/4 of an inch off? Does it really matter in the big picture? No plebe will ever get it right, it seems that we are destined for failure at whatever we do, so why worry about these little things, the un-tucked shoestrings, the dirt on the nameplate?* As I continued to fume with anger, Mr. Wyatt stopped, bent down, and picked up a speck of white paper that was on the floor. He held it up in front of us.

"Attention to detail," he whispered. He then looked over at me, as if he had heard what I had been thinking, "Ervin open up your *Reef Points* and read page 180 for me."

"Yes Sir," I replied as I pulled out my *Reef Points* from the top drawer in my desk. I turned to page 180 and I began to read:

> *The world supremacy of the United States Navy can be attributed to its constant state of peak operational readiness. This state of readiness is the result of the demanding standards of personal performance expected of all Naval Officers. At the Naval Academy, frequent room and personnel inspections are held to instill and ensure the individual's meticulousness and attention to detail that will be used in the fleet to hone the fighting edge...*

"That's enough," Wyatt said cutting me off. He once again softly said, "Attention to detail." He looked up at us and began speaking with a slight quiver in his voice, "Imagine that you are on an aircraft carrier. You are part of the deck crew. You are one of those people that I am sure you remember seeing in the opening scenes of *Top Gun*, the ones with the orange helmets who manage the organization of the aircraft and their take-off and landings onboard a carrier. You begin each day by lining up shoulder to shoulder with the rest of your crew forming a line that stretches across from one end of the carrier to the other. You and the rest of the crew move slowly across the carrier with one small step at a time. With each step you take, you scan the area in front of you looking for any small objects such as pieces of metal, plastic, etc., which must then be picked up off the deck. Halfway down the carrier you pass over and miss picking up a small metal screw. After your crew has finished, an F-18 that was on standby is now motioned for takeoff. The engines roar, the deck shakes, and the plane is shot off into the blue sky. The plane never makes it, though. It explodes within seconds from leaving the carrier. Not only is a million-dollar jet destroyed, but also two men have died, and potentially more lives could have been lost if that plane was part of a wartime mission. Later, you find out the cause of the accident, 'a malfunction in the engine had occurred due to a piece of metal that had been pulled in during takeoff.' It turns out that *that* small piece of metal was the same small piece of metal, which *you* had carelessly overlooked...

"*Attention to detail*," Wyatt continued forcefully.

"*It starts here ladies. In room 8315, and on this deck. Never forget that.*"

CHAPTER 7:

SUICIDE

TULLY, MR. PETERS, AND I pushed open the door to Room 8315 and stepped into the darkness. Mr. Peters opened the blinds shedding morning light into the quiet room. Suddenly, there was movement coming from one of the two beds.

"Ma'am, Sir…" A startled and half-asleep midshipman jumped out of bed and immediately stood to attention. He was dressed in regulation navy blue shorts and a white blue-rim t-shirt.

"Oh, we're sorry Erickson, I had no idea anyone was here," Mr. Peters said moving over to the bed. "Did you have an exam earlier today?"

"Yes, Sir," replied the plebe. "Physics, Sir."

"We are so sorry to wake you," I said as I grabbed Tully to back him out of the room.

"It's okay Ma'am," replied the semi-conscience, brain-washed plebe.

"This is Miss Ervin and her nephew Tully; they are here visiting," replied midshipmen Peters as he glanced over at Tully and me.

"This was my room when I was a plebe," I said as I looked around the darkened room. "I wanted to show my nephew…"

"Oh, it's okay ma'am you can still look around," the plebe said with a sleepy smile.

Tully re-emerged from the shadows and began to tiptoe around the small rectangular room.

"Thank you," I said looking down at the piles of clothes scattered across the floor. I walked around noticing a black uniform shirt draped across a chair, pant legs dangling off the side of the table, a hat on the top of the computer monitor, and both racks unmade (even though only one was being used). I was appalled. I didn't want to make the plebe feel bad; I mean after all we had just woken him up and he was technically on break. So I kindly said, "*Well*, I guess you aren't having room inspection today, huh?" I smiled at the plebe still standing at attention. Deep down inside of me, I wanted to rip the plebe apart—or at least try (I had never really had any training in the fine art of "being an upperclassman.")

His room, *my old room*, was a disgrace to the Naval Academy. I could not believe the state that it was in—the dirty clothes, the unmade bed, the disorganization, and the filth. I understood that the Mids were all on Spring Break, but a plebe's room was never supposed to be on break. I was also angry at the fact that Midshipman Peters had made no effort to criticize the state of the room. *Was I missing something here?* I was missing the fact that "attention to detail" was only used when you had to use it.

As I walked about the "unsat"[35] room, I realized that I should not be angry with the plebe, but rather with the system. The Academy's rules were that a plebe had the right to lock their doors at any time. There was no such rule when I had occupied the room.

Our rooms were never to be locked during the day. Doors were left wide open, so "attention to detail" was mandatory every day because every day someone was watching. After a while, "attention to detail" became so ingrained in us, that even if we could have locked our doors, our rooms would not have changed in appearance as if the door had been left open.

"Aunt Cathy, did you sleep up there?" Tully tugged at my shorts and pointed to the top bunk of a wooden bunk bed.

I had been so caught up in the condition of the room, that I had completely overlooked the fact that the room was not only unlike mine, in cleanliness, but also it had been completely renovated. The walls, the floors, the shower, and the windows were all new, as well as the desk and the beds. Against each side of the room was a multipurpose unit. The bed was like a bunk bed with a desk directly underneath of it. Shelving and cabinets were attached to the ends of the unit. The tiled bathroom was to the left of the entrance, and on the far end of the room were two large rectangular windows.

....

35 *Unsat:* Unsatisfactory; anything in the eyes of the upperclassmen that does not meet their standards; grades below a 2.0 GPA. "USNA Jargon," *Sppausnaparents.com,* https://sppausnaparents.files.wordpress.com/2014/10/usna-jargon.pdf

"No," I replied, "You see Tully when I was here the room was different. Now, It has new beds and desks in here," I moved closer to Tully, "Lily and I didn't have bunk beds. We had two separate beds, mine though was right here in this corner," I pointed to the bunk bed unit on the right. I turned around to face the center of the room, "We had a large desk in the middle here, and two chairs, one on each side."

Both midshipmen smiled as Tully peeked into the shower. I walked over to the shower and followed his lead. "Oh, and look at how nice these showers are? Did you know that my shower was so old that it had soap scum from 1845[36] still in the cracks of the tiles?" Tully looked up at me quite confused, but the other midshipmen laughed.

"And," I continued, "not only that, but the walls and the ceiling tiles produced so many dust bunnies that you would have to clean every day!"

"Dust *bunnies*!" Tully looked up and smiled as if seeing cotton-tailed rabbits hopping around.

"Oh yes, little balls of dust that collected all over the room, I would show you one, but this room is too brand new to have dust bunnies."

I turned to the plebe with a smile and said, "Well, it feels like my old room, but it sure looks different, and I must say these are pretty nice rooms they hooked you guys up with."

"Yes Ma'am—and I especially like my view from here!" replied the plebe as he turned his head towards the windows.

"I loved it as well," I walked over to the windows and pulled up the blinds. "Look Tully," I said picking him up so he could see over the window ledge. "See the tennis court down below? And now look to the left. See the water?"

"And look, Aunt Cathy, you can see the football field." As Tully and I continued to look out the window, I began to stare at the tennis court, then suddenly I let out a burst of laughter.

"What, Aunt Cathy?"

"Oh my gosh, the tennis court just reminded me of a very funny story."

"Can you tell me? *Pleeeease*, Aunt Cathy?"

....

36 The Academy was established in 1845.

I nodded my head yes as the midshipmen gathered closer. As the four of us stood looking out through the window, I began to tell a story that was sure to bring smiles to everyone…

Plebe Summer, Training, Day 35

Room inspections with Mr. Wyatt would continue throughout the summer. As the August wind blew cooler across the Yard, I had been hoping Mr. Wyatt would take after the seasons and begin to change, but to my disappointment, he did not. I tried my best to keep my shower scum-free, my deck polished, and my rack properly calibrated to the exact inch. I loathed Mr. Wyatt, and his constant visit to my room was just a constant thorn in my side. Why couldn't he be like the leaves, change color and fall off, out of my life? Instead, he held fast, waving his power and hovering over me.

Mr. Wyatt was specifically assigned to me, so his involvement in my training was mandatory. However, other 2nd Class midshipmen had stepped in and assisted in my training. One of them was Mr. Steinmann. Mr. Steinmann was a favorite among many of the plebes. He was tall, thin, and had a small patch of blond hair on the top of his shaved head. His extra-large wide smile and blue eyes softened his hardened face. He had come from the sands of Paris Island, a training facility whose fearsome reputation had made it famous. There he had earned the right to wear the "Globe and Anchor." He was a United States Marine and was proud of it.

Every aspect of Mr. Steinmann's character reflected his training and where he had come from. When he marched, his body was perfectly straight, in step, and never faltering. When he shouted cadence, his Marine Corps bark rolled out from the depths of his soul with command and confidence. His uniform was immaculate and worn with care. When he walked down the hallway, he walked with quiet, humble pride. His training style differed from the others in 34th Company. He did not yell, belittle, or constantly question us. He would simply talk to us and teach us what he knew.

I will never forget sitting in the hallway with a pair of my black shoes, a rag, and a can of shoe polish as Steinmann instructed us on how to get the perfect shine. He would sit on a chair in the middle of us, like a proud father with his children, and would tell stories of his boot camp days on "PI."[37] He would tell us of the sandflies that would get into his ears and eyes, biting mercilessly, while he stood for hours at attention. I would walk away from Steinmann, with not only a polished pair of shoes but more importantly with a polished sense of discipline.

I admired Steinmann for his leadership style, for he was able to find a balance between being serious and at the same time having a great sense of humor.

I remember this one day when I was on my way back from swimming lessons. I was wet and cold and rushing back up on deck before lunchtime formation. I squared the corner in front of the Watch Station, and as I pivoted to my right, I saw Mr. Steinmann and immediately stopped and stood at attention.

"Sir, Good Morning Mr. Steinmann, Sir!" I said loudly. I was praying that Mr. Steinmann wouldn't stop me because I hadn't read my three articles in the newspaper yet, and I was drawing a blank on all the information I was required to know for the day. I wasn't at all prepared. Suddenly he yelled "ER-VIN" in his famous Maine Corps bark.

"Yes, Sir!" I replied as I stopped again and stood at attention.

Mr. Steinmann looked at me with all seriousness and said, "Ervin, I hate to inform you of this, but your rack has committed suicide today!"

"Sir, Yes Sir?" I said with a confused look.

"Yes, an *unfortunate accident,*" Steinmann's smile spread across his face as he walked back to his watch post.

I continued down through the front shaft and then ran into my room. Immediately, I noticed the breeze rattling the metal blinds above the window and that the window was wide open. I glanced over to where my rack was, or where my rack should have been. My bed was completely gone. Only the wooden base was there. That probably would have been missing too if it hadn't been bolted to the deck.

I quickly put all the clues together: *Mr. Steinmann's words, an open window, and a missing rack.* I approached the window, hesitantly, afraid to look out. I glanced down to the green tennis courts and blinking

....

37   *PI:* Parris Island, Marine Corps Recruit Depot, Parris Island, South Carolina

my eyes in disbelief, I saw, my mattress, my sheets, my pillow, and my blanket all scattered across the tennis court.

I remember laughing at first, thinking it was funny how "*my rack had committed suicide.*" However, over the next couple of days, Mr. Steinmann continued to throw my rack out the window, and by the fourth time, the joke was getting old. Not only did I have to remake my bed each time, but also it was physically exhausting having to carry an old, heavy, sagging mattress up four flights of stairs. Sure, it's one thing if I could have walked, but I still had to chop and square corners.

Mr. Steinmann, however, enjoyed every minute of it. Each time I passed him in the hallway, lugging my mattress back to my room, he would make some smart comment followed by that smile.

"Not *again*, Ervin—that poor mattress must *really* be unhappy here!"

Or he would say, "I tried to stop him, Ervin. Really I did!"

Mr. Steinmann had gotten his point across. He was unhappy with the way my rack was being made, and this was *his* way of letting me know. He could have yelled at me, dropped me for pushups, or just ripped my rack apart (as the other upperclassmen would have done), but this was the unique training of Steinmann.

From that day forward, I worked harder at making my rack as perfect as I could. I never wanted to run up four flights of stairs with a mattress again, but more importantly, I never wanted to let Mr. Steinmann down again.

As Plebe Year moved along, I soon realized that Mr. Steinmann was the type of leader I wanted to be. He was tough, disciplined, and followed the corps values of the military. He carried himself with pride, pride in being both a Marine and a midshipman. He was committed to those underneath him, and he put others before himself. He taught from his heart and allowed his personality and his humor to shine through.

He could gain your respect and devotion, not by yelling, not by beating you into submission nor not by making you memorize useless quotes out of Reef Points, but by simply throwing a bed out of a window, by simply being Mr. Steinmann.

CHAPTER 8:

FAMILY

THE MIDSHIPMEN and I were laughing as I finished the story, both understanding the trials and tribulations of being a plebe. Tully was also laughing as he continued to stare out the window. I was glad he hadn't stopped to question what "suicide" was, glad that he was more focused on the fact that my entire bed had been tossed out the window.

"Well," I said looking at the plebe, "Thank you so much for allowing us to come into your room. It means a lot to me, and I am so sorry that we woke you up."

"You are welcome Ma'am," the plebe replied as he picked up a t-shirt off the floor, "Come back anytime."

Tully, Mr. Peters, and I said good-bye to the plebe. We walked past the multi-purpose furniture, stepped over the dirty clothes, and out of room 8315.

"So, what are we going to do now?" Tully asked quickening his pace down the P-way.

"Well, I wanted to go visit Mr. Wyatt for a little bit, okay?"

"Okay," Tully said running off ahead of me.

I walked over to the room that was right next to the watch station, the Company Officer's office. As I walked in, Tully followed with curiosity. Mr. Wyatt was sitting behind a large mahogany desk still talking on the phone. I placed a finger to my lips and motioned for Tully to sit with me on the coach that was across from the desk. Tully and I sat down and quietly looked around the room. I picked up one of the four yearbooks on the coffee table in front of us and opened it for Tully to look at.

"Gently," I whispered to Tully as he began to forcefully turn the pages. The Naval Academy's yearbook was called the "Lucky Bag" and was three-inches thick, filled with beautiful color pages. Tully had already found the Varsity Football Team's page. A page packed with shots of blue and gold jerseys, cheering fans, and Bill the Goat. *This should keep him occupied for a while*, I thought, as we waited patiently for Mr. Wyatt.

Within a matter of seconds, however, Tully was up, off the couch and walking out of the room. He looked back at me with the *"I'm-leaving-and-don't-try-to-stop-me"* look and then disappeared around the corner. *Great*, I thought, *it is probably not a good idea to let Tully roam 3rd Deck. Who knows what this kid will do—he does have a bit of his Aunt in him!* Actually, he had quite a lot of me in him: his sense of adventure, his determination, and his endless energy. I was so glad that he was part of my family; he had added so much to our lives in only four years, and I looked forward to the years to come.

Suddenly, as I was about to get up to retrieve my little plebe, he came stumbling in through the doorway carrying a large wooden object that was as big as him.

"What the...?" I said quickly getting up.

"Look, what I found Aunt Cathy," Tully said triumphantly. "It is a bullet from a tank." Tully was holding on to the wood with all his might. It was a replica of a bullet shell from a tank, used as decoration in front of the watch station.

"Oh, my gosh Tully! That is so cool! Now you better put it back before Mr. —"

Mr. Peters suddenly appeared in the doorway. "It's okay Ma'am," he said smiling down at Tully. "I was just showing him a few things."

"Thank you," I said as I watched in awe at the small boy still holding on to the heavy piece of wood. Finally, Tully put it down with a sigh and a wipe of his hand across his forehead.

"Phew, that is heavy," he said as he began dragging it back to the post. I glanced over to Mr. Wyatt who was still on the phone. I returned to my spot on the couch and Tully stayed in the hallway with Mr. Peters; there seemed to be more action on "Watch"[38] then in the Company Officer's room.

....

38 *Watch*: Mr. Peters was the "CMOW" Company Midshipman Officer of The Watch. "Watch" duty requires Mids to: Take charge of the area (post) and all government property; walk post on alert, observe everything within sight or hearing; quit post when properly relieved; give alarm in case of fire or disorder, be especially watchful at night, challenge all persons near post, and allow no one to pass without proper authority." "USNA Jargon," Sppausnaparents.com,https://sppausnaparents.files.wordpress.com/2014/10/usna-jargon.pdf

I looked over at Mr. Wyatt. It was a strange feeling to be sitting there as a "civilian" and as a "friend" to Mr. Wyatt. When I had found out that Wyatt was going to be stationed at the Naval Academy for three years of shore duty, I made sure to get in touch with him. He was married now to a wonderful woman and had been blessed with a beautiful son. He still loved the Navy evident by his active duty. He was also running an SAT tutoring business on the side, where he had discovered a new passion: teaching. He had taught me well, so I knew that his new endeavor would be successful.

I had filled him in on my past couple of years, backpacking through Europe, student teaching in New Zealand, climbing 19,000 feet to Mt Everest Base Camp in Nepal, teaching on a Navajo Indian Reservation, and my current business venture, EO-Challenge, a program I started where I combined education with outdoor adventure. Within our brief visits we often talked of our shared passion for education and of "the old Academy days." I enjoyed getting to know Jake as a person and not as an upperclassman. It was nice to be able to talk to him as friend to friend, and not as *plebe* to *Sir*.

As I waited on the couch, I continued to look around Mr. Wyatt's room. I immediately spotted something gold in one of the corners. It was a wooden pole with a small gold flag on the end. It was leaning up against the wall. The flag was unfurled, revealing the numbers 34 in blue lettering. I couldn't believe it! Mr. Wyatt had the guidon for 34th Company! Like a retired jersey hanging in a stadium, the 34th Company guidon had retired, but it had left behind a legacy that would not be forgotten.

Each company had a flag, called a "guidon,"[39] which was used to lead the company for various reasons. It was held high when marching through Annapolis on the way to a football game, it waved while marching past crowds of visitors during a dress parade, and it blew in the early morning breezes on our Company runs. At one time there had been a

....

39 37. *Guidon:* In the United States Army, Navy, Air Force, Marine Corps and Coast Guard, a guidon is a military standard that company/battery/troop or platoon-sized detachments carry to signify their unit designation and branch/corps affiliation or the title of the individual who carries it. A basic guidon can be rectangular, but sometimes has a triangular portion removed from the fly (known as "swallow-tailed"). "Guidon (United States)," *Wikipedia*, https://en.wikipedia.org/wiki/Guidon_(United_States)

total of thirty-six companies at the Academy, but now there were only thirty, due to the cutback in the size of attendance. Mr. Wyatt's pride in 34th Company was evident by his keeping of the 34th Company guidon. The flag was a reminder of his belonging to a family; a family he was proud of and would always be a part of. As I stared at the flag, I thought of 34th Company; they were my family too. I wondered where everyone was. The Naval Academy was our mother, and we had been separated after birth. We were now scattered across oceans and foreign lands. We would journey down different paths, but we would never forget where we had come from. There would always be comfort in knowing that you were part of a special family.

I began to think of one incident at The Naval Academy Preparatory School (NAPS); an incident in which I had felt this sense of a "special family" for the very first time.

Newport, Rhode Island: Naval Academy Prep School, 1993

My body was shaking from the inside out. My feet were cold, and my heart continued to race as I took a deep breath. I was standing in front of a closed wooden door. My fist was an inch away from it, ready to knock. I glanced down at my black uniform. Every tuck, every crease, every button was in place. Every piece of thread, every bit of lint had been removed. My shoes shined like chrome. I had spent hours polishing myself until I glowed with perfection, or at least with my idea of perfection. My uniform would be the first thing he would see, therefore it had to make a good first impression; an impression that would reflect my pride, my dedication, and my attention to detail.

As I tremored in front of the door, doubts began to creep back into my head. Once again, I was wavering back and forth like an untied boom on a sailboat.

"*I shouldn't be doing this.*"

"I have to… the other women are relying on me."

"*Am I making this something into more then what it is?*"

"No, this is a very serious matter."

"*I should turn back now.*"

"No, you shouldn't. You have moral obligations and values to uphold."

I tried to suppress my thoughts; I could not give them a chance to take over; I had a job to do. I had thought about this enough; it was time to act. I took a deep breath and knocked three times upon the door.

"Midshipman Candidate Ervin reporting as ordered, Sir, permission to come aboard?"

I stood at attention with my eyes fixed on the wood, waiting for a response, then suddenly I heard a deep muffled voice from inside. "Come aboard Ervin."

I turned the doorknob with my slippery hand. I stepped into the room and cautiously closed the door behind me. The room was small, just big enough to fit a desk and a few bookcases. I approached the wood desk in front of me. It was shinier than a polished pair of boots. Bronze pillars stood on the sides, aligned with the top of the desk. They shined as if they had been polished as well, and as I moved closer, I realized that they were bullet shells from a tank.

I glanced upwards towards a red glow coming from behind the desk. A flag the size of the wall was pinned at the corners. In the middle of the red flag, was a gold coat of arms—*a family crest.* It was not a shield of any kind, but rather a globe with an eagle and an anchor.

"Ervin, you may have a seat," said the man from behind the desk.

I left my position of attention and sat down in a leather chair facing the desk. I sat on the first four inches of the chair, with my back straight, and my hands folded in my lap.

I looked across at the man. He reminded me of a bulldog. He was sitting at his desk slightly hunched over, with huge arms resting underneath broad shoulders. It looked as if he had no neck, as I noticed his bald head motionless upon the buttoned collar of an olive-green shirt. He had an eager look in his eyes. Whether it was an eagerness to attack or an eagerness to listen, I was unsure. I was sure of one thing though: he was *not* smiling.

"Let's begin by having you tell me what you told Senior Chief Flora."

As he spoke, his lips curled up like a snarl. I looked into his brown eyes and began to speak, my words spilling unsteadily from my mouth, "First of all, Major Parrino, I want to apologize for jumping my Chain of Command.[40] I know I should have talked with my Company Officer first, but I found it too difficult to approach him on this matter. I needed to talk with a woman and someone I felt comfortable with, so that is why I went straight to Senior Chief."

As I said this, the Major nodded his headed understandingly. "I'm just glad that you went to someone. Usually in a matter like this, Ervin, people are too afraid to talk. I applaud you for your courage. Courage, Ervin, is not just being brave. When we think of courage, many of us think of it like charging an enemy bunker amidst gunfire, despite personal injury. Courage is also moral and mental strength to do what is right, even in the face of personal and professional adversity, standing up for what is right when others do not. I know this must be uncomfortable for you right now; I know it is difficult."

"Yes Sir."

"Well, before you continue, let me just tell you that I think of each of you here as one of my children. I feel that it is my duty to protect you, to see to it that none of you are hurt in any way, and that is why I am genuinely concerned right now."

I looked into the Major's eyes as he spoke, and I could tell that he was speaking from his heart. I no longer saw a bulldog, but for the first time, I saw him as a person—as a father—a father showing concern for one of his daughters. I smiled and continued talking, now feeling more at ease.

I took a deep breath and began, "This all began about a month ago in Lt. Conrad's English class. We had just finished reading a novel and our class was now focused on the discussion of the book. One day our discussion centered on a particular scene in the book in which the main character loses her virginity. Lt. Conrad singled out midshipmen Candidate Abby Mitchell and me, the only two females in the class,

---

40 *Chain of Command*: Everyone in the military has a chain of command. The chain of command is used to issue orders (downward) and to ask for clarification and resolve problems (upward). The military chain of command is such an integral part of military life. "Basic Training Chain of Command," *Military.com*, https://www.military.com/join-armed-forces/basic-training-chain-of-command.html

and began asking us questions." I paused. The Major nodded his head reassuringly, urging me to continue.

"Lt. Conrad asked us if we could explain to the class how a man can tell if a woman is a virgin or not. He continued to ask questions that not only offended us but also embarrassed us, questions you would not openly discuss among a room full of immature males. Lt. Conrad did not even act professionally; he laughed as if enjoying the fact that we were being verbally violated. To make matters even worse, our classmates joined in with the interrogation. Midshipman Candidate Mitchell and I were speechless and offended. During the next day in class, Lt. Conrad showed us a video on female circumcision performed in certain tribes in Africa. The video was not only graphic, explicitly showing what happens, but it had no connection to the novel. Once again, Midshipman Candidate Mitchell and I sat in silence feeling uncomfortable, embarrassed, and violated."

As I spoke to the Major, I began to get angry as I thought about Lt. Conrad. I could picture his face: his pallid, chapped lips cracking as he smiled; his wire-rimmed glasses wrapping around his bony face. I could hear his taunting laugh and see his blue Air Force uniform. The more I thought about him, the angrier I became.

"I am appalled," the Major said as eyes filled with anger, "and I apologize for what has happened. I promise you that Lt. Conrad will not get away with this."

"Thank you, Sir."

"This will not get easier for you, however."

"What do you mean Sir?"

"You will have to testify in front of the Captain, and you will probably go through some interrogation from the Academic board."

"Yes Sir."

"I will move you and midshipmen Candidate Mitchell into a different English class, though, so I am sure that will be some relief."

"Yes Sir. Thank you, Sir."

"Thank *you*, Ervin, for speaking up. I am glad that this has been brought to our attention, and as you know, others are now beginning to speak."

I began to think about Senior Chief Flora who I had first turned to. After listening to my story, she told me of a confrontation that *she* had

had with Lt. Conrad a while back. She had never mentioned it before to anyone.

"I will be letting you know when we will be meeting with the Captain. Until then, try to concentrate on your sports and academics. This will all be taken care of, I promise, so you can rest assured."

"Yes Sir."

"By the way, speaking of sports, how is your volleyball team doing?"

"Good sir, we have a tough team and Senior Chief Flora is a great assistant coach!"

"Well, that is good to hear. As you know, Senior Chief is there for you on and off the court; you make sure to maintain communication with her. Your company officer has been informed of all of this as well, so you have a network of support."

"Thank you, sir."

I began to think of Senior Chief Flora and how comfortable I felt with her; how much I trusted her. When Abby and I decided that we needed to tell someone about what had happened, without hesitation, I went straight to Senior Chief.

I had come to know "Senior" (as the volleyball team called her) on a different level than the other Napsters, and the recent drama that was unfolding only deepened our friendship.

Senior Chief Flora was a beautiful Mexican woman with dark skin and eyes. Her thick curly black hair was always braided neatly, and her lips painted with a touch of pink. She had worked her way up the enlisted ladder in a man's Navy with determination and discipline. She was tough, smart, focused, and her character was built on the military's values and her strong morals.

She roamed the Prep School hallways focused and intense, unapproachable, and intimidating. The sound of her raspy voice blaring over the intercom made all of us cringe as we awaited the storm that her angry voice would stir among the airwaves.

I first met Senior in the early weeks of NAPS Indoc.[41] She gathered all the females for a mandatory meeting, *all twenty of us*, and discussed certain "female issues" that we would soon be encountering: the changes

....

41 *Indoc:* Short for "Indoctrination," which was NAPS version of Plebe Summer.

in our bodies due to the high level of stress and physical activity, how to maintain proper behavior and modesty in a male-dominated workplace.

I immediately liked and respected Senior from the start. She was straightforward and honest. She was proud to be a woman and never held her standards lower than a man's. She was tough, strong, and confident. She carried herself with pride, strength, and she demanded respect. She was professional and treated us as adults, holding us to a higher standard. Senior Chief Flora was everything I had hoped a woman in the military was, and she was everything *I wanted to be.*

Throughout the year I had the privilege of getting to know Senior on a deeper level. She was the assistant volleyball and basketball coach. She not only helped at practices and accompanied us on road trips, but she became a den-mother to all the girls, taking us under her wing. She was tough on us but allowed her soft side to shine through. She would invite us to her home for Belgian waffle sundaes, joke around with us at practice, and would talk with us as "one of the girls."

When she was on duty as Officer of the Watch, I often laughed at the reaction in my company as a certain phrase crackled through the intercoms:

"This is Senior Chief Flora!"

The guys would cringe and groan as the woman of their nightmares was taking over the ship. For me, it was like hearing a mother's voice and it filled those nights with comfort and joy. It would make my day because I knew that before lights were turned out for the night, Senior Chief would be joining my friends and me for prayer time.

When the incident with Lt. Conrad happened, Senior Chief and I reached another level of friendship. She was more than just a mother away from home; she was truly a kindred spirit. It felt as if God had sent me one of his angels to watch over me, and He had disguised her in a Navy uniform.

As a mother, she protected and watched over me. As an officer, she gave me an example of leadership. As a friend, she encouraged and listened to me.

As I thought about Senior, I looked at the man in front of me. A man who had the same qualities and character as my "Navy-mom." I had never met the Major until now, but I knew who he was. He was second in command at the Prep School, our XO: "Executive Officer." He was the officer that scared us. He walked the hallways with intensity in his eyes and seriousness in his step. No one ever feared the Captain, but we all feared the Major.

The Major demanded respect, and we gave it. He demanded perfection, and we tried to achieve it. His room inspections were brutal and by the end of the year, they had become legendary. Room Inspections were held on Friday nights when our liberty was supposed to begin. Liberty, however, *had to be earned*, and we never seemed to earn it until Saturday morning. We were held captives on Base until every single room met the XO's expectation. While other college freshmen were enjoying their Friday nights with parties, beer, and freedom, we were on our hands and knees scrubbing decks, polishing drainpipes, and measuring the folds in our beds. The Major epitomized discipline and attention to detail. He was known for taking the attention to the extreme and for his legendary room inspections, often taking out a paperclip and scraping out dirt from a crevasse in the corner of your room.

Uniform inspections were just as tough. We polished our hardest, trying to shine with perfection. *Major's perfection.* If there was one thing I learned from the Major, from the very beginning, it was that the Marines were different from the other officers. They were a different breed. They seemed to demand more and held their standards higher. They walked with more pride, shined with more perfection, and expected more out of you. I soon learned that it was an honor to be a Marine, for they were *the best.*

Major Parrino had never met me before the incident, but he had always known who I was. I had left an impression on him during the first few months at NAPS. He saw me dropped for push-ups once, with a smile on my face, and took notice of my energy, spunk, and enjoyment in physical challenges. He nicknamed me "Sunshine," and I was told by the other officers that I was the only one they had ever known that could make the Major smile. As I was now finding out, there was another side to the Major, the soft side or rather the emotional side. (*We would never call a Marine "soft."*) I was beginning to see that the Marines stood apart in another way; they genuinely cared for the people within their command. They treated them like family, caring for them, guiding them, and ultimately giving their life for them. I felt like I had a father away from home. I knew I would be taken care of.

The major cleared his throat, pulling me away from my thoughts and back to the present. "I apologize for this Ervin; I guess you can look at all of this as a learning experience. Not only are you learning about yourself and the strength of your character, but you are also learning about the different types of leaders there are. With each leader you meet, take the good and throw away the bad; build yourself as a leader in this way." The major paused and then softly said, "Thank you again for coming to me. Do you have any questions for me?"

"No Sir, thank you, Sir. I appreciate you listening to me and believing me."

The Major lowered his head and then looked up at me, his brown eyes reflecting the strength and firmness in his voice, "Ervin, you are *one of mine*. I will *not* let anything happen to you."

With a sailor's knot in my throat and tears held at bay, I got up from my chair and stood at attention. "Sir, Permission to shove off?"

"Permission granted Ervin."

I wanted to reach out and hug the Major, but I knew that I had to keep my military bearing[42] and my professionalism. I just wanted to express what I had been feeling for the past half hour, and what I had felt when my thoughts had drifted to Senior Chief. I wanted to thank them for being there for me in one of the most critical times in my life. A time when I was on my own, separated from my family and friends; a time when I was still in the process of growing and trying to find out who I was; a time when I was learning about the new life I had chosen for myself.

I took another glimpse at the large red flag with the gold coat of arms; a flag that represented my new family. As I walked out of the room, the image of the globe and anchor stayed in my mind as did the words of the Major and the thoughts of Senior.

....

42 *Military Bearing:* Bearing is the way you conduct and carry yourself. Your manner should reflect alertness, competence, confidence, and control. An officer who exhibits bearing is one who is in total control of his emotions, posture, and general outward appearance. Discipline and self-respect are the keys to bearing. "Marine Corps Leadership Traits," *Officercandidateschool.com*, https://officercandidatesschool.com/2012/10/12/marine-corps-leadership-traits-bearing/

As I opened the door to leave, I turned and gave the Major one of my smiles; he smiled back. From that point on, I never felt alone. For the first time I was okay with having my family 500 miles away from me, for I was now part of a new family; a new family that would continue to nurture, guide, and protect. I would not be the person I am today if it hadn't been for Major Parrino and Senior Chief Flora.

CHAPTER 9:
NEVER LEAVE
A MAN BEHIND

"PRETTY COOL, HUH?" Mr. Wyatt said, noticing that I was staring at the guidon. Like a gentle breeze, my mind blew from one family's flag to another, leaving the memory of Major Parrino and returning to the present.

"I made sure to get the guidon when they got rid of 34th Company. I just couldn't let it go; It's a piece of history."

"I know what you mean. It was a great company. *Membership has its privileges,*" I said quoting the company motto. "It *was* a privilege, although as a plebe my attitude had been quite the contrary, and I must tell you, Jake, that I never liked you very much!"

Mr. Wyatt laughed, "Oh, I know! it was hard to deal with you too, Ervin, but somebody had to do it!"

I smiled at the fact that I had been Mr. Wyatt's "problem child."

"So, what about 29th Company? How are your Mids doing this year?"

"We're hanging in there; it has been a rough year. There have been so many changes since you were here, Cath. It's been a challenge because we just can't discipline like we used to."

"I think I just got a glimpse of what you are talking about, Jake. The plebe in my old room had his door locked and his room was a mess. I can't believe that is allowed."

"Not like the good ole days, right Ervin!" Wyatt smiled with the wink of his eye. "There are many things that have changed, some for the better and some for the worse. It's been rough here in 29, and my performance as a company officer has been under heavy scrutiny. We are considered "the black sheep" of the brigade because of all the trouble that my Mids have managed to get into. I am so worried about my "fit-report."[43] The marks on the paper, I fear, will not be good even though I am a good company officer. I have just been dealt a bad hand."

"Jake, you are a *great* officer, and I am forever grateful for what you taught me. I will never forget how you helped me during *my own* "perception problem." During that difficult time, you had said to me that *you knew who I was*, despite what others *had perceived*. Jake, *Mr. Wyatt*, I know who you are, and you will make it through this."

"Well, thanks Ervin, and we did work hard to straighten you out, didn't we?"

"We sure did!" I said smiling. We both paused realizing that we shared more in common than just the 'blue and gold."

The silence we found ourselves in did not last long as a small burst of energy bolted through the door.

"Oh my gosh, Aunt Cathy, guess what?"

"What, Tully?" I replied to the small ray of light that was illuminating the somber room.

"Mr. Peters took me around the deck!"

"He did?" I said excitedly, "Well that was very nice of him!"

"Uh-huh, and I saw a picture of an airborne ranger, and a submarine... and I... I helped him on watch we had to walk around and make sure everything was okay... midshipmen Peters is my friend."

As I listened to Tully talk about the new friends he made, the pictures, the bulletin boards, and the bathrooms, I realized how happy he was here. I watched him talk; his sparkling blue eyes, his laughter, his cute-4-year-old expressions. *This right here*, I thought, *this complete joy. His happiness, this is what makes this all worthwhile.* Sure, it was hard to be back on the Yard, it was hard to open the door to some painful memories that I had locked away, but I had given the key to Tully to unlock them, and he was worth every minute I was back and every memory that was released.

....

43 *Fitness Report:* A Fitness Report (FITREP) is an evaluation form used by the United States Navy and United States Marine Corps. Navy officers are given Fitness Reports, while Navy chief petty officers (E-7 to E-9) are given "Chief EVALs" and Navy sailors E-6 and below are issued Evaluation Reports (EVALs). "Fitness Reports," *Wikipedia,* https://en.wikipedia.org/wiki/Fitness_Report

"Here Tully, I have something for you," Mr. Wyatt quickly opened his desk drawer. Within seconds, Tully was at Mr. Wyatt's side staring up at him with the "I am so cute, please can I have it" face.

"This is an official Navy pin that you can wear on your coat." Mr. Wyatt handed Tully a tiny gold pin of the Naval Academy Emblem[44].

"Thank you, Sir,"

"I have a feeling that one day, you will make a fine Naval Officer," Mr. Wyatt gently patted Tully on the back.

Tully looked up at him mischievously and said, "Well—I want to be in the *Army!*"

Tully had learned that uttering the "A word", especially at the Academy, could get him quite a reaction.

"What!?" Mr. Wyatt yelled.

"Please, don't tell me you like Army," Mr. Wyatt said pretending to be angry.

"Go *Army*, Beat *Navy!*" Tully replied quickly backing towards the door.

"Why you—" Jake lunged towards Tully, who squealed with delight and bolted out into the hallway. Jake and I ran after him and soon captured the blasphemy-speaking boy who had taken cover behind Mr. Peters at the watch station.

"Do you know what an upperclassman would do if he heard you saying that?" Jake said as I lifted Tully into my arms. "He would… well, I am not sure, because I don't think a plebe would *ever dare* to say such a thing. I must say, Tully, you are a brave little boy, but I am going to warn you, you better not go around the Yard yelling that again, okay?" Jake smiled at Tully and rubbed his head. Tully was shaking with laughter as I kissed him.

"Okay buddy, so where should we go now?"

....

44 *Navy Emblem/Seal:* The coat-of-arms, or seal, consists of a hand grasping a trident, a shield bearing an ancient galley ship coming into action, an open book (representing education), and a banner with the motto "Ex scientia tridens," meaning "from knowledge, sea power." Designed by Park Benjamin, Naval Academy Class of 1867, the seal was adopted by the Navy Department on Jan. 25, 1899. "USNA Seal," *Usna.edu*, https://www.usna.edu/PAO/faq_pages/Seal.php

"I want to see John Paul Jones's crypt," Tully said sliding down out of my arms. Jake looked over at me with a raised eyebrow.

"He knows about John Paul Jones?"

"Of course he knows about him, right Tul? Tully nodded his head with pride as if he knew the man personally.

"Who was he, Tul? Now, remember, he wasn't a pirate because that would mean he was bad, but rather he was a—"

"He was a privateer!" Tully replied confidently.

"You are correct, and can you tell me, Tully, why he is so important? He is the "Father of the…"

"Navy!" Tully shouted.

"You are correct again," I said bending down to hug him.

"Yes Mr. Wyatt, Tully knows all about good ol' John Paul, about pirates, privateers, cannon balls, and the great sea battles of long ago."

I looked at my nephew with pride. Not only did Tully have a good memory, but he also had a strong interest in the Navy, as well as in pirates, and therefore the story of John Paul Jones had become one of his favorites.

"Well, I think we are going to shove off here sir," I said to Mr. Wyatt. "Thank you so much for having us up here. Tully, what do you say to Mr. Wyatt?"

"Thank you, Sir," Tully said hugging Jake around the leg.

"And what do you say to midshipmen Peters?"

Tully turned towards Mr. Peters and placed his hand to his eyebrow and saluted. "Thank you, Sir."

Midshipmen Peters smiled and saluted him back, "You are a great soldier, Tully."

"Thank you, Mr. Peters," I said, "I wish you all the best of luck here, and I know that you will make a great Naval Officer one day."

"Thank you, Ma'am, and you and Tully are always welcome up here on deck!" midshipmen Peters replied returning to his post at the watch station.

Tully and I waved goodbye to Mr. Wyatt, Mr. Peters, and the other midshipmen who had gathered around to say goodbye to us. We walked through the double doors, back down the plebe ladderwell, and out of 8th Wing.

I reached down and patted Tully on the back. "I am so glad that you got to see where I lived, Tul, and that you got to meet some people that were in my family."

"Yeah, but I am your family," Tully replied confused.

Taking what I learned, "never leave a man behind," into the next Arena—two of my Navajo students

"I meant my Naval Academy family. The Academy is like a big family that I was blessed to be a part of. You are my real family, Tul, and I am so glad that you are my nephew, my godson, and my best buddy—I wouldn't want anybody else!"

Tully looked up at me and smiled, "It was fun up on deck, can we go back?"

"Not today. We have other places to explore, but when we come back we can go up again!

I still could not figure out what I had been afraid of back up on deck. I was beginning to feel better after visiting with Jake, but there was still something in the pit of my stomach that would not go away.

Tully walked away from 29th Company with a sense of happiness and excitement. He had made new friends, friends that were *real* midshipmen, he had explored a secret area that was off-limits to civilians, and he had a small taste of life at the Naval Academy.

I walked away from 29th Company with a sense of pride yet at the same time sadness and loss. I felt proud as I walked through the deck, proud that I had been there, that I had been a plebe, that I had made it. Yet at the same time, I felt the loss of 34th Company, not only the loss of the physical company itself but also the loss of a family, the people of 34.

I looked down at Tully and smiled at my new family. I loved him so much, and I would give my life for him. As Tully held on to my hand, I knew that he had felt it. Being part of a family, whether you were born into it, or whether you joined it, was a feeling like no other in the world. He felt accepted and loved. Tully knew he would never be alone. I would always be there for him, and I promised to nurture, guide, and protect him. He was not only a blessing to me and my family, but I knew that one day he could be a great addition to another family, if he chose to join. I had vowed to never push the military on Tully, but I had promised to plant a seed. I only wanted him to be happy. Firefighters, policemen, and pirates were high up on his list, so I knew that the SEALS and the Marines would have some competition down the road.

Tully and I walked out from under the shadows of Bancroft and into the bright summer sun. We crossed the road and headed across a parking lot next to a building similar in structure to Bancroft. It was called "Dahlgren Hall"[45] and home to the Navy Ice Hockey team. I decided to bypass stopping in, for Tully had already been in Dahlgren. There was a small eatery inside where we would often come to enjoy a piece of "Navy Pizza." We continued through the parking lot, past 6th Wing, and towards a set of steps that continued along the rest of the south side of Bancroft. Suddenly, Tully saw the steps and immediately darted off without me.

"Wait up for me Tully," I said. "I don't want you leaving my side. We're a team; we stick together." Tully quickened his pace and took off running up the steps.

"*Tully!*" I yelled running after him. I never let him out of my sight. He had a "no fear" attitude and a thrill for danger. I was angry that he wouldn't listen at times and would take off unexpectedly. He was like a jet on a carrier; one minute right there in front of you, the next minute, a trail of smoke. My little "blue angel"[46] required a serious talk.

"*Tully!*" I said angrily as I caught up to the tired jet. I took his hand and knelt beside him.

"Tully, I am very upset. You left me back there all alone. I thought you wanted to be a good Naval Officer. Well, there is something very important that you must always remember."

"What, Aunt Cathy?"

"You must never leave a man behind."

"What do you mean?"

"Well, what if you were an officer in charge of a platoon of men, and let's say you are escaping from the enemy—well suddenly, one of your men gets hurt as you were running away—you are a good officer so you would go back to get him. *You never leave a man behind.*

....

45   *John A. Dahlgren* was appointed a midshipman in the U.S. Navy in 1826. Over a period of 15 years, from 1847 to 1862, he designed and produced several large-caliber naval guns including a boat howitzer and the eponymous Dahlgren gun—which would later become the most common cannon mounted on board U.S. Navy ships during the Civil War. Thus, he is called the "Father of Naval Ordinances." "John Adolphus Bernard Dahlgren," *Naval History and Heritage Command,* https://www.history.navy.mil/

46   *Blue Angel:* A word play on the Navy's Blue Angel which is the name given to their acrobatic show planes. The planes are F/A-18 Hornets and are painted navy blue and gold. In 1946, the Chief of Naval Operations, Admiral Chester Nimitz, had a vision to create a flight exhibition team in order to raise the public's interest in naval aviation and boost Navy morale. "Significant Events in Blue Angels History," *United States Blue Angels,* https://www.blueangels.navy.mil/history/

"Oh," Tully said quietly as his breathing slowed down.

I knew he was listening. I had established good communication with Tully at a young age. When I had something important to tell Tully, he would listen with remarkable attention. I would say to him, "*Tully, I have something to tell you*," and he would immediately hop up onto my lap and look me in the eyes. I could always see the innocence in his eyes, as he tried to understand something that was beyond his comprehension. What was amazing was his ability to make connections or to want to understand. He would show empathy, compassion, and a sense of wonder all within a softly spoken, "*Oh.*"

As I looked into his eyes, filled with soft blue, I desperately wanted to tell him about James Albert Graham, so that he would understand. It was a story that I had been told, which had helped me to understand, but a story, I decided, that Tully would have to hear when he was older. A story, that if told right now, would just fill his head with images of fighting, guns, and death. So, I decided to tell him another story.

"Tully, did I ever tell you about the time that I got in trouble for leaving a man behind?" Tully grabbed my hand, as I stood up.

"No," Tully said as we moved under the shadow of an area of Bancroft that connected the 6th Wing to the 4th Wing.

"Well, this story happened during Plebe Summer. You know the time when we were trained really hard?"

"With Mr. Gumery?" Tully questioned.

"That's right, with Mr. Montgomery, our Platoon Commander who was one of our toughest upperclassmen. Well, at that time, I had two friends who shared my room with me. One roommate was Lily Sinclair, who you already have heard about, and my other roommate was Anna Summers. Anna was a nice friend, but sometimes she was hard to live with. She had a hard time keeping up on our company runs, her uniform was always a mess, and she was very forgetful.

Well, every day during Plebe Summer, our companies would have to line up to go to lunch. It was called "Noon Meal Formation."[47] All

....

47 *Noon Meal Formation:* The entire brigade assembles each weekday at noon, then marches into lunch before crowds of tourists. Noon meal formations began in 1905, born from the tradition of mustering troops in the Civil War. Formations were once a way to keep account of midshipmen. They still call, "All present or accounted for," but the tradition has become more about pageantry. Tim Prudente, "Pageantry, tradition and jitters: Noon meal formation returns to the Naval Academy," *Capital Gazette Newspaper*, https://www.capitalgazette.com/education/naval-academy/ph-ac-cn-meal-formation-0324-20150323-story.html

the companies would meet here on T-Court." I pointed out towards the large courtyard across from where we were standing. "From 34th Company, we would have to run out of 8th Wing, across that parking lot, up the same steps we just climbed, and then line up in rows *right exactly* where we are standing now.

So anyways, on this one particular day, Lily, Anna, and I had just barely arrived in time for formation. We were so relieved that we had made it in time, that we didn't even notice that Anna was not wearing her cover[48]. In the Navy, we call a hat, a "cover." It was our Dixie cup hat—you know Tully, the white hat that I have given to you."

"Oh, the hat I wear when I play plebe?"

"Yes, that's the one," I said smiling at the thought of our unique playtime together.

"Well, suddenly," I said continuing, "Anna realized that her head was missing something, so she whispered to me that she had forgotten it. She got so scared at the thought of getting in trouble that she suddenly ran out of formation. Lily and I couldn't believe that she was going to go *all the way* back to her room to get her hat! She would miss formation and get in trouble with the upperclassmen!

As soon as Anna left, Mr. Montgomery walked past my row. As if he had radar, Mr. Montgomery stopped and turned towards me. Then he noticed the space where Anna should have been, and said angrily, "Ervin, where is Summers?"

Now, remember, we are called by our last names, so Montgomery was asking where Anna was. I quickly replied, "Sir, she forgot her cover and went back to get it, Sir."

Montgomery then moved right up into my face and said, *"What?* She forgot her cover?"

I then said, "Yes, Sir," hoping that Anna wouldn't get in trouble but instead of being mad at Anna, Montgomery was mad at me. Now, Tully, why do you think he might have been mad at *me*?" I looked down at Tully who was listening very intently.

"I don't know Aunt Cathy."

....

48　*Cover:* Name given to a Navy uniform hat. Sure, it is easier to say "hat," but it actually makes sense because a hat "covers" your head.

"Well, at first, I didn't know either. I thought it was because at that time I was going through a "perception problem" in which the upper-classmen were trying to correct my behavior as a plebe, and someone always seemed mad at me for something or other.

Well as I was trying to figure out what I did wrong this time, Montgomery looked me deep in the eyes, and said, "Ervin, why didn't *you go with Summers* to get her cover?"

'I don't know, Sir,' I had said.

I'll never forget how Montgomery's face became red with anger, and how he yelled for everyone to hear, "Ervin, *you never leave a man behind!*"

I bent down and looked into Tully's eyes. "Montgomery was teaching me a lesson that day. He wanted me to know that when you are in the military, one of the most important things to remember is to remember your friend next to you, to never leave him or her behind."

I looked out toward T-court, pausing as I thought of Anna and Mr. Montgomery.

"So, buddy, let's get going to see John Paul Jones," I said standing up.

"I will never leave a man behind," Tully said reaching for my hand.

I smiled at Tully, "Good, and neither will I."

As we continued down the sidewalk, on our way to the chapel, I began to think of how a few days after that incident in T-Court, I had come across a story, which reinforced the lesson Montgomery was trying to teach me.

* * *

It was a hot summer day in South Vietnam on June 2, 1967. A captain in the Marine Corps by the name of James Albert Graham was hiding quietly in a clear paddy in the province of Quang Tin. He was Commanding Officer of Company F of the 2nd Battalion, Fifth Marines, First Marine Division. His mission, called UNION II, was to launch an attack on an enemy-occupied position, with three companies, A D, and F. One company would stay in reserve, while Company F was to be the leading company.

As they began their attack, the enemies spotted the Marines and began bombarding the area with mortar and small-arm gunfire. The rain of fire continued to shower down upon the Americans, inflicting a great number of casualties. The hardest to be hit was Captain Graham's 2nd platoon in Company F. Not only were they wounded but also, they were pinned into a position where they were unable to evacuate the wounded.

Captain Graham bravely formed a small team of men to go and destroy the first machine gun position. He was able to take over the first enemy position, thus relieving pressure on his 2nd platoon and enabling the wounded to be evacuated. Captain Graham and his small force of brave men continued the assault on the second machine gun position. Despite, being injured twice, Captain Graham continued the attack while personally accounting for 15 enemy kills.

As the Eastern sun began to set, the enemy position remained invincible to the Captain's relentless attempts. Soon, Captain Graham's ammunition ran out, and he ordered the remaining men in his small team to retreat to friendly lines. Knowing full well, that if he left, he would have a chance for survival, he chose instead to stay with one of his men who could not be moved due to the seriousness of his wounds. In his last radio transmission, Captain Graham reported that he was being attacked by a force of 25 enemy Vietnamese.

Captain Graham died that day while protecting the man he chose not to abandon—the man he did not leave behind.

CHAPTER 10:

ROW 51

I LOOKED AHEAD at the Chapel[49] dome we were quickly approaching, as my little Blue Angel continued to speed along. I stared at the dome as I thought of my faith, and how God never leaves us behind. In fact, he sent his son Jesus to remind of us that.

"Come on, Aunt Cathy," Tully said as he continued to pull me along, not wanting to leave his man behind.

"I'm coming Tul," I said quickly, "I just was enjoying the view of the Chapel dome! Look at it Tul," I said stopping and pointing up to the sky, "Isn't it so beautiful?"

Tully stopped for half a second, glanced up, and quickly said, "Yes, now come on Aunt Cathy?"

I could understand Tully's sense of urgency. After all, there was a real privateer waiting for us.

Leaving Bancroft behind us, we crossed a small street and continued along a sidewalk leading to the front of the Chapel. The morning was warming up as the sun climbed higher in the sky. It was a perfect day to be at the Academy, a day that would rival one of the postcards at the Visitor Center. The yard was dressed for inspection. It was wearing Spring, its best uniform, and drops of dew had created the perfect shine. As we walked, I kept one eye on Tully and one on the chapel dome. The magnificent dome was framed by a bright blue sky. The closer we got to the chapel, the smaller I felt. Soon the blue-green copper dome was hovering 210 feet over us. The golden cupola glowed from the sun's touch as we approached the front entrance. Tully and I began climbing up the granite steps.

....

49 *Chapel*: The historic Main Chapel at the center of the Yard—and its landmark dome— are symbolic of the vital role that moral and spiritual guidance plays in the development of Midshipmen into naval officers. "Chaplain's Center Home," *Usna.edu*, https://www.usna.edu/Chaplains/index.php

"Why are these here?" Tully asked pointing to the large, mounted anchors flanking us on both sides.

"Those are real anchors from a Navy ship called the "New York." They put them here to remind everyone that our faith in God is like an anchor, it keeps us from floating away. It reminds us that Jesus wants us to stay anchored to him, to do what is good and be a good person."

Tully and I continued up the steps and through two 22-foot-high bronze doors. As we walked in through the portico, I dipped my hand in a large font of holy water and blessed myself. Tully, seeing me do this, blessed himself as well. We quietly walked into the sanctuary. I looked ahead of us at the long center aisle of blue carpet, a tempting runway for my little Blue Angel. I checked my side to make sure Tully was still there, for it was unusually quiet. This was the first time that I didn't hear any engines running.

I watched Tully as he walked with his head tilted back and his eyes reflecting the blue from inside the chapel. My first time in the chapel had taken my breath away. I knew that the feeling would be even more overwhelming for a child. The granite and gray brick walls with the rows of high arched windows, the endless sea of polished wooden pews, the illuminated dome of light, the feeling of grandeur and the presence of peace—it was a sight that could touch the heart of a man and plant the seed of faith in a child. I was praying that Tully would feel the presence of God in this chapel.

Tully and I walked to the center of the chapel where the sanctuary extended out to the left and right, forming the configuration of a Latin Cross. I lifted my head upward. We were underneath a dome of white. There was a crown of arched windows circling the dome, creating a mural of pale blue sky. It looked as if the dome was touching the Heavens, touching God like a Michelangelo fresco. Lights, like diamonds, sparkled against the dome's inside surface. My eyes hovered in the dome, circling around the different busts of famous figures that filled in the space between the windows. They stood as pillars representing the races of man in civilization. I immediately recognized the proud figure of Tecumseh, the great Indian chief. My gaze fell from the dome and landed on a marble ashlar with the carved words, "Eternal Father Strong to Save."

Below the ashlar was a stained-glass window with Christ walking upon the waters of a raging sea. The light shining through the window painted the waters in a mix of deep blues and stormy grays, and the figure of Christ illuminated in brilliant golds and yellows. This window had always been my favorite. When I looked at it, I felt as if my life was like the troubled waters. At times I felt alone in a raging sea. At these times, it was my faith, it was Christ, who calmed the storms and gave me strength, serenity, and encouragement.

Two marble columns framed this window and helped to guide the eye down to the alter underneath. The alter was protected in an arched cove of marble walls. The smooth walls were made of rectangles of sand and beige colored marble. I turned around and looked back down the main aisle to the chapel entrance. Above the choir loft and suspended from the 85-foot ceiling was a 12-foot-long ship. It was a common practice in Europe to hang a "votive ship" in a place of worship. It sends a message to the people that God protects seafaring men and women and brings them safely to a place of anchoring. The ship hanging in the Chapel was designed after a Flemish carrack,[50] but to me, it had the perfect makings for a pirate ship with its wooden hull, large canvas sails, and hoisted red flag.

"Tully," I said pointing at the ship, "there is the Pirate ship I was telling you about!"

"Oh my gosh," Tully said as he looked at the hanging ship.

"Is it real?"

"No," I said with a smile, "But it is designed after a real one. It would be too hard to fit a real Pirate ship in the chapel; it would be too big!"

"I would like to have that ship!"

"I wish I could give it to you, Tully, but it belongs to the Naval Academy."

"I could play in the bathtub with it!"

....

50   *Carrack:* A three or four-masted ocean-going sailing ship that was developed in the 14th to 15th centuries in Europe, most notably in Spain and Portugal. In their most advanced forms, they were used by the Portuguese for trade between Europe and Asia starting in the late 15th century, before eventually being superseded in the 17th century by the galleon, introduced in the 16th century. "Carrack," Wikipedia, https://en.wikipedia.org/wiki/Ca

"Now, that would be cool wouldn't it," I replied as I thought of Tully's aircraft carrier that often sailed on the seas of bathwater.

"Aunt Cathy is that John Paul Jones' ship?"

"No sweetie, that is just a model of a ship. John Paul Jones's ship was a real ship, and it was called the 'Bonhomme Richard.'"

"Oh," Tully said with his interest beginning to shift, "Can we go see John Paul Jones now?"

"Definitely," I replied with enthusiasm, "First, I would like to say a prayer by that candle. Would you like to say a prayer with me?"

"Yes," Tully replied as he took my hand. We walked back down the center aisle until we came to a pew where a single candle was mounted. I turned around, genuflected towards the alter, and walked into the pew directly behind the candle. I knelt, my knees feeling instantly at home upon the plush velvet cushion. Tully knelt beside me. My arms rested on the pew in front of me—Row 51—the only pew in the church that is roped off and kept empty of visitors. Empty, except for one candle. A candle that was always kept lit. I could smell the melting wax and feel random waves of heat brushing past my face. The plain white candle stood alone, held up by a black stone candle holder adorned with red and white carnations.

As I lowered my head in prayer, Tully quietly whispered, "What is this candle for?"

I looked up at the candle and paused for a moment as emotion began to overwhelm me.

"This candle, Tully, is the POW-MIA candle. POW stands for 'Prisoner of War,' and MIA stands for 'Missing in Action'. This candle is always kept lit and stands alone in this one row because it honors our military men and women that are either prisoners in another country, or that are missing. It is a reminder for everyone who comes in this chapel, to pray for these men and women; to remember that there are brave soldiers all over the world that have not made it home yet. We pray that God will keep them safe and bring them home to their families.

"Why are they prisoners?" Tully asked reaching towards the candle.

"Well," I replied pulling Tully's arm back, "they are prisoners because they were caught by an enemy. They were protecting our country and doing their jobs, their mission. The enemy wants to stop that mission, so they try to kill or capture that person."

"Oh," Tully replied with sadness in his voice.

I bent over and kissed Tully. "Why don't we say a prayer for all those men and women that are POW's?"

As I bowed my head in prayer I began to think back to the time when "POW" became more than just a common term, more than just an image on a black flag. I thought back to when "POW" took on a name, a face, and when it forever changed my life…

USNA Chapel. Notice the POW candle on the left hand side.

Plebe Summer, Training, Day 41

I poked my head out of my room to see a train of velvety blue bathrobes slowly disappearing around the corner of our hallway. It was silent in the hallway, except for the scuffing of slippers across the shiny deck. I grabbed my rifle placing the barrel against my right shoulder while holding on to the butt of the gun with my right hand. A month and a half of Plebe Summer had gone by, but the constant stress and anxiety had not.

"Quick Lily, everyone's already leaving," I said nervously, picking up a small, folded piece of paper.

"I've just got to grab my piece," Lily replied as she heaved the heavy rifle onto her tiny shoulder. I flicked off the lights and propped the door open.

"Ahh, the window," I said realizing I had left mine open.

"I've got it," Lily said as she quickly closed it.

"Thanks, let's go," I said taking a deep breath. "Oh, do you have your *thought*?"

"Yeah, thanks," Lily replied waving a small piece of paper in her hand. After the experience of having Anna as a roommate during the first set of Plebe Summer, I was now more careful to not leave anything behind.

Lily and I had to run in order to catch up with the rest of the plebes. Surprisingly, no detailers had spotted our undisciplined sprint down the hallway. Usually, there was always a detailer lurking around somewhere, watching every single move you made.

Lily and I caught up to the slow-moving train of plebes as it was inching its way around the corner. Once around the corner, the silent train split into two and began lining both sides of the hallway. I felt exactly how the plebe in front of me looked, exhausted. My shoulders were probably slumped over like his from the weight of the ten-pound rifle. It ends up feeling like thirty pounds when you factor in the extra weight of stress that builds up during the day. We were dressed for bed and sleep was knocking at our doors but being a plebe would continue until your head hit the pillow.

The train stopped and like an assembly of robots, we all turned and faced into the center of the hallway. With my back inches from the cinderblock wall and with my rifle at my side, I extended out my left arm, holding on loosely to a small piece of paper.

As I concentrated on the gold emblem on the bathrobe across from me, my squad leader walked by yanking the piece of paper out of my hand and adding it to his collection. I thought of what I had written on the paper.

"I can do all things through Him who strengthens me. Philippians 4:13." It was my mandatory "Thought of the Day;" a requirement by all of the

plebes which was collected each evening before Taps.[51] The "thought" gave our upperclassmen a brief glimpse into our heads. For me, the "thought" was a way to bring closure to my day. I usually wrote Bible scripture, which gave me strength and focus for the next day.

I had been going through a painful change and darkening of my spirit. The torment from Mr. Montgomery was getting worse, and I couldn't figure out why. I was giving 110% as a plebe. I loved the physical training and always wanted more of it. I was trying to learn everything that was thrown my way and believed in what I was learning. *Why then, was Montgomery so tough on me? Why was I always singled out?* His hatred for me was more than just my inability to recite "Man in the Arena." It went beyond that. *Why?* Over the past month and a half, Montgomery had crept into my head and had become my worst nightmare. It was my faith that gave me comfort and gave me strength. Montgomery was breaking me down, but my faith helped me to find my inner strength, and the fight within me to stand back up.

As the squad leaders collected the thoughts, I remained at attention with my eyes in the same spot, locked on the gold emblem. I did not dare look around. The slightest flinch of my eyeball would be considered a "lack of bearing." I pushed my heels closer together as I tried to get a perfect forty-five-degree angle in a pair of foam slippers. My left arm was now at my side with my thumb lined up against the imaginary seam on my bathrobe.

I could feel someone watching me; I knew that someone was watching me; there was always somebody watching. Every movement, every breath, was closely monitored. I learned to keep my body stiff, to tighten up every muscle, to control the urge to fidget. I would pick a crack in the wall, or a button on a shirt to stare at; I would stare at it until my eyes became unfocused until everything became a blur. The emblem, I had been focusing on, was now a blur of gold. Within my head, I began to say the "Man in the Arena" one last practice run before Mr. Montgomery came, before the dreaded command of, "Ervin! 'Man in the Arena'—*go!*"

....

51 *Taps:* The official military Taps is played by a single bugle or trumpet at dusk, during flag ceremonies and at military funerals by the United States Armed Forces. "Taps," www.usmemorialday.org, https://www.usmemorialday.org/taps

"It is not the critic who counts, not the one who points out how the strong man stumbled or how the doer of deeds might have done them better. The credit belongs to the man who is actually in the arena, whose face is marred with sweat and dust and blood..."

Suddenly I heard the voice of an upperclassman yell, *"Count!"* Like trained dogs, we all immediately snapped our heads to the right.

"Off!" was then shouted. Our heads snapped back to the front individually, one right after another, as if dominoes. With each turn of a head, a number was yelled. The count started at one and ended at thirty-three. Every plebe was present and accounted for.

With my eyes now locked back on the gold emblem, I began to hear the familiar slow-paced stride coming from the other end of the P-way. It was Mr. Montgomery. Instantly, fear and anxiety began to batter me like ocean waves against a tied up dingy. His presence alone was enough to demand discipline and respect. I straightened my back and tightened my fist. His voice, slow and serious filled the hallway.

"I will be reading you a passage from the Good Book tonight," he paused, "and each night for the rest of Plebe Summer." The suspense began to build as I wondered what the "Good Book" was.

"Does anyone know what the *Good Book* is?" Montgomery questioned as he paced back and forth through the hallway. I timidly stuck my closed fist out in front of me.

"What Ervin?"

"Is it the Bible, Sir?" I said with hesitation.

"No, Ervin," Mr. Montgomery replied. He held up the book for all of us to see. "The Good Book is a book that contains all of the people who have received the 'Medal of Honor,' the military's highest-ranking medal. It is a collection of stories; stories, which exemplify honor, courage, and commitment. They are stories that I want all of you to remember."

"Great," I thought. "More information to memorize." Not only was I disappointed that it *wasn't* the bible, but I was also upset that it was more work for all of us.

As Mr. Montgomery passed in front of me, I looked at the blue-covered book that he held reverently in his hands. He stopped in the middle of the P-way, leaned against the bulkhead,[52] and quietly opened the book.

"Rear Admiral James B. Stockdale of the United States Navy, " Mr. Montgomery began softly, as he gazed upon the white pages. The words penetrated the silence that his presence had instantly created. Mr. Montgomery continued to read the citation with an intensity and passion that immediately spoke right to my heart. Mr. Montgomery continued, going beyond the printed pages in order to explain the details of the citation. I listened as the story of an amazing man began to unfold:

> *The date was the ninth of September, 1965. James B. Stockdale was the Commander and the senior pilot of Air Wing 16 flying combat missions off the "USS Oriskany," in south Hanoi, Vietnam. His mission was to take out the Thanh Hoa Bridge. For weeks, the attacks had been unyielding as his A-4E Skyhawks dropped 500-pound bombs on the bridge. Despite this continuous onslaught, the structure was unable to be destroyed and soon became a symbol of resistance for the North Vietnamese.*

> *On this particular day, a new plan of attack was put into effect. The mission had been altered in which 2,000-pound bombs would replace the 500-pound bombs and would hang from the F-8 bombers as well as from the attack planes. However, at the last minute, the mission was abandoned due to zero-zero visibility over the bridge.*

> *Despite the disappointment, Stockdale continued with the secondary targets in mind, boxcars along the railroad between the villages of Thanh Hoa and Vinah. Unfortunately, Stockdale never finished the mission. He was shot down by enemy gunfire and within a matter of seconds, he was injured, alone, and in enemy territory.*

....

52 *Bulkhead:* Nautical terminology for a wall-like construction inside a ship or airplane, as for forming watertight compartments or strengthening the structure, and thus what a midshipman would call a wall.

Stockdale was immediately captured by the Vietnamese and taken to Hoa Lo prison, where he would spend the next seven and a half years of his life as a prisoner of war.

At Hoa Lo, Stockdale had a new mission: to stay alive and to assist others in staying alive. Stockdale became the leader in a Prisoner of War Resistance. Not only did he establish a prisoner's code of conduct[53], but also he established communication with the other prisoners through clandestine means. The whole concept of this code of conduct was based on the "prisoner next door," placing prisoner unity over selfish interests.

Stockdale embodied this code by his personal sacrifices and unselfish attitude. The Vietnamese aware of his resistance and his leadership role were relentless with the physical and mental abuse they continuously put him through. Stockdale was tortured fifteen times, he was in leg irons for two years, and he was in solitary confinement for four years. When the Vietnamese extortionists tried to force him to participate in propaganda exploitation, Stockdale resisted through self-mutilation. In one incident, he cut his head with a razorblade; in another, he beat himself with a wooden stool until his eyes swelled shut. At one point, he had even managed to smash his face against a brick wall. Due to Stockdale's self-mutilation, the extortionists were unable to proceed with TV filming. The disfigured and un-presentable prisoner had made it clear that he would not be exploited.

There were times when the extortionists had caught Stockdale during a resistance. For example, there was an incident where a hidden note had slipped out of Stockdale's pants and had been found. Upon the interrogations that followed, Stockdale inflicted a near

....

53   A code of conduct similar to the *Code of Conduct*, presented on April 17,1955 by Presi-dent Eisenhower, which contains six statements of principles that Americans in the military must believe in and must live by. "Military Code of Conduct," *Vetshome.com*, http://www.vetshome.com/military_code_of_conduct.htm

mortal wound by slicing his wrists with shards of glass. This action of self-sacrifice saved the purging and death of those lives that could have been uncovered by the note that had been found. This action and all the actions that had preceded it eventually caused an end to the physical and mental torture toward all Prisoners of War.

By Stockdale's heroic action, at great peril to himself, he earned the eternal gratitude of his fellow prisoners and his country. Rear Admiral Stockdale's valiant leadership and extraordinary courage in a hostile environment sustain and enhance the finest traditions of the U.S. Naval Services.

Mr. Montgomery stopped speaking. The words "valiant leadership and extraordinary courage" seemed to hang in the air as we all stood at attention in complete silence. Mr. Montgomery kept his head down with his eyes fixed on the pages of the Good Book.

The loudspeaker in the P-way began to crackle with static and soon broke our trance. We all joined in singing the song that was now flooding the P-ways throughout Bancroft Hall.

Now, sailor men in battle fare,
Since fighting days of old,
Have proved the sailor's right to wear
The Navy, Blue and Gold

Beat Army Sir.

At 2300 hours every night, "Navy Blue and Gold" was sung, bringing an end to another day in the life of a midshipman. To plebes, this simple song was a comfort. The demands of the day; the rates[54], the chopping,

---

54 *Rates:* Term used to describe certain minimum requirements expected of all plebes. They consist of information that a plebe is held accountable for; information which they are tested on constantly throughout the day by all upperclassmen. Rates consist of information out of *Reef Points*, the professional topic of the week, the menu for the next meal, the Officers of the Watch, major events scheduled for the day, formation calls, conversational knowledge of three newspaper articles, the number of days until important dates such as First Class Graduation or the Army Navy game.

and the push-ups, were over for now. It was a chance to sleep it all off, to put the worries aside, and to prepare for the start of a new day.

Tonight, however, "Blue and Gold" signified something even greater for me, something that would have a profound impact on my life. It signified the fact that here we were as plebes trying to prove our right to be a part of the United States Naval Academy. In the big picture though, we were being prepared to prove our worthiness as a person in the military. I began to think of those who had proved their right to wear *much more* than simply the Blue and Gold. They were the ones who went beyond the call of duty proving their right to wear the Medal of Honor.

As I laid in my bed that night, I thought of how I had first thought Mr. Montgomery's "Good Book" was the bible. Ironically, in many ways, *it is like the Bible.* The Bible is a collection of stories that embody the teachings of Jesus Christ and is a guideline as to how we should live our lives as Christians. The Good Book is a collection of stories of individuals who embody everything a military person should be. They embody certain values such as courage, honor, and commitment. They embody certain spirits such as enthusiasm, patriotism, and heroism. Most importantly, they embody the greatest act of love, giving their life so that others may live.

Like Christ in the Bible, the men and women in the Good Book are our guidelines. They are examples of how we should live our life. We should look to them for guidance each day, whether it is in times of peril or in times of great joy. They are what inspire us to be the best person that we can be.

As I drifted back to Tully and the Chapel, I began to think of the story that I had heard; the story that I would tell others, as Mr. Montgomery had told to me; the story that would have a continuous impact upon my life.

I opened my eyes and stared at the candle in front of me. The yellow flame danced quietly. The memory of those POW's would always stay lit, and as the candle flame, that memory would continue to burn in the hearts of those who understood.

I looked over at Tully, who was still kneeling beside me. "Tully, I want to say one last prayer out loud and then we can go, okay?"

Tully smiled as I softly recited the Navy Hymn,

Eternal Father strong to save,
Whose arm hath bound the restless waves,
Who bid the mighty ocean deep,
Its own appointed limits keep,
O hear us when we cry to thee,
For those in peril on the sea.

Amen.

The words "for those in peril on the sea" continued to echo in my heart. I knew that *those in peril* were classmates of mine, they were POW's, and they were MIA's. They had all taken on a similar job, a job that involved great risk and danger, a job they were willing to sacrifice their lives for. We will never know how many are still in peril across various seas, but what we do know is that their memory is being kept alive and will never be forgotten.

As I watched the candlelight dance, I pictured a POW, his face marred with sweat and dust and blood, lying alone upon a cold dark floor, bruised and beaten. I then pictured Admiral Stockdale, with his head held high, and with the Medal of Honor pinned upon his chest; a medal that he had unquestionably proven the right to wear. I quietly whispered, "thank you," as I lowered my head over Row 51.

CHAPTER 11:

12 KILLS

I LOOKED AWAY from the POW candle to see Tully walking away from Row 51 and down the center aisle. I quickly made the sign of the cross and walked out of the pew.

"Okay," I said catching up to Tully, "Let's go find John Paul Jones, the most famous of all privateers!"

"Where is he Aunt Cathy," Tully asked looking around the corner.

"We have to go underneath of the Chapel to where the crypt is."

Tully and I pushed open a smaller set of wooden doors to the right of the main doors, ran down a flight of steps, and exited the Chapel. The sunlight greeted our squinting eyes as we walked down another set of stairs. We were now eye level with the foundation as we pulled open a heavy metal door.

Tully and I stepped into the thick darkness, as silence crept in around us. The room was circular with green marble flooring and black and white marble pillars. A circular walkway was separated from the center of the room by a rope. In the center, on a sunken marble floor, rested an ornate marble structure. The indirect and dim lighting around the room created a theatrical feel.

"Where is he?" Tully whispered.

"John Paul Jones is right in there," I said pointing at the sculpture in the center of the room, at center stage. The work of art had been crafted by a French sculptor who had used black and white Royal Pyrenees marble. Green coral garland decorated the top of the sculpture, while bronze dolphins supported it from underneath.

"In there?" Tully questioned moving closer to the rope.

"Yes, that is called a 'sarcophagus.' It is like a coffin." I said staring at the twenty-one-ton sculpture.

"But I can't see John Paul Jones, where is he?"

"He is in there, Tully, but remember how I told you that John Paul Jones lived a long time ago and that he died. Well, this is where he is buried. You can't see him because his bones are just left inside of there."

"Why?" Tully quickly asked.

"Well, he died a long time ago, so there wouldn't be much left of his body, but people wanted to honor him by burying him in this special place, this crypt under the chapel."[55]

"Why?"

"Because he was one of the best officers in the very first Navy of our country. It was called the 'Continental Navy'. He fought and defeated the British ships, and he received the first gun salute from another ship that recognized the United States as a country. So that is why we call him the 'Father of the Navy.' See this gold writing here on the floor? It says:

> John Paul Jones, 1747–1792;
> U.S. Navy, 1775–1783.
> He gave our Navy its earliest traditions
> Of heroism and victory.
>
> Erected by the Congress, A.D. 1912.

"Did John Paul Jones go to heaven?" Tully asked as we began walking clockwise around the tomb.

"Yeah, uh… I am sure that God was happy with him. He was a good and brave man who fought and died for our country," I replied quickly, trying to answer the difficult question.

Little did Tully know that John Paul Jones had more history than just being "a privateer" and a "brave Naval Officer." This quick-tempered Scotsman had gotten his start in the French Navy, where he had killed his crewmembers for fear of mutiny, changed his name, John Paul to John Paul Jones, and moved to the American Colonies to escape his pending execution in France. Nevertheless, despite these shortcomings,

....

55   The corporal remains of John Paul Jones were interred into the crypt beneath the Naval Academy crypt in 1906 in a ceremony presided over by President Theodore Roosevelt. From the point of his death in 1792 until then John Paul Jones' remains had been in a grave in France, where he died. "Crypt of John Paul Jones, *Usna.edu*, https://www.usna.edu/Chaplains/virtualTour/crypt.php

he had the makings for the perfect privateer. Tully had recently become fond of pirates, almost to the point of obsession. I introduced Tully to John Paul Jones to counteract the pirates, with a real-life example of a privateer.

Tully outside the crypt of John Paul Jones

"Tully! Look over here," I pointed Tully in the direction of a small alcove that displayed memorabilia. Tully and I approached a white marble bust of a man in uniform.

"This is what John Paul Jones looked like," I said to Tully pointing at the bust. Jean Antoine Houdon had sculpted the bust from life in 1781.

"Oh," Tully said looking up at the realistic portrayal. You could almost see the courage in his eyes, the intensity upon his pressed lips, and the devoted patriotism upon his chest.

"Where is his sword," Tully asked noticing that the bust had no arms.

"Over here, Tul," I said as I guided him to the next alcove.

Tully stared at the shiny bronze sword encased in a box of glass.

"Where is his gun?" Tully asked as he walked over to the next alcove.

"I don't think they have his gun here, Tully, but look here," I said pointing at another glass case. "These are all the medals John Paul Jones was awarded while he was in the Navy."

Tully looked in the case for two seconds and they turned and walked away; he had spotted something more interesting near the entrance of the crypt. I followed him over to a small table near the entrance. Behind the desk was a Marine guard standing at attention. The darkness of the room and the positioning of the light had hidden him, and therefore Tully and I had walked right by him upon our entry.

"Hello, Sir," Tully said to the statuesque Marine.

"Hello," the Marine replied with hardly any movement.

"Are you here to see John Paul Jones too? Well, he is inside there," Tully whispered with intensity as he pointed to the sarcophagus.

A smile cracked from the face of the Marine.

"Tully," I said, holding back a laugh, "He is here to guard the crypt."[56]

"Why?"

"This is a very important place and not only is the Marine here to guard the tomb and all of John Paul Jones' possessions but also he is here to show respect and honor to the Father of our Navy."

Tully smiled up at the Marine and gave him a salute. The Marine saluted back with a reverence that seemed to echo that of the room.

....

56   As of January 6, 2006, a Naval Academy tradition that lasted 155 years has come to an end: The Marine Corps sentries who guarded the gates and the crypt of Revolutionary War Capt. John Paul Jones have been withdrawn and sent to war. The four dozen Marines were released from their security duties in a ceremony on Friday and are being replaced by Navy enlisted personnel. The Marines have provided security at the gates and for dignitaries' visits and special events on the academy campus since before the Civil War. They also performed largely ceremonial duties, including standing guard outside the crypt of Jones, one of the founders of the Navy. "After 155 years, Marine sentries removed from Naval Academy to be sent to war." *Free Republic*, https://freerepublic.com/focus/f-news/1558096/posts

Tully and I said goodbye to John Paul Jones and walked out of the hallowed crypt. The crypt was difficult for a child to understand and I was now worried that the visit had been disappointing for Tully. I knew that he had wanted to see John Paul Jones as he had pictured him in his imagination, an image of a privateer, not a marble coffin.

As we walked away from the Chapel, Tully could not stop talking about John Paul Jones. He continued to ask me about his tomb, about his sword, his uniform, and if he had killed any bad pirates. I realized that the dark crypt, with its mysterious atmosphere, polished memorabilia, and honored remains of the privateer *did after all* have an impact upon my nephew.

"Aunt Cathy, I want to go to heaven so I can see John Paul Jones."

I looked down at the small example of innocence and said, "You will get to see him one day Tully."

Tully and I continued walking across campus, heading due north toward the Severn River. We crossed Stribling Walk, an area of trees, grass, and brick pathways that provided access from Bancroft to the west side of campus. The Yard was bathing in light and the air was hanging lazily in the sky. We were surrounded by well-groomed patches of green grass and clipped bushes. Large pink and red tulips[57] lined the walkways, like companies of plebes standing at attention and lined up in perfect rows.

I pointed out the lacrosse field, Dewey Field, to our left and McDonough Hall and Luce Hall to our right. We crossed a road and walked over to the edge of the choppy Severn River.

"Let's go look at the sailboats," I said leading Tully along a wooden dock. The dock lined the perimeter of a small harbor. The dock hugged the water and was attached to the Robert Crown Sailing Center, a wooden building that was home to the Navy Sailing Team.

Tully and I stood in front of a row of sailboats bobbing beside the dock. Their tall masts rocked back and forth mechanically in the wind. They appeared lifeless with their sails put away. I closed my eyes and took a breath of the moist air. I became wrapped up in the familiar

....

57   The Academy spares no expense on the upkeep of the Yard, even importing their tulips from Holland!

smell of rotted wood, saltwater, and tar. I opened my eyes and smiled as I took notice of the "lasers," the unusually small sailboats that were directly in front of us.

"Hey Tul, would you like to hear a funny story?" I sat down and hung my legs over the edge of the dock.

"Yes!" Tully said sitting down beside me.

"Well, now that you have learned about a famous *privateer*, I am going to tell you a story about two famous *pirates*." Tully's eyes widened and his smile stretched from ear to ear.

"In fact," I continued, "See these small boats right here? The pirates had actually sailed in one of these!" I began to tell my swashbuckling story about a pair of pirates that once ruled the high seas of the Severn...

Plebe Summer, Training, Day 48

Like Montgomery's nightly readings from the "Good Book," there were certain moments during Plebe Summer that you actually enjoyed and even looked forward to. It was 13:30 on a Tuesday, and I was closing in on another one of those moments. I had just taken off my white works and had folded them neatly, placing them alongside the dock at the Sailing Center. I was wearing my regulation blue and gold bathing suit, and our mandatory navy-blue baseball cap.

What an awesome day for sailing, I thought as I looked up into the clouds. I began to drift away as my body soaked up the warmth, relaxing me and clearing my mind of all thoughts. I felt a gentle hand on my shoulder as my roommate, Lily, brought me back down.

"Hey, let's go grab a boat," Lily said with her mischievous smile. "You're my partner, right?"

"Definitely," I said clipping on my helmet. We walked down the wooden pier and onto a dock covered in green plastic grass. Lined up in orderly rows were small white sailing vessels. The hull of the vessel was about the size of a kayak with room enough for two people. Immediately Lily and I ran over to one. We flipped the boat over onto its bottom and began to piece together the large puzzle. The mast had to be put into place and the sail had to be rigged.

As I grabbed a hold of the mast, I looked out across the Severn. The water was a palette of blues; Sapphire, cobalt, and turquoise covered the canvas. The sunlight sparkled on the tops of the waves that were splashing against the dock. There was a symphony of sounds surrounding us; cries from seagulls swooping overhead, beating canvas battered by the wind, and sloshing water striking the sides of the boats. The music soothed and calmed me until it was interrupted by the voices of our instructors.

Tully in a Laser sailboat at Visitor Center

They were newly ordained Ensigns[58], fresh out of the Academy and now officially part of the Navy. Their first assignment, or should I say *Tour of Duty*, was "Plebe Summer Sailing Instructor." They had a tough job; one that required a lot of time and effort, a lot of time in the sun and a lot of effort driving around motorboats. The instructors all wore the same uniform: Oakley sunglasses, navy blue collared shirts, khaki shorts, and canvas shoes. Their bodies were relaxed from the hours spent on the water and bronzed from the hours exposed to the rays.

"Navy's finest," I thought to myself as two instructors strolled by talking and laughing loudly.

....

58 *Ensign:* The lowest ranking officer in the Navy. Graduating from the Naval Academy promotes you to either the rank of an Ensign in the Navy or a Second Lieutenant in the Marine Corps.

As they approached us, they stopped talking and glared over at Lily and me. "What are you two waiting for?"

Before we could even answer, they both rolled their eyes and continued on their way.

"This Class of '98 is the worst class yet," mumbled one of the instructors.

"Yeah, tell me about it," whined the other one, "They seem to be getting slacker each year."

As their conversation faded away, Lily and I resumed our work on the boat. Suddenly Lily looked up from the knot she had been struggling with, "What are ya doing Cath?"

"Just looking."

"Looking at what?

"That instructor over there. I know her." I had suddenly recognized Ensign Schmitt, an arrogant blond who had been one of my cadres at the Naval Academy Preparatory School in Newport, Rhode Island. A "cadre" was a midshipman who spent four weeks out of their summer up at NAPS training recruits. This training was called "Indoc," and it was a smaller version of the Academy's Plebe Summer. Ensign Schmitt and I had never hit it off well up at NAPS. For some reason, we had a mutual dislike for each other. I began to get nauseous at the thought of having to deal with her again. I glanced over at Lily with a look of disgust.

"Another one of the Navy's finest," I moaned as I looked down hoping not to be noticed.

Ensign Schmitt pranced over to us with her neck strained and her nose pointing to the sky.

"Ladies, let's get the boats rigged, okay?" she said with an over-dramatic sigh. "I don't have all day or the patience to put up with *you!*" She said crossing her arms. I could feel her ice-cold eyes looking straight at me.

"Aye-aye Ma'am," I said loudly as she strutted back to her motorboat.

"Oh, she's really happy to see ya Cath," Lily giggled.

"Yeah, imagine how happy I am." I took a deep breath preparing myself for more harassment.

"Wouldn't it be funny if she asked you to recite the 'Man in the Arena?'" Lily said laughing.

I couldn't help but smile at her clever comment, "Yes, that would definitely make my day!"

My reciting of 'Man in the Arena' was becoming quite a common occurrence in 34th Company. My roommate, along with every other plebe, knew of my struggle with it and with the continuous Montgomery harassment that went along with it. I am sure many of my classmates empathized with me, but I knew for a fact that most of my classmates never even bothered to memorize the passage. They knew that they would never be asked to recite it; they knew that they would only ever hear:

"Ervin! 'Man in the Arena'—*go!*"

"We better get moving here," I said nervously as I looked around. The dock was almost empty, and the Severn was rapidly filling up with boats, boats whose captains had obviously paid attention during the briefing. Earlier that afternoon, we had been shown a demonstration video at the Sailing Center. The intent of the video was to teach us the lesson for the day. I found it helpful in the sense that it gave me extra time to study my *Reef Points*. Instead of paying attention to Sailing 101, I concentrated on the small Navy-blue book that I always kept with me. Whenever there was an extra minute or two in our daily routine, *Reef Points* was always pulled out. It was a common sight to see a plebe with their head lowered and *Reef Points* opened. Mine was often opened when standing in line, waiting in my room, or during instructional time—say for example a sailing lesson.

Fortunately, lasers are such tiny boats that their "How to Assemble" instructions were not too complex. However, for me, the hard part was trying to remember how exactly the knots were supposed to be tied. Even the metaphors that were used to help us figure it out always seemed to just make it worse. For example, when tying a slip knot "the bunny (being the end of the rope) had to go around a tree then through a hole." My bunny always managed to get lost. By the time Lily and I had finished tying the ropes in place, I had invented at least five new knots.

Hey, I figured if *the knot holds, then why worry about how it was tied.* (If you are a sailor, please ignore that last line!) Luckily, for Lily and me, the knots somehow managed to work.

After the mast went up, the sail rigged, and the boom tied in place, we were ready to shove off. We took our positions—Lily at the rudder and I in charge of the sail. A small gust of wind pushed against the canvas sail and in no time, we were drifting slowly away from the dock. I adjusted my helmet strap and tightened my yellow life jacket as I looked ahead to the bobbing buoys that were beckoning us in their direction.

The smell of the saltwater lingered in the air; I could taste it in the wind that blew across my face. I was excited as I looked out across the water to see the bay spotted with tiny white sails. As I felt the warmth of the sun shining its gold upon me, I thought to myself that this was the first time that Plebe "Summer" actually felt like *summer*. For a moment I was transported to Bethany Beach, a Delaware beach where my family and I had spent many of our summer vacations. However, I was slapped by reality when a shrill whistle cut through the air. I turned around to see our sailing instructors speeding rapidly towards us in their motorboats. Their shirt collars were flapping in the wind, and the sun was glaring off their Oakleys. With one hand on the wheel and the other in the air, they were motioning us in the direction of the orange buoys that were floating about in the water. Our training for today was to practice figure eights around the marked course. Our instruction earlier on the fine art of sailing was now to be put into action.

Lily, who was sitting to my left, held on to the wooden lever that moved the rudder back and forth. The "rudder" was like the steering wheel on a car; it guided the boat in a certain direction. I held on to the ropes, pulling them or loosening them depending on the amount of wind that was caught in the sail. The "sail," like an engine, was the power behind the boat. It harnessed the wind, which was the engine's fuel. The wind would hit our sail on either side, shifting the sail away from us or bringing it towards us. The sail, which looked like a giant white shark fin, was attached to a horizontal metal bar called the "boom" and a vertical bar called the "mast." The boom was at the same level as our heads when we were sitting. When the sail would catch the wind, it would pivot the boom around, causing Lily and I to duck to avoid being knocked over. We were constantly ducking, moving the rudder, switching sides, and pulling ropes. It was like a dance, in which you had to be in sync with your partner in order to make it work. In no time at all, Lily and I were waltzing across the water. However, after the third figure eight around the course, we both decided that we had had enough. We figured that we had mastered the skills fairly well and that it was now time for something new.

I reached over the side of the boat and ran my hand through the cool, inviting water.

"Ya know roomy, it's a perfect day for swimming," I said to Lily, as I looked up with an evil grin.

"I was just thinking the same thing," she replied playfully, "and I was noticing how *warm* Peter and Andrew look over there." Lily pointed at a boat to the right of us. "They may need to be *cooled off*, what do ya think?"

"They do look warm and I'm sure that they could use a bit of refreshment," I said with a devious laugh. Lily and I steered away from the buoys, quickly changing our course.

"Ready about!" I commanded. I was preparing us to "tack" or in other words to put the front of our boat through the eye of the wind[59]. The wind punched our sail, Lily turned the rudder, and in no time at all, we were facing our target.

"Full speed ahead!" I shouted as our boat sliced through the choppy water. The waves banged against the sides of our boat creating a hollow rhythm, a cadence that helped keep our course steady. I held the wind captive while keeping my eyes fixed on our enemy target.

"Hey Sinclair," I yelled deeply, imitating an upperclassman, "are your eyes in the boat?"

"Yes Ma'am!" she replied. As a plebe, we were required to always have our "eyes in the boat." This meant that we had to keep our eyes looking straightforward. Any movement of our eyeball away from that fixed position was considered a lack of bearing and a lack of discipline.

Soon we were closing in on our targets. I noticed Peter and Andrew casually glance over at us unaware that our boat was heading straight for them.

"Hey Lily." I pointed towards our target. "Look at the guys." Lily turned her head as she held tightly on to the rudder.

....

59 *Eye of the wind:* A sailing term referring to the direction in which the wind is coming from.

"They don't seem a bit worried, do they?" Lily said squinting into the sun.

"They probably think that we're just having a problem tacking," I replied as I pulled on to a rope. We were closing in rapidly on our target, with our boat only a few feet away.

"Mind your helm!" I yelled to Lily noticing that our boat was steering slightly to the left. Lily quickly adjusted the rudder as we approached the boat.

"Hey boys," I said angelically. Peter's and Andrew's eyes widened with worry and before either one of them could utter a word, their bodies jarred with the impact. The sound of metal colliding with metal was heard all around us. The two boats crunched and scraped until the boys' boat tipped over onto its starboard side[60].

"What the—?" was heard as both boys tipped along with the boat.

Within a few seconds, there was a large splash followed by Lily yelling out, *"Man overboard!"*

I laughed as I looked at the boys' sail, which was now lying parallel on top of the water. Lily quickly turned the rudder as I grabbed a hold of the ropes to pull the slack in.

"Mission complete!" I said as I slapped Lily a high-five.

"I think I like this training much better," she said retying her brown hair into a ponytail.

"So do I," I said smiling. We both turned around and laughed at the sight of the two baldheads bobbing up and down in the water screaming profanities into the salty air.

We turned our attention away from the boys and looked in front of us at all the other unaware boats doing their exercises like mechanical robots.

"We've got a whole fleet to pick from," Lily said pointing ahead of us. Like pirates thirsty for another kill, Lily and I decided to continue our attacks. After about twenty minutes, we had successfully destroyed four ships, and we were closing in on our fifth.

"Let's get those two over there—it looks like Anna and Beth," yelled Lily pointing ahead of us.

....

60 *Starboard Side:* Sailing term, referring to the right side of a boat, where as the "port side" refers to the left side.

"Enemy straight ahead. All hands-on deck," I said as we both ducked under the swaying boom. After tacking and holding our course steady, in no time at all, we were only inches from the port side of Anna and Beth's boat.

"Hey, girls, are you enjoying the day?" Lily asked innocently as we pulled in for the kill. Now up until this point, we had been using a ramming technique to destroy our enemies. We would come out of nowhere and surprise the boats, and thus, the enemies had no time to react before the big collision. This method had been successful until the other plebes began catching on. Before long, our sneak attacks were no longer a secret. The other plebes would spot us coming and immediately change direction so that their boat would end up parallel with ours. Instead of a massive collision, the two boats would just brush sides.

Well, unfortunately, Anna and Beth had caught on and were now quickly steering away from us, lessening our opportunity to ram. Nevertheless, it did not take long for Lily to come up with a new plan of attack. As we approached Anna and Beth, Lily put her new plan into effect.

"Cath, pull our boat alongside theirs as close as you can," Lily yelled as she began to stand up.

"O… kaay," I said hesitantly. I caught the ledge of the other boat and began to pull the two boats closer together, shortening the gap.

"Hey, how's it going guys," I said casually looking over at the confused girls.

"What's going on?" asked Anna. Her eyes widened with panic as she looked at Lily.

"Oh my gosh," I screamed, looking up to see Lily with one leg in our boat and the other in the girls' boat.

"Hold on Cath," Lily yelled as she grabbed a hold of the girls' mast. I shifted to the other side of the boat to keep our boat from tipping. Lily was now hanging from their mast and rocking their boat back and forth. Before the girls had time to react, Lily gave a forceful push with all her strength as she simultaneously jumped back into our boat. I watched Anna and Beth's boat capsize in one swift motion. I looked up to see Lily, who was now hanging on to the mast of our teetering boat. I felt like the driver in a getaway car as I pulled away from the scene of the crime.

"*Yeah!*" we both yelled as we pulled away from the sunken ship.

"Well, let's chalk that one up for another kill," I said as we watched the girls struggling to flip their sailboat back over. Suddenly, I noticed the outer edge of our sail, called the "luff," beginning to buckle due to a lack of wind. I quickly yanked the rope pulling the luff taut. I also noticed that we were drifting away from the other plebes and decided that we needed to change our course before we missed other prime opportunities to attack.

"Stand by to come about," I sounded out. "Left 30 degrees rudder," I said glancing over to Lily.

"Left 30 degrees rudder, aye," Lily replied, pulling the rudder's lever towards her. "The rudder is left 30 degrees, Ma'am."

"Very well, steady on this course."

"Steady on this course, aye Ma'am."

Lily and I were using the "sailing lingo" that we had been taught and were putting it to the best use yet!

Lily and I continued our attack on the *Fleet of Plebes* for about another twenty minutes. We had the attack well mastered and as we looked out to see an increasing number of heads bobbing up and down in the Severn, we knew it had been successful. If Blackbeard would have been alive, we would have made him proud. Luckily, our classmates weren't too angry at us for using them as targets. They were grateful for the opportunity to cool off in the water… or so we believed.

Lily and I had just completed another kill, when…

"O… Oh…," Lily said softly. Lily had her head ducked under the boom that was behind us. I turned my head around towards the sail. I didn't have to duck under the boom, as she had done, because there was a window in the sail positioned right near my head. All I had to do was look through the window to see what was behind us. As I looked through the small triangular piece of clear plastic, I noticed a motorboat hydroplaning across the surface of the water and heading straight for us.

"Here comes the Navy's finest," I said, noticing two Ensigns onboard. "Damn the torpedos! Full speed ahead!"[61]

Suddenly, a static voice shot through the salty air. "Hey! You two! Out of your boat now!"

I looked over at Lily who was now looking at me. "Oh well, it was fun while it lasted."

"Yeah, and lucky for them we haven't figured out how to capsize a motorboat," Lily said laughing.

"Out of your boat, NOW," the voice boomed, "You two are going to shore immediately!"

Lily and I stood up in our laser and climbed aboard the motorboat that was now pulled up beside us. Both Ensigns had their sunglasses propped upon their heads and their hands on their hips. I was *so happy* to see that one of the ensigns was Ensign Schmitt. The corners of her mouth were curved upwards as she tried to hold back her pure pleasure in the catch she just made. We had been caught and the snake was now taunting us with delight.

"Oh, wait until your detailers hear about this one," Ensign Schmitt hissed as she glanced down at us with her piercing, beady eyes.

The other Ensign grabbed the megaphone and yelled into it, "You should never mess with us, *ever!*"

As Lily and I rode back to the dock in silence, I couldn't help but smile at the sight of a few white sails still lying face down in the water.

"Oh, you think this is *funny* Ervin?" Ensign Schmitt said glaring at me. "Soon you won't be laughing, you can count on me to make sure of that!"

After the motorboat had pulled up alongside the dock, Lily and I got out and were then ordered to get into our uniforms. Once we were

....

61 Admiral David Glasgow Farragut (1801-1870) entered Mobile Bay, Alabama, on August 5, 1864, in two columns, with armored monitors leading and a fleet of wooden ships following. The lead monitor *Tecumseh* struck a torpedo and began to sink, causing the rest of the fleet to back away from the mine-infested waters. At the time, Farragut was watching the battle while lashed to the rigging of his flagship *(USS Hartford)*. Alarmed, Farragut shouted, "What's the trouble?" The *USS Brooklyn* answered, "Torpedoes!" Farragut shouted back, "Damn the torpedoes! Full speed ahead!" In the end, Farragut's fleet defeated Confederate Admiral Franklin Buchanan and the last open seaport on the Gulf of Mexico fell to the Union. "David G Faragut," American Battlefield Trust, https://www.battlefields.org/learn/biographies/david-g-faragut

dressed in our white works, we were then ordered to stand at attention in the parking lot beside the dock. As Lily and I stood in silence, I
began to wonder which detailer was going to pick us up today. Usually,
at the end of a training session, one of our detailers would retrieve us
and march us back to Bancroft. Today, our fate would be in the hands
of this detailer. If Mr. Montgomery, Mr. Nash, Mr. Trevor, or Mr. Wyatt
came, we were surely dead. I began to pray for Mr. Steinmann to come.
I knew that Steinmann would be the most understanding with us, or at
least he would be the most tolerant.

I turned my head to the left and began scanning the approaching
road for any familiar faces. Suddenly my heart skipped a beat; there in
the distance I saw a familiar sight. It was a man with a very slim and
tall physique. His walk was more like a march in which his body was
as straight as a board and his head was held high. The way he carried
himself reflected pride and control. He looked like a machine; his body
was hard and his movements unfaltering.

"Thank you, God, it's Mr. Steinmann," I said out loud.

Lily and I both watched in suspense as Mr. Steinmann marched over
to the Ensigns who had been lounging in the motorboat. As soon as
Ensign Schmitt saw Mr. Steinmann, she stood up and immediately
began relaying all the details of our little escapade. She first pointed to
us, I wanted to wave to Mr. Steinmann but changed my mind consid-
ering it inappropriate, and then she motioned to the water and the
other plebes. Her hands were flying all over the place, trying to keep
up with her mouth. It felt like Lily and I were in a game of charades
as we watched trying to figure out what Ensign Schmitt was acting
out. It wasn't too difficult though, because she was over-dramatizing
everything. The whole time Ensign Schmitt's charade was going on, Mr.
Steinmann stood silently with his arms crossed and his head nodding
up and down. Every now and then, he would glance toward us, and
from where I was standing, I could not quite tell if he was angry or
disappointed. Whatever he was though, he was not happy.

"I'm beginning to think that we shouldn't have done what we did," I
whispered to Lily barely moving my lips.

"Don't worry roomie, Steinmann will take care of things," Lily replied
barely loud enough for me to hear.

"I'm not so sure of that anymore. I mean look at him, he looks pretty upset."

As I looked at Steinmann, I began to get upset at myself. The last thing I wanted to do was disappoint him. Mr. Steinmann was one of the few upperclassmen that I respected and trusted. He was the type of leader that *I* wanted to be. He was tough and disciplined, yet he knew how to laugh and have fun. He had gained my respect from day one when he told us his Paris Island stories, and he had maintained my respect as he continued to nurture and teach throughout the summer. (Even if his teaching involved throwing my rack out of the window.) Mr. Steinmann could smile the largest smile I had ever seen, a grin that went from ear to ear. As I stood in the Sailing Center's parking lot, I wondered if I would ever see that smile again.

Lily and I continued to wait until the rest of the plebes had finished their exercises. I pulled out my *Reef Points* and began my daily task of trying to memorize "Man in the Arena." As I read the portion that says, "who errs and comes short again and again," my mind began to wander, and I kept thinking of what Lily and I had done, and the more I thought of it, the more I regretted it.

Soon the fleet of wet plebes returned to the dock. We received a barrage of laughs and smirks from our classmates on our march back to Bancroft Hall. Once we were back in 8th Wing, we were all instructed to immediately go to our rooms and change into PEP gear, which was our blue rim t-shirts, our navy shorts, and our running shoes. We all knew that "PEP gear"[62] meant physical torture. I knew that this had been coming, and I felt bad knowing that Lily and I were the ones to blame for the extra PT[63].

Lily and I had just gotten into our room when suddenly, "Ervin, Sinclair, hit a bulkhead *now!*" Mr. Steinmann's Marine Corps bark shot through the P-way.

Oh great, I thought, *here it comes.*

"Get out here *now!*" Steinmann continued to bark.

....

62 *PEP:* Abbreviation for "Physical Exercise Program." PEP gear, therefore, was what was worn for any physical exercise. This outfit consisted of a blue-rimmed t-shirt, navy blue mesh shorts, white socks, and running shoes.

63 *PT:* "Physical Training"

Lily and I ran out of our rooms, squared the corner, and yelled, "Go Navy, Sir!" we squared another corner, "Beat Army Sir!" we yelled even louder. We then pounded our hand three times against the *bulkhead,* did an *about-face,* and then *braced up* at attention. In other words (civilian translation), we hit a cinderblock wall, turned around 180 degrees, and then pressed our chin down onto our chest while standing at attention.

I noticed the angry faces of Mr. Wyatt and Mr. Steinmann only inches away from us. It felt like two grenades had just been rolled into our P-way and Lily and I were trapped with nowhere to run for cover. We stood frozen in fear, waiting for the explosion to happen.

"What in the hell were you two thinking today?" Mr. Steinmann boomed.

"Do you know how bad you made us look in front of those Ensigns?" Mr. Wyatt banged.

"They informed us that you not only blew off your lesson but that you also risked the safety of the other plebes,"

"Why am I always dealing with you, Ervin?" Mr. Wyatt hollered an inch away from my ear. Both of them continued to explode at the top of their lungs for a good five minutes, and then all of a sudden, they just stopped. My ears continued to ring in the silence. After a long pause, after the smoke had cleared, Mr. Steinmann approached me and said softly, "So how many kills did you get Ervin?" I paused for quite a long time. *Did he really just ask me that?* I thought to myself. It was like I had just been killed, and now suddenly I was being resurrected.

With hesitation I replied, "Ahh... twelve, Sir."

"Twelve! Excellent job you two," Steinmann said, smiling the smile that I never thought I'd see again.

"I think that twelve is a record," declared Mr. Wyatt.

"Why don't you two get back in your there and change into some dry clothes," Mr. Steinmann said pointing to our room.

Lily and I were unable to move, as we stood in our room dripping saltwater onto our meticulously waxed floor. We were both in shock and disbelief trying to sort out in our heads what had just happened. I was barely able to speak.

"What the—" I said looking over at my roommate and my partner in crime.

"That was crazy," Lily gasped, hardly able to speak, "I thought for sure we were…"

"Dead!" I said finishing her sentence. Relief swept over my entire body as I quickly changed into my dry PEP gear.

That afternoon, we continued our plebe training schedule without the PT punishment I thought we would receive. Not only were we *not* being punished for our Severn River attacks, but at evening meal that night, Mr. Wyatt and Mr. Steinmann acknowledged us. They announced to the entire Company of our accomplishments; that we had "single-handedly taken out twelve enemy ships and pissed off two of the most disliked Ensigns on the Yard."

While congratulations were being passed around to us for our "twelve kills," Lily and I sat in shock. With our "eyes in the boat," we were unable to look at each other. However, I did not need to look at her,

For I knew that her smile, like mine, was as big as Mr. Steinmann's, and that she may have even lifted her chin a little bit higher, as I had done.

CHAPTER 12:
MACDONOUGH

THE WIND BLEW and rattled the boat rigging against the hollow masts, creating the sound of ringing bells. I couldn't stop smiling as my gaze remained locked on the small sailboats. Now when I looked at them, I no longer saw a sailing craft, but rather a vessel of memories that would forever bring a smile upon my face.

As Tully and I left the dock, I thought of a passage that I had memorized back during those Plebe Summer days, "Qualifications of A Naval Officer" by my favorite privateer, John Paul Jones. In the passage Jones says, "It is by no means enough that an officer of the Navy should be a capable mariner. He must be that, of course, but also a great deal more. He should be as well a gentleman of liberal education, refined manners, punctilious courtesy, and the nicest sense of personal honor."

"Tully, John Paul Jones had once said that not only should you be a good sailor, but more importantly you should be a good person with good manners, who is nice to other people. Do you think Lily and I followed the good example of John Paul Jones?"

"No," Tully said laughing.

"No, we didn't and luckily no one got hurt. Lily and I may have acted like pirates, but we made sure that we did not hurt anyone. It would not have been nice to hurt any of our classmates. I wonder if John Paul Jones was looking down from heaven laughing at the sight of all those wet plebes floating in the water, or if he was planning to drop Lily and me for push-ups!

Tully and I continued to laugh as we left the dock. Soon images of pirates and privateers disappeared from my mind as I focused on the large building across the street.

We walked to the front of Macdonough Hall[64], a massive building that towered over us like all the other buildings on the Yard. It was dressed in the mandatory uniform of gray granite stone and on its head wore a cover of patina copper. It was a mirror image of Dahlgren Hall, which, like Macdonough, was connected to Bancroft. Its shape resembled an airplane hangar, long and rectangular with an arched roof. The arched roof and its location near the water once had a great purpose, back when the Naval Academy was born.

At one time, the water's edge was at Macdonough's doorstep. Macdonough, along with a few of the other buildings, would usher in large sailing vessels out of the murky Severn River and under its arches to be repaired. Under the arched roof was a network of walkways built around the perimeter. Men would work high above the resting giants, laboring tediously among the wood and the canvas.

Today if you enter Macdonough Hall, you will not look upon wood planks lining the deck of a ship, but rather upon the wood planks that line the basketball court. You will not smell saltwater from the Severn River, but rather chlorine from the water in the two fifty-meter pools. You will not hear the hammering of nails echoing from up above, but you will hear the hammering of leather in the boxing ring or on the volleyball court. You will not see men sweating off pounds from the lifting of wooden masts, but rather from the lifting of iron weights.

Macdonough Hall houses the water polo team, the soccer team, the lacrosse team, the boxing team, the gymnastics team, and the volleyball team. Besides being a training ground for six of the Academy sports, part of Macdonough is called Misery Hall, and it is here that Macdonough has a different purpose. You could say Misery Hall continues Macdonough's tradition of years ago—the tradition of repair. Today, however, broken ships do not enter through the arches, but

....

64   *Macdonough*: Entering the navy as a midshipman in 1800, Thomas Macdonough saw service during the U.S. war with Tripoli (1801–05). When war broke out with England, his major assignment was to cruise the lakes between Canada and the United States. When enemy ground forces threatened Plattsburg, N.Y.—the U.S. Army headquarters on the northern frontier—Macdonough's foresight and painstaking preparation for battle paid off. On Sept. 11, 1814, his 14-ship fleet met the British in the harbour and after several hours of severe fighting forced the 16-vessel squadron to surrender, thus saving New York and Vermont from invasion. "Thomas Macdonough," *Britannica*, https://www.britannica.com/biography/Thomas-Macdonough

rather broken bodies do. Ankles needing to be wrapped, muscles needing to be iced, bodies needing repair after a day of beating from sports, or from the other physical demands of the Academy.

I pulled open the heavy wooden door in front of me and stepped into a place that smelled of sweat, dirt, and chlorine.

"Where are we?" Tully asked as he began to look around.

"Macdonough," I quietly replied. As I stood still looking up into the arched ceiling of Macdonough, I began to think about the first time that I had sailed under Macdonough's arches. I first came to know Macdonough, and thus the Academy, in the summer of 1992. I was a sophomore in high school attending Navy Volleyball Camp. Not only was I introduced to the head coach of the women's volleyball team, but I was introduced to the Academy. I remember sweating away those summer days of Camp in the 3rd-floor sauna of Macdonough while dreaming the nights away in the halls of Bancroft. plebe summer was in full swing by the time Volleyball Camp had started. Before going to bed each night, I remember hanging out of my windowsill watching columns of newly shaven plebes march by. I would sit wrapped in the cool salty air, restlessly wondering what it would be like to be a plebe.

At the end of Camp that first summer, a seed had been planted. The head coach had approached me with an invitation to play for her team. I was a sophomore at the time, so I was quite taken back and honored by her invitation. *This was the Naval Academy, and this was a Division I team. Was this coach serious?* I had thought. I was scared by the idea as well; somehow I knew that I would end up accepting the offer and that a rough road would lay ahead of me. I liked challenges, and I liked the fear that went along with them.

I spent that summer and the following one building my skills and building a good reputation with the coach. A year later, I had been accepted at NAPS, the Naval Academy Preparatory School. A year after that, I was standing back in McDonough wearing blue and gold and the number "3" upon my back. I remember feeling like that little girl at summer camp; the little girl who had dreamed of becoming a part of Navy. And here I was— for real—and this was no summer camp.

Tully and I continued to walk through Macdonough. I had the strangest feeling like I was that little girl from four years ago and at the same time feeling like that woman I had dreamed of becoming. The smell was home to me; the sweat and chlorine lingered around instantly bringing me back to this place of comfort. I looked down at the blue carpet and proceeded to follow it as it led us to a set of brown stairs. Tully and I climbed up to the second level and walked into an entrance just beyond the staircase. We passed the water-polo pool on our left, and the soccer team's locker room on our right. After passing a set of showers, I turned to my right and stopped in front of a solid metal door.

"What are we doing Aunt Cathy?"

"I am going to get us a volleyball to play with!" I punched three small buttons on the lock in a specific order and then pushed open the heavy door. Tully and I walked into a small narrow room filled with another familiar smell to me—the locker room smell. Musty jerseys, sweat, and dirt all mixed into that unforgettable odor. It smelled of pain, of loss, of triumph. I moved to the left of the long wooden bench in the middle, which paralleled the length of the room. Light from a high window at the back end of the room illuminated the bright blue walls.

I walked across the rubbery floor passing by walls of yellow metal lockers. I came to a locker with a piece of medical tape stuck to it. I did not recognize the name written on the tape.

"This was once my locker room, Tully, and this locker had been mine. When I was at the Academy, I played on the volleyball team."

"Where is your uniform?" Tully asked peeking into small holes on the locker doors.

"I don't have the uniform now, someone else does. I don't play on the team anymore. I can tell you what it looked like, though; it was a gold jersey with a navy-blue number 3 on it and a pair of navy-blue shorts."

"Did you win?" Tully asked walking around the room.

"We did win some games, but we lost some too. But we did *beat Army* and that was all that mattered!"

"Did Lily play with you?"

"No, Lily did not play volleyball. She played in Navy's Drum and Bugle Corps, the marching band. But I had other friends that were on the team. There was Sarah; she was an upperclassman. She was a great player and really took care of me like I was her younger sister. Then there was Ally; she was an upperclassman also and was our toughest player.

She motivated me to give 100% every day. I was lucky to be on a team with such great players. Playing sports at the Academy is important Tul; you make new friends, it teaches you teamwork, and it helps take your mind off being a plebe!

As I described to Tully what it was like to play volleyball for Navy, I began to feel like I was back again and in no time at all, I was standing in front of that locker not as Aunt Cathy, but as #3...

Academic Year, September

It was a hot Indian Summer afternoon, and I was preparing myself for battle; a battle that would hopefully score more than *twelve kills*. This time, however, the battle would not involve pirates, the Severn River, or angry Ensigns.

I was standing in front of my locker undressing. With each article of clothing that I freed myself from, I felt an incredible sense of relief. It was as if I was taking off weights that had been strapped to my body. The necktie was always the first to come off. It was a small piece of black material shaped like a "w", which wrapped around the buttoned collar of your shirt. I un-velcroed the necktie and began to unbutton my black long-sleeved shirt. I hung up the stiff shirt meticulously on a hanger, knowing the time it had taken me to iron it the night before. As I undid the silver buckle on my belt, I slipped out of my black leather shoes. After carefully folding my pants along the creases and hanging them on a hanger, I grabbed my shining shoes and placed them at the bottom of my locker. My body felt free, released from a binding hold.

As I continued to undress, I could feel the cold from the room rush through my body, adding to shivers from the nervousness. I quickly put on my navy-blue spandex shorts and grabbed the gold jersey from my locker. I placed the jersey on and felt the number 3 slide down my back. I alternated feet up on the bench and carefully tied my shoes, making sure they felt just right. I undid the braid that my hair had taken the shape of and gathered it up into a ponytail. I closed my locker and then took one last look around the room.

My nervousness was pacified as I looked at the blue and gold balloons attached to my locker and the banner hanging above. The banner read

"Go Navy!" As I stared at the banner, I was in awe. There were times at the Academy when I would stop in amazement, and think, *Oh my gosh, I am actually here.* This was now one of those moments. I looked down at the NAVY lettering across my jersey. I continued to stare in disbelief, trying to let the reality of it sink in. During times like this, when the reality would hit home, I would gain a sense of pride in where I was and of who I was. Since July 1, this pride, like waves on an ocean, had never ceased and never would.

On my way out of the locker room, I grabbed a mesh bag filled with volleyballs and walked away with "Go Navy" pounding in my head.

I quickened my pace down the hallway, past the water-polo pool, and up a flight of stairs. In no time at all, I was standing on the volleyball court located on the top floor of Macdonough. I dropped the bag of volleyballs, untied the cord, and pulled out one of the soft leather balls. I tucked it under my arm and walked over to the net, which had been stretched across the center of the court. Brown metal bleachers were to the right of the court, and a row of fold-out chairs lined the left side of the court.

I sat down on the plastic tile floor, placed the ball by my side, and began to stretch. As I straightened my legs to touch my toes, I looked at the large arched window in front of me. The window took the shape of the arched roof and had a view of the Lacrosse Field and the water. The area in front of the window was home to the Boxing Team. There was a roped-off ring in the center, with punching bags to the left, and mirrors to the right. Smaller arched windows lined both sides of the gym, stretching back into the gymnastic area, which at the moment, was separated by a large hanging curtain that spanned across the width of the gym.

I continued to stretch, laying my back and my head down against the floor. Soon, I could hear the voices of the other girls, echoing from below. As I listened to their chattering and giggling voices, I thought of how happy I was to be a part of a team. Not only did I enjoy playing my favorite sport, but also I enjoyed sharing that love with others. Every one of us shared a bond, a bond that went beyond ranks. We were respected and treated equally, whether plebe or Firstie. Some of my teammates were just that—teammates, and nothing more. Others, however, were more.

There was 1st Class Ally Warner. Ally was the greatest volleyball player that I ever played with. She was fast, strong, and smart. She was confident but never came across as intimidating. She made you feel that you belonged playing beside her, even though you knew that she was at another level. She was a natural leader who could motivate you by just being around her. She was always positive, always encouraging, and always had a smile on her face. She was a tomboy and was not afraid to show how tough she was. The greatest thing about Ally, though, was the fact that she had kept me motivated to play when I had wanted to throw in the towel.

I had been recruited as a "setter." A setter is similar to a quarterback on a football team, in the sense that they are responsible for running the different kinds of plays. The setter position does not require a lot of height, and thus perfect for my 5'4 and 3/4" size. It requires speed, endurance, and aggressiveness, for the setter's job is to get to the ball no matter where it is on the court and *set* it up for the hitters (the position that does require height). When I arrived at the Academy, my volley-ball world was turned upside down. Within the first week of practice, I found out that I would not be playing the position of setter but rather as a "back-row specialist." Back row specialist was a less glamorous role than quarterback; I would be the one in charge of digging[65] up the hard-hit spikes from the back line. I was the best setter in high school; I had planned to be the best setter for Navy. I felt betrayed by my coach, especially when I found out that all along, she had me in mind for this other position. I continued to ask my coach for a chance to play setter, but she had some "loyalty" to the girl that was already in the position. To make matters even worse, the coaches "pretended" to work with me

....

65　*Digging:* Volleyball digging is essential for having a successful defense. The job of a volleyball digger is to prevent the ball from hitting the floor after being spiked by the opposing team. To dig, the volleyball players must anticipate the spike and be prepared to quickly dive in any direction. Volleyball players with quick contracting muscles are able to move faster, using their strength and flexibility to get low to the ground in order to dig out a hard hit. Volleyball diggers must be able to move laterally, forward, and backward explosively at full range of motion. "Volleyball Digging," *Myosource.com*, https://myosource.com/volleyball-digging/

on setting, it felt as if they were trying to pacify me. I never felt like they really wanted to work with me, it was as if it had been set in stone that I would be the back row specialist.

Ally was the one that understood my frustration; she saw how hard I pushed myself in practice hoping to push myself back into the setter position. She was the one, not the coaches, who made me understand and want to do what was best for the team, and if the team needed my quickness and speed in the back row, then that is where I would give my 110%.

Another great teammate of mine was 2nd Class Sarah Johnson, an all-around player who had become like a sister to me. I had met Sarah in my senior year of high school. She was a plebe at the time and had been assigned to "drag" me around the Naval Academy for a few days. I instantly gained her respect when I chopped alongside her and participated in all her other plebe duties. (Something a drag is not intended to do!) She instantly gained my respect as I witnessed a strong female midshipman, who was tough both on and off the volleyball court. We quickly developed a friendship and before I knew it, Sarah was by my side on a road trip to Newport. She had decided to drive up with my parents and me upon my entering into the Prep School. Not only was she a friend, but also, she became a support.

It wasn't long before I was playing beside her in Macdonough. I was honored to be on her team. She was a strong, and competitive player who could play all positions. It was her strength of character that I looked up to more so than anything else. There was a tragic accident that took place while I was at NAPS, in which Sarah's strength ultimately shined through.

It was a cold and dark day. I was standing with my Company in an unlit hallway at the Naval Academy Prep School listening to an announcement over the intercom. A silence surrounded all of us as a solemn voice slowly echoed throughout announcing that just that night, outside of Annapolis, four midshipmen had been in a car accident as they were on their way home from the Army-Navy football game. It had been storming that night and a tree had fallen onto the car resulting in the deaths of three of the midshipmen. One of the midshipmen was Sarah's best friend. I was shocked and overwhelmed with sadness as the name was announced, followed by the playing of Taps. I will never forget how different Taps sounded that night. As the notes from the solitary trumpet pored through the intercom, it profoundly affected me, for now death had become tangible. I hadn't known Sarah's friend very well, but that didn't matter. She was a Napster—she had shared a common bond with me. She was on the volleyball team, and I had met her when I was Sarah's drag.

Sarah's spirit could have died with the death of her greatest friend, but it didn't. Sarah continued on, she continued to be strong and brave in a time of great weakness. She remained focused on her goals and steadfast in achieving them. She never left a man behind; she took care of all her friends and kept the memory of her greatest friend alive. She was proud to be a part of Navy, and Navy was proud to have her.

As I looked up into the arched roof of Macdonough, my eyes focused on the American Flag proudly hanging from one of the metal support beams. Like the American flag, Macdonough was a symbol of pride, protection, and freedom. I was proud to wear number 3, to represent the Naval Academy. I was proud to be part of a team and was honored to share the court with players like 1st Class Ally Warner and 2nd Class Sarah Johnson.

Macdonough was also my protection. I felt shielded under its arches and allowed to let my guard down. Macdonough gave me the chance to be me. For a few hours every day, I was free from being a plebe. I was able to leave "Plebe Year" outside of the gym. My whole focus was on volleyball. When I was on the court, I didn't need to memorize "The Man in the Arena," instead I needed to memorize the different plays I had to run. I didn't have to worry about my uniform being "properly tucked" or "free from lint," instead here I wore a uniform that I could get dirty and leave un-tucked as much as I liked. I didn't have to worry about saying "Go Navy!" because I was required to; instead, I was screaming, "Go Navy!" because I wanted to.

I remember how just walking by Macdonough in the mornings on my way to classes was such a comfort, because I knew that at 15:00 it would be "my time." When I stepped under those arches, it was my time not my upperclassmen's time. My escape into Macdonough was a chance to breathe, to repair myself from any of the day's disappointments, and to pump myself up for the next day. McDonough restored my spirits. I could be that little girl again running around on the court, like at volleyball camp, with only one care in the world, to have fun and to play my heart out.

As I continued to stretch, players and staff slowly dwindled into the gym. In no time at all, the sound of leather banging against the court was echoing throughout the third floor. Shoes squeaked, voices chattered with girl talk, and excitement bounced from one player to the next. The afternoon light faded, as beams of light slowly fell from the arched windows. Fans began to take seats in the stands as the opposing team arrived in warm-ups, and game faces. I could not wait to start playing even if it meant playing a new position. I was ready to do what I loved.

As I walked on the court, I walked on with a sense of gratitude. I would be forever grateful to Navy volleyball, to Macdonough Hall, for it had given me pride, protection, and freedom. Day in and day out, I had sailed under its arches with broken spirits, and day in and day out, my spirits had been repaired and restored, for whatever battle the next day would bring.

CHAPTER 13:

HUNGER PAINS

"WHERE'S THE VOLLEYBALL?" Tully asked pulling me back to the present as Macdonough continued to whisper *pride, protection, and freedom.*

I reached over and pulled a ball out of a large, netted bag. Tully grabbed the ball and like a wind-up toy, sprung from the locker room. I raced Tully up to the 3rd floor, embracing the butterflies that fluttered into my body. *I don't think these feeling will ever leave me,* I thought, *the Academy has imprinted my heart and my spirit.* I had been feeling these feelings all day—the nervousness, the fear—yet the more time I spent on the yard, the feelings of pride and courage had begun to flutter above the butterflies.

Tully and I reached the top of the stairs and walked into the gym. The gym was empty, but somehow, I could hear the cheers of a crowd, the rattling of the boxing bags, and the squeaking of volleyball shoes. I walked onto the volleyball court and motioned for Tully to come with me. However, Tully had spotted a large pit of foam blocks in the gymnastic area. He looked at the pit, waiting for me to give him the go-ahead. I told him to wait for me as I walked off the court. I looked back out across the gym and placed the soft leather volleyball down. I guess the volleyball lesson would have to wait for another day.

"So why do they have this?" Tully asked as he leaped into the large rectangular pit.

"It is for the Gymnastic Team," I replied as a small head re-emerged from under gold and blue cubes of foam.

"The gymnasts use this to land into, so they don't hurt themselves. See the hanging rings up there?" I pointed to the suspended apparatus above Tully. "They swing on them, practicing their routine, and then they land into the pit."

"Oh," Tully said struggling to get free from the spongy foam. With nothing solid to grab a hold of or push himself up from, he began to get frustrated at his lack of ability to move.

"I got you, Tully," I said jumping in after him. Tully laughed at the sight of his aunt acting like a kid, although it was nothing new to him. I was the one adult in Tully's life that was not really "an adult." I was the one to dress up and play "Plebe" or play "Fireman", I was the one to slide down the slides, swing on the ropes, and play in the sandboxes. I was a child at heart and a playmate in the heart of Tully.

After lifting Tully out of the pit, I pulled myself out and looked at the clock. It was a little after twelve. *We had better get a move on*, I thought, Tully and I had a lot more to do and see.

"Alright, Tul, one more jump, and then we should get going!"

Tully walked back to the end of a small-carpeted runway perpendicular to the pit. He took off in a quick burst of speed as if taking off on a carrier. He leaped off the edge of the pit and belly-flopped into the soft cubes.

"Excellent job," I said as I clapped my hands. As I bent down to pull him out of the foam, a sudden noise startled me.

"Excuse me, that is off-limits!"

I turned around to see a man with gray hair quickly approaching us. He began to speak louder, "This is off-limits to the public; you must leave now!"

"Oh, we are sorry Sir," I replied as I walked towards the man. I noticed his Naval Academy collared shirt, the shirt civilian employees of the Naval Academy wear. I realized that the man was the security guard for McDonough.

"I am an Alumni," I said proudly, "I was just showing my nephew around." The man looked at me unconvinced. My youthful face, long blond hair, and feminine persona made disbelievers out of many whom I would share my past with.

"I don't care who you are," the man replied annoyed, "the head coach of the gymnastic team gave orders that this area was to only be used by gymnasts.

"Yes Sir," I said as I took hold of Tully's hand, "Thank you, Sir."

Despite our play time being cut short, I was grateful for the time we had. McDonough had once again restored my spirit.

Tully and I descended the stairs to the first floor. We walked past the basketball court, the trophy cases, and then pushed through a set of large wooden doors leading out of the east side of McDonough, the side in which the vessels of long ago would enter in through. As Tully and I sailed back out into the bright sunshine and balmy air, I decided to follow the road along the backside of Bancroft.

"Where are we going now?" Tully asked as he looked up at the towering giants closing in on us. We were walking between the 7th and 5th Wings of Bancroft. The gray granite walls, the copper roofs, and the rows of blue-green trimmed windows were all around us.

"I thought maybe we could go to the Visitor Center."

"Can we go to the Gift Shop?" Tully asked knowing that the Visitor Center was connected to the Gift Shop.

"Yes," I said, smiling at the fact that no matter how many cool things we did today, nothing could compete with the Gift Shop. Tully became excited as visions of toys, model airplanes, and footballs danced in his head.

"Can you buy me something since I have been a good boy?" Tully asked with a soft politeness in his voice. I looked down at the very smart boy who knew what buttons to push with his Aunt.

"Oh, *so you think* you have been a good boy, *huh*?" I replied with a laugh.

"Yes," Tully said lifting his chin up in pride.

"Well, I think you have but remember that the day is not over yet. We have much more to see. So if you can continue to be good, and disciplined, and brave, then I will buy you a gift, okay?"

"Okay," Tully said happily knowing that I had taken his bait.

"Oh, my gosh," I said suddenly changing the subject. "We are at King Hall."[66]

....

66   *King Hall:* King Hall is the dining facility for the Brigade of Midshipmen. It is named in honor of Fleet Admiral Ernest J. King, Naval Academy Class of 1901, Chief of Naval Operations during WWII and one of only four men to hold the rank of Fleet Admiral. Optimum efficiency is the only thing that can prevent utter chaos when more than 4,400 people sit down at one time for dinner at 392 tables spread over a 55,000-square-foot area. Hot meals are served to all within five minutes, reflecting the efficiency that exists in King Hall. The staff in the academy's Midshipmen Food Service Division plan, prepare and serve more than 13,500 meals per day." "King Hall, USNA, https://www.usna.edu/PAO/faq_pages/KingHall.php

"What, Aunt Cathy?"

"This, right here," I pointed at a pair of doors to the right of us, "This is King Hall! Here let me show you."

I opened the heavy doors, which led into a small vestibule. I walked over to the next set of doors and held open one of them for us to peek inside.

"Look," I said to Tully, pointing through the opening. Tully and I looked into a room filled with rows of large rectangular wooden tables. It was an endless sea of brown tables and chairs, blue tablecloths, and neatly arranged centerpieces. The tables were arranged on both sides of a center aisle that stretched back to the central area of the room. The room then branched off to the right and the left, with more tables and more chairs. The room was shaped like the letter "T."

"This is where the midshipmen eat their breakfast, lunch, and dinner," I said as I noticed a small woman pushing a large cart with metal shelving.

"It is so big," Tully said slowly moving into the room.

"It is, isn't it!" I replied, "All of the midshipmen eat at the same time—all 4,000 of them!" I watched as another woman with a hairnet and an apron on, rolled a large metal bin of apples and oranges across the aisle.

"The cooks and workers here," I said pointing to the women, "do such a great job. They work so hard to make sure that all 4,000 midshipmen get their food fast and hot!"

As I stepped forward into the room, the King Hall smell came rolling in like a strong wave. The smell of food, the musty building, and the recently bleached tables not only made me hungry, but my stomach began to stir with anxiety.

"The midshipmen call food, "chow," and as a plebe, we had to do something called a "chow call."

"What's a chow call?" Tully asked moving slowly over to one of the tables.

"It is where plebes have to make announcements in the hallway for the upperclassmen. You have to yell the menu out as loud and as fast as you can. We were responsible for all menus: breakfast, lunch, and dinner! It's called a chow call because we had to *call* out *chow* for every-one to hear."

"Was it fun?" Tully asked.

"Well, I didn't think chow calls were fun, but there were other Academy traditions that were a lot of fun. Do you know what a *tradition* is, Tully?"

Tully shook his head no.

"A tradition is something like when we go cut our Christmas tree down at that farm every Christmas: it is something special that we do every year as a family. Well, the Naval Academy has many traditions that date back to hundreds of years ago, and no other school has these traditions."

As Tully and I walked down through King Hall, I continued to explain chow calls, as well as a few other Academy lunch-time traditions...

Academic Year, September

I was standing in the doorway of my room with butterflies in my stomach. They were new ones, replacing the ones from the night before that had fluttered in when I had stepped onto the volleyball court at McDonough Hall for our game opener.

My right hand was spread out on the inside of my white combination cover,[67] pressing the top of it to my side. I looked down at my watch—11:54 and 55 seconds, 56... 57... 58... I took a deep breath and I bolted straight out into the hallway.

"Beat Army, Sir!" I yelled, squaring the imaginary corner in the middle of the hallway, turned to my right, and ran a few steps to the end of the hallway. I abruptly stopped, did an about-face, and jolted my body into at-attention. I looked across from me and saw Anna standing at the other end of the hallway. From my peripheral view, the hallway appeared free of detailers, but I knew that they were there; I could feel their presence. I took one large breath, clenched my fists, and then immediately began yelling as loud and as fast as I could:

"*Sir you now have five minutes until noon meal formation. Formation goes outside. The uniform for noon meal formation is Summer Whites.*

....

67 *Combination Ccover:* White hat worn with uniforms such as Summer Whites. https://www.usna.edu/UniformRegs/Chapter2-DescriptionOfUniforms/working-blue.php

The menu for noon meal formation is chimichangas, picante sauce, Spanish rice, whole kernel corn, relish tray, white bread, margarine, assorted cookies, vanilla milkshake, milk, and fruit punch. The command duty officer is Captain Lane, United States Marine Corps. The officer of the watch is Midshipman Lieutenant John, brigade adjutant. All hands are reminded to shut off all lights, running water, electrical appliances; lock all confidential lockers, and open all doors. Time, tide, and formation wait for no one. I am now shoving off. Five minutes, sir!"

Before I could even take one step, let alone recover from my lack of oxygen, I felt the presence of a tall figure behind me.

"Ervin, what are we having for breakfast tomorrow?" The thundering voice and tall presence belonged to Mr. Ross, Mr. Wyatt's roommate, and friend, and thus an enemy of mine.

"Sir, the menu for morning meal tomorrow is orange juice, grape juice, assorted cereals, sausage links, pancakes, maple syrup, margarine, breakfast croissants, fresh fruit, yogurt, milk, and coffee, sir!"

"Ervin, how many days until my ring dance?"

"Sir there are 262 days until your ring dance."

"Okay, Ervin, shove off."

"Aye, Aye Sir," I said as I quickly left to form up with the rest of my classmates who had already left the building.

As I ran to the ladderwell, I looked across to see Anna surrounded by a mob of upperclassmen. They were yelling at her for some reason. Somewhere in the loud jumbled burst of her chow call, they had found a mistake. Maybe she had left out mentioning, "whole kernel corn," or maybe she said, "lemonade" instead of "fruit punch." Maybe she didn't yell the chow call fast enough or loud enough. Maybe she hadn't been at the proper form of attention. Whatever the case was, she was taking a beating, and she would continue to be harassed up until the last second before formation.

I could feel Anna's pain. Like "Man in the Arena," I was in a constant battle trying to master the perfect performance of a chow call. It was a very rare occasion when I was not harassed or asked to start over repeatedly. In fact, at one point, my squad leader, the infamous Mr. Wyatt, assigned me to "ping-pong ball chow calls." It was his creative way to combine punishment with practice.

A "ping-pong ball chow call" was just what its name implied. The ping-pong ball (being me) would bounce back and forth in a fun and fast-paced game! I had to do a chow call for each minute, starting at "ten minutes until formation" until "one minute until formation." Also, as if this were not enough, I had to go to a different chow call station each time, alternating with stations on the deck above me (stations that didn't even belong to us but rather to 36th Company.) I had ten stations in total to get to, and I had ten minutes of yelling to do in between. There was, however, one advantage of a ping-pong ball chow call. By bouncing around from one station to the next, I ended up covering everyone else's chow call and thus my classmates would continue to reap the benefits of having a *problem child* in their company.

The daily stress of chow calls would eventually lessen for me as I began to gain confidence and discipline. I even began to understand the real reason for performing chow calls. At first, I thought chow calls were simply intended to add stress to a plebe's life and to provide a wake-up call for the upperclassmen. I found out, however, that there was more to this shouted-menu-wake-up-call. According to our "Plebe Training Manuel," chow calls were intended to "train fourth class to retain information and develop a poise and a command voice under pressure." Not only did I have chow calls for this specific training, but I had "Man in the Arena" as well.

As I ran away from my chow call station, after the go-ahead from Mr. Ross, I heard the dreaded voice of Montgomery behind me.

"Hold it, Ervin. You're not getting off that easy." Mr. Montgomery approached me as I froze to attention.

"Why don't you tell me how many days I have until my graduation."

"Sir, there are 266 days until your graduation, Sir!"

"How many days until the Army-Navy Game?"

"Sir, there are 87 days until we beat Army, Sir!"

"What we are having for dinner—*two* days from now."

"Sir, the menu for evening meal—*two* days from now—is linguini with clam sauce, scalloped ham, and potatoes, carrot coins, whole wheat bread, margarine, jello with whipped topping, salad bar, milk, and assorted drinks, Sir!"

Mr. Montgomery continued to fire away unable to shoot me down. Like a good enemy, though, he knew my weakness.

'Man in the Arena'—*go!*"

"Sir, it is not the critic who counts, not the one who points out how the strong man stumbles or how the doer of deeds might have done them better, the credit belongs to the man who is actually in the arena, whose face is marred with sweat and dust and blood, who strives valiantly, who errs and comes short again and again. Who know the great enthusiasm, great devotions and... and..."

Suddenly, once again, my mind went blank.

"... and..." My ship had taken a direct hit, and I was drowning.

"Enough, Ervin! You are making me mad. Just get out of my sight and down to formation."

"Aye-aye, Sir!"

I ran away demoralized and angry at myself. *Why can't I ever get it right!* I was tired of failing, and I was tired of my whole life being wrapped up in this stupid phrase. If this was what the Academy was about, I was done with it. Who cared about "developing a poise and a command voice under pressure," I was tired of the stress over stupid stuff, tired of people like Mr. Montgomery, and tired of yelling off menus for food that I never got to eat.

As I ran down the ladderwell, I wondered if Anna would make it down alive. She had taken a beating as well. I placed my cover on my head and pushed through a set of glass doors. The high noon sun pierced my eyes, and a warm touch of air brushed my face. I quickly walked over to my squad and slid into the space next to Lily.

After all the midshipmen were present and accounted for, we were dismissed from formation. I quickly made my way with the other plebes toward the doors of King Hall. I walked into King Hall, smelling what I had just been yelling in the hallways of Bancroft. As I smelled the greasy fried chimichangas, I thought of how knowing what was for chow, did not necessarily mean liking what was for chow. I made my way to my squad's table, as my stomach gurgled with anxiety.

I was ahead of the other plebes in my squad, so I knew that I had first dibs on what seat to take. It would have been to my advantage to choose the seat closest to the non-harassing upperclassmen and other plebes. However, I choose to take the "hot seat." The hot seat was located at the end of the table, and to the immediate right of the squad leader (who sat at the head of the table). If you were in the hot seat, not only were you the target for rating, harassing, and abuse but also you were responsible for preparing the table for your upperclassmen. Every plebe was supposed to take turns in the hot seat; however, it was often left empty for the unfortunate one that arrived too late to the table. Today I had decided to take the hot seat, even though I had had it yesterday. *I had just been destroyed by Montgomery, why would I be back for more attacks?* I was unaware of the fact that taking the hot seat was an indication of the confidence that was building inside of me.

As I placed my cover on the shelf underneath the solid wooden chair, I began to prepare the table. I reached down and pulled off sticky cellophane that was wrapped tightly around a silver platter of tomatoes, lettuce, and cheese. I untwisted the ties on the bread bags, placed spoons in the dishes of Picante sauce, and opened the milk and juice cartons.

As I stood, waiting nervously for everyone to arrive, I reviewed the information I would soon be dishing out.

Today's *main menu* would consist of: three articles from the newspaper ("read with the ability to hold an intelligent discussion"), a list of the major sporting events on the Yard, the three purposes of the aircraft carrier, a description of five types of naval aircraft and five types of Marine aircraft, the ordinance, engines, speed, range, and crew of the F-14 Tomcat, and etiquette involving respect for the flag.

The *side dishes* consisted of: "Table Salt,"[68] "Laws of the Navy,"[69] and any other useless memorized sayings from our *Reef Points* book. Also,

....

68   *Table Salt:* Absurd responses to questions that must be memorized and recited out loud when asked the specific question. Found in *Reef Points* of course! For example: "How long have you been in the Navy? All me bloomin' life, sir! Me mother was a mermaid; me father was King Neptune. I was born on the crest of a wave and rocked in the cradle of the deep. Seaweed and barnacles are me clothes. Every tooth in me head s a marlinspike; the hair on me head is hemp. Every bone in me body is a spar, and when I spits, I spits tar! I'se hard, I is, I am, I are!"

69   *The Laws of the Navy:* Twenty-seven laws written by Admiral R.A. Hopwood, R.N. which contain "words of wisdom that few of you will appreciate fully now, words which you may wish you had heeded twenty years from now." *Reef Points* (p.60–64) For example: "The 3rd Law: Take heed what ye say of your seniors, Be your words spoken softly or plain, Lest a bird of the air tell the matter, And so ye shall hear it again."

to wash it all down, I could be asked anything from the past that I had been taught. Of course, I couldn't forget what was present at every meal, a *special dessert* just for me, the recitation of "Man in the Arena."

As I waited to dish out what information I could remember, my stomach groaned with the pain of hunger and with the pain of nervousness. I was nervous about the upcoming event that was about to take place. I had decided to perform a tradition which involved "one wild and crazy plebe, and one unaware and despised detailer."

As I stood nervously fixed at attention, King Hall was rapidly filling up with white uniforms funneling in from various corners. The familiar smell of King Hall lingered in the air as the sounds of hungry midshipmen echoed throughout the endless sea of wooden tables. Attention was directed towards the center of the Hall. The Chaplin's prayer and the Brigade Commander's announcements soon silenced the rumbling of hungry stomachs.

As we took our seats, carts rolled past our table and large metal trays were handed off. I took one of the trays of chimichangas, pulled off the cellophane, and offered the tray to Mr. Wyatt, who passed the tray on, insisting that "a good leader allows his men to eat first." As I sat on the front four inches of the heavy, wooden chair, I continued to pass trays, bowls, and containers around the table. As the food found its way around back to me, I filled my plate, even though the food would never be touched. I straightened my back as I looked across the table. I noticed Mr. Wyatt looking back at me. I could see his lips moving but I could not hear his words. I was blocking him out as I tried to focus on the mission at hand.

Should I do this? I reconsidered. *Will I be able to get away with it? Do the other plebes remember that today is the day, and if so will they help me out? Okay,* I thought to myself as I took a deep breath. *I better do this, now or never.*

I quickly glanced to the right. *Good,* I thought, *Mr. Shen is over at the next table, in the same seat he always sits in, and it looks like he is busy enjoying his lunch.*

I looked to the left. *Perfect,* I thought, looking at a clear plastic pitcher filled with liquid.

I was just about to make a move when suddenly my moment was ruined with the voice of Wyatt forcing its way into my ears.

"Ervin! I asked you a question! How many torpedo tubes does the Los Angeles Class submarine have?"

As if a robot, I quickly replied, "Four, 21-inch tubes, sir."

He then proceeded with the interrogation, "Unique to this class of subs, is its separate sonar system. Where is it located and what does it do?"

"Sir, it is located on the sail, and it is used for under-ice maneuvering as well as allowing maneuvering through minefields, Sir."

Mr. Wyatt continued down his endless list, "Name three types of torpedo-tube launched weapons."

I ignored the question.

"Ervin, answer the question!" Mr. Wyatt's face began to redden.

Once again ignoring Mr. Wyatt, I pushed myself away from the table and jumped up out of my chair. Before anyone had time to realize what was going on, I grabbed the pitcher of liquid and moved to the table to the right of me. With one twist of my wrist, I dumped the contents of the pitcher over Mr. Shen's head. A scream shot out, followed by the clanging of an empty plastic pitcher hitting the floor. I took off running as chairs screeched across the floor. From the sound of it, the other plebes had remembered, they were forming a blockade with their chairs allowing more time for my escape.

I slammed open one set of doors, then another set, until I was out of King Hall. I ran across the street, past Mitcher Hall, and through the familiar doors that led into the 8th Wing. I had four flights of stairs ahead of me to climb; I took a short pause, and then in a mad burst of energy I sprinted up to the top. I had always been fast, and I had been running up steps now since plebe summer, so I had more of an advantage over Mr. Shen. (*And I had set up a blockade.*) However, I still did not like the fact that I had an angry upperclassman at my heels, so the sooner I got to my room, the better. It felt like I was playing tag, and my room was base. Luckily, things had gone as planned, and I made it to my room with plenty of time to spare.

A few minutes later, an out-of-breath midshipman staggered into my room.

"Sir, you look *pretty in pink*," I said holding back a smile. The red Kool-Aid that had been in the pitcher had transformed Mr. Shen's white uniform into a lovely shade of pink.

Mr. Shen was so angry that all he could do was point a wet, sticky finger at me. All I could do was smile, for I knew that I had successfully completed the tradition called a "wildman." Because my wildman was a success, respect from the other detailers would soon be bestowed upon me. If my wildman had been a failure, I would have been subjected to whatever punishment determined by Mr. Shen, and there is no telling what that might have been since I was already on his "hate list."

I stood in my room enjoying the feeling of beating the enemy for the first time. I felt empowered. I was ready to take on anyone—well anyone besides Mr. Montgomery. The anger in Mr. Shen's eyes matched the anger in his voice. "You have made another mistake, Ervin. You will pay for this! I am not one to mess with!"

It *had* been a mistake to pick on Mr. Shen. Unfortunately, I found out after the fact that he was not one to appreciate Academy tradition. By choosing him as a target, my life became even more difficult as a plebe, but that was the risk that I had taken. I knew there would be consequences for my actions, but I did not want to sit back for fear of repercussions. I wanted to fight.

The "wildman" was a chance to be me, not Midshipman 4th Class Ervin, but rather that crazy wild child; a girl full of mischief, energy, and who was always ready to take a risk. By being a plebe, there were times when my spirit felt as if it had been tamed and my body harnessed. During this Academy lunchtime tradition, we were allowed to run wild, and that is just what I did!

I had missed eating chow that day, however, the look on the face of an upperclassman dressed in pink was well worth a little hunger pain!

CHAPTER 14:
THE GIFT

"AUNT CATHY, I'm hungry!" Tully said as we weaved in and out of the sea of wooden tables.

"So am I," I said, still feeling the hunger pains and the anxiety twisting my stomach in knots.

Tully and I walked out of King Hall, and away from the memories of dreaded chow calls and pink upperclassmen. I lifted my head grateful for the command voice and courage that I had been fed during meal time. Like the spice from a chimichanga, the taste would remain on my tongue.

"Hey, I have an idea," I said as I grabbed Tully's hand, "Let's go eat lunch down on the *rocks*."

"What is the rocks?" Tully asked as I quickened my pace.

"It is an area, where large rocks have been put down next to the water. It would be a nice place to sit down."

The "rocks," aka the "seawall," had been constructed for the prevention of erosion. Some of my earliest childhood memories consisted of picnics at the seawall with my mother, father, and my two brothers. I remember sitting on the warm, sun-soaked rocks, dangling my bare feet at the water's edge, with a peanut butter jelly sandwich in one hand, and a skipping-rock in the other. As my parents watched us play along the rocks, they entertained the thought of one of the boys attending the Academy, maybe Lindsay, the older of the two, the extremely intelligent and quiet son, or maybe Paul, the baby of the family, the rambunctious child with a no-fear personality. Little did they know that the Academy seed they had planted grew within the platinum blond wearing the yellow summer dress, the middle child, the stubborn one with endless energy and a wild spirit.

Tully and I took a left turn at 8th Wing and followed a sidewalk that passed LeJeune Hall on the right, and Ricketts Hall on the left. Ricketts Hall was used as a dorm for the visiting sports teams, dorms for the enlisted, and as a home for the Athletic Association. As we rounded the corner, Tully stopped immediately, for there on a patch of grass in front of him was a real airplane.

"That is an A-4 Phantom," I said as Tully sprinted towards the retired plane. Without ducking, Tully ran under the nose of the plane. He touched the wheel from the landing gear and then looked up at the belly of the plane. He ran through its long shadow and checked out the back wheels.

"Can I get up there?" Tully asked pointing to one of the wings.

"Sure, but no walking around if I put you up there."

I lifted Tully and placed him upon the edge of the wing. The gray metal had been warmed from the sun. I looked at Tully above me, as he slowly stood up with balance and determination. He smiled with pride as if he was the pilot and had just returned from a successful mission. He stood for a while making sure that anyone who passed us would take notice of the "pilot."

"Look at that, Aunt Cathy!" Tully had spotted another retired hero, a black submarine that was resting about 30 feet away from the plane. I reached up to get Tully who quickly leaped into my arms. I let the impatient boy down, who sprung from my arms and over to the bullet-shaped vessel.

"This is a submarine, a ship that travels underwater," I said as I approached the immortalized metal. The black paint had been chipping off, and patches of rust were spreading like a virus as it sat in an ocean of grass. Despite its sad predicament, it was somehow still able to convey its power and legacy. You could almost imagine it lurking through deep waters, with its echoing sonar, and its destructive torpedoes, sneaking upon unaware victims.

The black metal was hot, as I noticed Tully quickly pulling his hand back. He had been looking for a place to climb up, but quickly changed his mind.

"Does it have guns like the airplane?" Tully asked circling the sub.

"No, it fires torpedoes."

"How many torpedoes does it have?

I looked down at Tully, or rather at my mini version of Mr. Wyatt, and replied, "I am not sure, but I will find out Sir!"

Tully smiled and looked at his Washington Redskin's lunchbox I was holding.

"Hey, Tul, let's go eat our lunch, okay?"

"Okay, but can we come back and see the airplane again."

"If we have time, Tul, but we still have more to see!"

Instructing Tully about the A-4 Phantom

I was about to cross the street to get over to the seawall, when I noticed that Tully had left my side and was sitting upon a set of steps in front of two cement walls that formed a "V." The wall contained a map of the Naval Academy, with a list of building names and each with its corresponding number on the map, and a red "You are here" arrow. I pointed out all the places that we had been to, trying to give Tully an overall picture of the Academy.

"So, Tully do you want to go down to the *rocks* to eat our lunch?"

"No," Tully said sitting down on the steps.

"Oh, come on! It is so nice on the rocks," I replied disappointedly. I had been looking forward to sharing one of my favorite childhood memories.

"I want to eat lunch here," Tully said as he reached up to me for his lunchbox.

"Okay," I sat down next to Tully and handed him his lunchbox. "Let's see what goodies Grandma packed for you today!"

Tully placed the lunchbox on his lap and opened the latched lid. He poked around and pulled out a green plastic bottle and a bag of orange goldfish.

"Juicy-Juice and goldfish," I said smiling at one of his favorite snacks. "Let me see what other goodies you have in there!" I leaned over his shoulder and spotted a bag of Oreo cookies.

"Oreos! Grandma gave you Oreos, you lucky duck!" Tully picked up the bag and hid it in his lap.

"Grandma loves me!" Tully said with an air of prestige.

"She does! Don't worry, Tul, I don't want any of your Oreos but maybe you could share your apples with me?"

Tully quickly gave me the bag of apples, relieved he wouldn't have to fend for his Oreos, as he usually did with Grandpa, the cookie monster in the family.

"Oh Tully," I said looking across from where we were sitting. "I must say you did pick a nice spot to have a picnic! Look at our view from here." I pointed to the view across the road. You could see the newly constructed Visitor Center with its wall of glass windows, brick walkways, and benches near the water's edge. From where we were sitting, we could see the Severn River as well as the easternmost portion of the Annapolis City docks. The seawall was not in our view; however, I must admit that Tully's picnic spot was just as good. Either this 4-year-old had a pretty good idea of picturesque views or his stomach had told him that it was time to eat.

We both sat quietly wrapped in the warmth of the sun, the gentleness of the breeze, and the soothing sound of the seagulls. We watched as one car after another drove by, slow cars carrying tourists, fast cars carrying midshipmen, and shiny cars carrying officers. We watched as midshipmen ran by—some running fast, others running slow, some looking scared, others looking relaxed. We watched as tourists entered and exited through the glass doors of the visitor Center, some walking out with nothing, others walking out with much more.

I looked over at my nephew who had one hand in the bag of goldfish, and the other holding on to the bottle of juice. He shook the bottle and deciding there were a few more precious drops left, took one last slurp of the cherry-flavored juice.

"Hey Aunt Cathy, I want to do a *wildman* on *Grandpa*!"

Tully laughed with delight as he pictured his beloved father figure with a wet head drenched in cherry juice.

"That sure would be fun, Tul! Maybe we could get him when we have one of our big water balloon battles!"

Tully smiled as the two of us reminisced of our water balloon battles in which Grandpa was always our main target. It had become quite a common occurrence that my father had taken over the role of the enemy. He was the brunt of all tricks and pranks, and the words, "Let's get Grandpa," was now a common household phrase.

Tully and I continued to laugh as we pictured Grandpa running around with a wet head. As Tully continued to eat his lunch, I closed my eyes resting in the warmth of the afternoon sun. The cool moist air was blowing in from off the water as the chatter of seagulls drifted in and out. There was a certain feeling that Annapolis had. It was peaceful yet restless, simplistic beauty yet complex splendor, superficial pageantry yet profound ideals.

I heard the snap of the metal lunchbox being closed. I looked over at Tully, who had black cookie crumbs circling his entire mouth.

"Okay, so where should we go now?" I took a napkin out of the lunchbox and wiped Tully's blackened mouth.

"The Gift Shop," Tully said pointing across the street to the Visitor Center.

"Let's go," I said taking Tully's hand to cross the street. As we approached the main entrance, I stopped and looked at the wall of glass on the eastern side of the building.

"Come on Aunt Cathy," Tully said pulling my arm towards the doors.

"Hold on, I just wanted to take a good look at this building. Did you know that it is brand new and that when I was here, it was just a pile of dirt? I remember the construction workers coming in and building it."

"Did the workers put up work cones?"

"Yes, they sure did Tully! In fact, they had the really big work cones," I replied trying not to laugh. Ever since Tully was 2 years old, he had a fascination, *rather an obsession*, with work cones. We never could quite figure out why. Maybe it was the fact that they symbolized control; the workers could keep out traffic and people away from their work area with one simple cone. Whatever the case was, Tully had quite a collection of toy work cones at home. He even had a real life-size work cone, thanks to the city of Annapolis. (*Midshipmen do not lie, cheat, or steal. But sometimes they "borrow!"*)

Tully pulled on my hand, guiding me towards the entrance of glass. The whole east side of the Visitor Center was a wall of glass that rose from the floor to the second story. Not only did it provide a great view of the Severn River, but you felt surrounded by the water, like a ship out at sea.

As we entered, the Gift Shop was immediately in front us. Brightly colored sweatshirts, toys, footballs, mugs, and hats bombarded us from all directions. There were blue and gold pom-poms, red and olive-green bumper stickers, t-shirts with the Academy emblem, and sweatshirts with the Globe and Anchor[70]. There was a barrel full of soft, stuffed-animal goats with blue and gold horns, which immediately caught Tully's attention.

"There's Bill the Goat! I like Bill!" Tully picked a goat up, kissed it, and then placed it back into the barrel. Within a matter of seconds, he was gone and was standing in the toy section. He began rummaging through the square bins of toys, bouncy balls with airplanes inside, rubber duckies with Dixie cup hats, and Bill the Goat key chains. Suddenly he spotted a small metal plane; It was a tiny replica of a Blue Angel.

"Oh, my gosh," Tully said as he pulled the packaged plane down off the metal hook. His face lit up as he held the tiny jet in his hands.

70 *Globe and Anchor:* The Eagle, Globe, and Anchor is the official emblem and insignia of the United States Marine Corps. The Eagle is the symbol of the United States, and it proudly carries a streamer in its beak that bears the motto of the Corps: *Semper Fidelis* (Always Faithful). The Globe signifies the worldwide commitment of the Marine Corps and its areas of responsibility. Marines serve in any time or place. The Anchor, whose origin dates back to the founding of the Marine Corps in 1775, represents the amphibious nature of the Marines' duties and emphasizes the close ties between the Marine Corps and the U.S. Navy. "USMC Emblem," *Hqmc.marines.mil*, https://www.hqmc.marines.mil/hrom/new-employees/about-the-marine-corps/emblem/

"Look, Aunt Cathy, it's a Blue Angel!"

"That is way cool," I replied. "I think we may just have to buy it! What do you think?"

A smile stretched across *my angel's* face, "I think we should!"

We walked through the obstacle of clothing racks until we came to the checkout counter. A pleasant older woman with white hair greeted us. "Hello," she said as she straightened the navy-blue silk scarf around her neck. "Oh my," she said as she glanced down at Tully. "We have a real soldier here!"

Tully smiled up at the woman whose ears and wrists glistened with gold jewelry. I paid for Tully's gift, opting not for a bag, knowing that the gift would soon be flying alongside us.

As we left the gift shop, Tully spotted a display near the Information Desk. He ran over to it and stood on his tiptoes trying to see what was inside. The display was about a foot taller than Tully and was the size of a small rectangular coffee table.

"Aunt Cathy, lift me up," Tully ordered, "I want to see it."

"Please!" I ordered back as I picked him up.

We both immediately looked down into the display.

"Oh, my gosh," Tully said as he pointed to the six tiny model Aircraft Carriers lined up along one side of the display. The Carriers were in a painted blue ocean. Green plastic landmasses were scattered throughout the ocean.

"What does this say?" Tully pointed to a small label that was pinned to one of the green islands.

"It says, 'First wave of attack, 0755—Wheeler Field.'"

"What about this one?" Tully asked pointing to another label pinned onto a tiny ship.

"It says, 'First wave of attack, 0800—USS Arizona,'

"Tully," I continued, "This is the attack on Pearl Harbor."

"Oh," Tully replied. "I saw Pearl Harbor!"

"Yes, you did see part of that movie,'

I circled us around to the other end of the display.

"See, a long time ago, the Japanese attacked our American Navy Base on an island called Hawaii. It was a surprise attack, Tully."

"A surprise?"

"Yes, the Americans had no idea that the Japanese were going to attack. This attack was very sad."

"Why?"

"Well, we lost a lot of American soldiers, they died trying to fight back against the Japanese. The United States then decided to go to war with Japan."

Tully looked down into the clear glass, with sadness upon his face. "Why did they attack us?"

"Well," I paused trying to figure out how to explain the Japanese alliance with Germany, the United States' oil embargo to Japan, our financial aid to China, and the unwanted presence of our Pacific Fleet in Hawaii.

"Sometimes countries don't get along, and they want to start a fight so that they can do what they want."

Tully continued to look at the tiny paper-clip size airplanes lined up on the decks of the 6 carriers. "Are these the Americans?" Tully asked pointing to the planes.

"No, those are the Japanese. Do you see the small red circle on the wings? That is the symbol for Japan."

"All of these are Japanese?" Tully pointed to the six carriers.

"Yes, they are all Japanese. The planes left the carriers early in the morning and flew to the Islands of Hawaii. The Americans were just waking up, when suddenly the sky was filled with planes, torpedo planes, bombers, and fighter planes. The American soldiers fought back, but the Japanese were too strong. The Japanese attacked for two hours and destroyed 21 American ships, 188 airplanes, and 2000 American soldiers were killed. It was a sad day for America, but we fought back and now we are no longer enemies with Japan. They are now our friends."

"Aunt Cathy," Tully began squirming to get down from my arms.

"Yes, Tul," I said as I landed my little jet.

"Can I play here?" Tully asked as his Blue Angel took off across the Hawaiian Islands.

"Sure, but just for a few minutes."

At home, Tully would often reenact battles with his fleet of ships and plastic army men. It was too hard for him to resist playing now. He had a battle that was already set up and a brand new plane ready for action!

As Tully began to play, I noticed the room darken. I looked outside to see a fleet of clouds that had overtaken the sun. The darkened room and the sound of Tully's aerial attacks kept me thinking about Pearl Harbor. I had memorized the date—*December 7, 1941*. I had been forced to memorize the date. I had known that it was *"A day that would live in infamy."* I had learned about the attack, and the history leading up to the attack. I had learned about the numbers, the numbers of ships, the numbers and types of planes, and the numbers of American soldiers killed. I had learned the names, the names of the ships, the names of the Commanding Officers, and the names of the islands and the airfields. I had learned what was in this display. I had been forced to learn it, but now I understood it.

As I stood in front of the display, I remembered a story where Montgomery had shown us that in the darkness and infamy of Pearl Harbor, there was a strength of character, resilience of country, devotion to duty, and love of fellow soldier, that had shined through.

Academic Year, October

It was another day in the life of a plebe, and another day of failing at "Man in the Arena."

I had just returned from the firing range with the rest of the 34th Company plebes, where we were practicing for our certification on the M-16 semi-automatic machine gun and the 45-caliber handgun. We were tired and hot and soon found ourselves lined up at another firing range—*Montgomery's firing range*. Bullets shot out from his mouth, as my ears continued to ring from the ongoing live fire.

"Ervin, 'Man in the Arena'—*go!*"

"Sir, it is not the critic who counts, not the one who points out how the strong man stumbled or how the doer of deeds might have down them better. The credit belongs to the man who is actually in the Arena, whose face is marred with sweat and dust and blood, who strives valiantly, who errs and comes short again and again, who knows the great enthusiasms, the great devotions, and spends himself in a worthy cause… who… if wins knows the triumph of high achievement… and… and…"

I could not finish. My words hung in the thick air as darkness once again filled my spirit. I had failed again.

"*Stop,* Ervin, that's enough. I don't want to waste any more of your classmates' time. We could stand here for another hour, and I am sure you would continue to screw it up. When will you see that you are not only failing yourself, but your classmates as well? They have been punished enough for your failure, so this time you will just be punished. I want you to write out "Man in the Arena" 340 times, and have it to me by tomorrow evening. Is that understood?"

"Sir, Yes Sir!" I replied holding back my tears and wondering how in the hell I would be able to complete my new task.

Mr. Montgomery disappeared into his room and reappeared in the hallway with the "Good Book."

"Ervin, when was Pearl Harbor?"

"Sir, December 7, 1941, Sir!" I replied as my voice quivered from the aftershock of the earlier hit.

"Correct. I am now going to tell you all another story from the Good Book, and as always, I expect it to be ingrained in your pathetic minds. Is this understood, Ervin?"

"Sir, Yes Sir!" I felt like I was the only plebe standing in Montgomery's firing range. *Why was I taking all the bullets? Why were my other classmates always free to escape?*

Montgomery began his story:

> *It was December 7th, 1941, a day that would live in infamy. Many heroes shined through on this dark day in December. One such hero was a young man, only 20 years old, from Springfield, Ohio. His name was James Richard Ward; he was a Seaman 1st Class[71] in the United States Navy. This young man was only the third-highest rank in the Navy.*

71   *Seaman 1st Class:* He has three stripes on the left sleeve of his dress uniform and while he has a rate—Seaman 1st Class, the rank for the E-3 pay rate in the Navy—he's probably training for one of the many ratings that will be his profession throughout his enlisted career. The duties of a Navy Seaman 1st Class may be many, but they often fall into one of two categories: either he's a student learning his Navy job or he's a seagoing janitor. The 1st class seaman rank is often the reason those nice, clean Navy ships look that way. "Navy Seaman 1st Class Duties," *Chrono.com,* https://work.chron.com/navy-seaman-1st-class-duties-13325.html

He may not have had strong experience at sea, but he did
have a strong sense of his duty. Seaman Ward was on board
the battleship, "USS Oklahoma," amid the onslaught of the
Japanese attack. The Oklahoma was hit with three torpedoes
and instantly began to sink. The ship darkened with the
loss of electricity and the spirits of the crewmembers were
darkened by the death surrounding them. The crew was
ordered to abandon the ship, but Seaman Ward 'remained
in a turret holding a flashlight so the remainder of the turret
crew could see to escape, thereby sacrificing his own life.[72]

A light pierced through the darkness on that December day.
Seaman Ward was that light. His strength of character,
his sense of duty, and his love for the man beside him.
Seaman Ward received the Medal of Honor and received the
gratitude of a nation during this time of infamy.

Montgomery closed the Good Book as we all committed another
one of his stories to memory. What I committed to memory was more
than just a story. The image of Seaman Ward holding a flashlight and
giving light to others on that December day would always stay with me.
This simple young man would be a reminder of the person I should
strive to be like; one who knew the "great devotions," one who "spent
himself in a worthy cause," and one who undeniably gave others the
gift of life. I began to realize that there were times when *I was failing
my classmates, times when I left them in the dark.* I knew that one day I
could be in a position where I would need to be that light, where their
life may depend on it.

I was willing to give the gift of life, but for right now I needed
to see that "Man in the Arena" was the "gift" I had to give.

....

72 "Ward, James Richard," *Naval History and Heritage Command,* https://www.history.navy.
mil/our-collections/photography/us-people/w/ward-james-richard.html

CHAPTER 15:
ANGEL IN CAMOUFLAGE

"THANK YOU FOR MY GIFT, Aunt Cathy!" Tully said as he continued to shoot down the Japanese. His plane had been single-handedly defending the Hawaiian Islands and re-writing the outcome of Pearl Harbor.

"You're welcome," I said patting Tully on the back. "You deserve it, you have been such a good boy."

"Well how about we leave the Hawaiian Island and fly your plane on another mission?"

As we left the Visitor Center, I began to wonder about the tourists who would come as we had done. How many of them would understand? How many of them would be unable to get past the exciting images or the bright colors in the gift shop? How many of them would walk away with more than a bag of gifts? How many would stop at the small rectangular display and take time to understand that it was more than just *a day that would live in infamy*, that it was a day of indebtedness? How many would walk away with a bag of gratitude, gratitude for those that gave a gift of life.

Tully and I continued along the sidewalk that led away from the Visitor Center and out towards the seawall. As I looked out to the sparkling water, I took a deep breath of the moist air. It was mid-afternoon and I could feel the strength of the sun's rays as drops of sweat trickled down the middle of my back. I looked down at my little Blue Angel, who had been slowing down and was now at minimal cruising speed.

"Would you like to fly your plane to the *rocks*, Tul?"

"What rocks?"

"The rocks that make up the seawall. The seawall is a huge row of big rocks that are fun to climb on! Remember, I wanted to eat lunch there. Grandma and Grandpa used to take me there when I was your age to have picnics. It's just a fun place to play."

"Okay!" Tully replied as he quickened his speed.

The seawall consisted of a pile of large boulders that formed a barrier between the entire east side of the Academy's grounds and the water. Back in 1885, sediment had been deposited on the east side of the Academy to enlarge the area, and thus a barricade was established to hold back the Severn's waters. The seawall offered the best view of an Annapolis sunrise.

Tully and I left the sidewalk and followed the road until we came to the start of the seawall; we immediately hopped a wooden barrier that separated the road from the rocks. In no time at all, the two of us began a balancing act along the unsteady and unevenly spaced rocks.

"Tully, you have to go slow. It is easy to twist an ankle. There are large openings between the rocks."

Tully immediately stopped at the edge of one large boulder looking down into a deep crevasse, "What's down there? I hear something."

"Oh, that's cool, isn't it Tul, see the water comes up underneath some of the rocks here and makes a noise as it splashes inside there."

"It looks like a little cave, Aunt Cathy."

Tully and I sat down with our feet dangling over the edge of the rock. We watched as the waves splashed in between the spaces in the rocks, creating a hollow rhythm as the water disappeared into the small caves. A salty mist sprayed our faces, and our legs were cooled with gentle splashes. White foam clung to the sides of the rocks as small fish bobbed in and out of the small pools of water.

"Did you know Tully, that the sun rises right across from the seawall here?"

"No."

"And it is one of the prettiest sunrises I have ever seen!"

"Really?"

"In fact, as a plebe I got to see the sunrise every morning!"

"Why?"

"Well, every morning we had to come out here for PEP!"

"Why?"

"PEP was our 'Physical Exercise Program.' We were woken up by our detailers at 5:15 when it was still dark out, and we were taken to this field right over here." I pointed to the turf field directly behind us.

"What happened next, Aunt Cathy?"

"Well, we lined up with the rest of the plebes from the other companies, and in the middle of the field, there was this big wooden platform. And guess who was on the platform?"

"Who?"

"A Marine! He had a big megaphone, and he would stand up there and shout out commands. We would follow him as he led us through different exercises, like jumping jacks, pushups, and sit-ups. The detailers would walk around us making sure we were doing the exercises right and that everyone was trying their best. I remember working hard at PEP, sweating and in pain, and wanting to stop but that Marine would keep us motivated.

I remember this one day when he stopped us in the middle of an exercise, and he made us do an "about-face." We all turned around to see the most amazing sunrise ever! The sun was like a big red ball of fire sitting on the water and the whole sky was pink and orange. The Marine shouted out, "Hoo-yah Mr. Sun!" Then, all the plebes yelled back, "Hoo-yah!" That sunrise made you forget about the pain; it made you glad that you were up exercising because if you hadn't been, you would have missed the beautiful *gift* that God had painted across the sky."

My other angel in camouflage, then at the age of 9...

...and now as a soldier in the US Army.

I began to think about PEP and the Marine that motivated us to endure the physical pain at such an early hour and even come to enjoy it. I thought of one Marine in particular, who had been my sunrise in a time of pain, he had motivated me to endure.

"Hey Tul, do you want to hear a story about a Marine that helped me out one time, like the Marine that helped us all during PEP?"

"Yes!" Tully replied wiggling closer to me on the rock.

I looked down the long expanse of the seawall and over across the water to an area of forested land. "Do you see those trees, Tully, way over there?" I pointed out across the water.

"Yes!"

"Well, that is where my story takes place. Where God had sent down one of his angels and dressed him in camouflage!"

Together we looked over at the dense patch of trees as I began my story...

Plebe Summer, Training, Day 15

The small, covered pontoon boat rocked violently against the waves of the choppy Severn River. I was huddled inside with about twenty of my classmates. We were all quiet and cold from tightened nerves, from the 8:00 am chill, and from the occasional splash of river water from above us. We were dressed in our BDU's[73] and had our heads resting upon the padded orange life vests around our necks. It had only seemed like minutes ago that I was shouting out the morning chow call, and now I was feeling that morning chow with every rock of the boat. With each sway of the boat, I became more grateful for passing up on the pancakes and sausage links that had been offered, opting for cornflakes. The boat pitched against the waves for the entire crossing of the Severn River.

....

73   *BDU's:* The Battle Dress Uniform (BDU) are fatigues that were used by the United States Armed Forces as their standard uniform for combat situations from the early 1980s to the mid-2000s. Since then, it has been replaced or supplanted in every branch of the U.S. Armed Forces, except for certain elements of the U.S. Coast Guard, which still use them as of 2013. The U.S. Navy currently authorizes wear of the BDU uniform at locations such as at the U.S. Special Operations Command and other ground-based naval units, such as Seabees. "Battle Dress Uniform," *Wikia.org*, https://military.wikia.org/wiki/Battle_Dress_Uniform

Approximately fifteen minutes after we had left the docks of the Naval Academy, our boat came to a stop on the opposite side of the river. We immediately funneled out of the boat trying to take control of our swaying body and wobbly legs. A column was formed as we lined up into our respective squads. With our backs to the Academy, now a faint mist in the distance, we looked ahead to a dense forest. Within a matter of minutes, our column of camouflage was following Mr. Montgomery down a dirt road at a slow and steady jog.

The canopy of heavy foliage soon muffled the bright morning sun, and the smell of moist soil and dew-dropped leaves filled the air. The smell was home to me. I had spent much of my early childhood exploring the small patch of forest behind our townhouse. By the time I was old enough to dress myself, I put aside the skirts in favor of pants. I had told my mother that it was too hard to climb a tree in a skirt. I would cling to a high limb and sit for hours up in the trees, listening to the forest sounds, and rocking gently with the wind. Now as I ran with the column of plebes, in the cool shadows of the trees, among the patches of sunlight speckling the fallen leaves, and surrounded by the music of the birds and chirping squirrels, I was excited to be in a familiar home. I was also nervous—I could sense a new challenge lurking in the shadows of the forest.

Suddenly, our column slowed down as we reached the top of a hill. There was an area to the left of the road, which had been cleared. We stopped and stood in formation waiting for our instructions. Our instructions came quick and clear: the Navy way. We were to choose to run in the fast, medium, or slow group.

I had always been a runner and felt confident with my ability. I also had scored the highest among the women in our company for our timed PRT (Physical Readiness Test). At the Prep School, I had earned the title of "Iron Woman" for three out of the four semesters; a title given to the top female athlete who had scored the highest in the PRT.

As the thought of "Iron Woman" raced in my head, and as I noticed that no women had stepped aside to run in the fast group, my decision had been sealed. As I left the side of my roommate and most of my classmates, I huddled up with a group of long-legged and lean men. They resembled a pack of anxious gazelles ready to flee. Our group was the first to go, and before I knew it, we were given the go-ahead by one of the detailers to begin. I took off with the pack, following a small trail that disappeared into the forest.

The trail winded through the sweet smell of wet bark and sun-ripened leaves. The pace was fast as trees blurred past me. Tripwire roots, stumbling rocks, and ankle-twisting pits covered the trail adding a test of agility to this test of endurance. Branches reached out slapping my face as thorn-covered vines clung hold of my socks, clawing into my ankles. Runners, like jumpy deer, passed me in quick blazes and disappeared in front of me. In no time at all, it seemed as if an entire herd had passed. I ran harder, as frustration set in. My chest tightened as my lungs fought with the lack of oxygen, and my thighs began to burn with acid. Sweat poured down my face as mosquitoes buzzed in and out of my ears. My brown t-shirt was soaked, and my thick camouflage pants had to be constantly pulled up from the added weight of sweat.

Fatigue was quickly setting in, but I had learned to ignore the signs. Every day you felt pain and over time you accepted it; it became as common as sounding off around a corner in the halls of Bancroft, so common that you would ignore it. You would stand up from the push-up position to see blisters burned from asphalt upon the palms of your hands. You would take off socks and see pruned feet covered in blisters. You would lie down at night and feel a throb from a twisted ankle or an inflamed knee. Your mind would keep going, pushing your body; a body that would have stopped a long time ago if it hadn't been for your head to get in the way. Our detailers were training our bodies and our minds. They pushed us until our bodies broke, teaching us to rely on our minds. They would continue to push, and if they succeeded in breaking your mind, then you were really in for it.

Fatigue *had* set in, and I ignored it. My body became loose and raggedy. I began to stumble on the rocks and trip on the roots. My ankles twisted and my knees buckled. Soon I came to a large slope leading down to a small creek. Halfway through the creek, my combat boots sank into an abyss of black mud. As I struggled to pull them free, the mud oozed its way inside. I crawled and pulled until I was on my stomach against the opposite embankment. I grabbed ahold of a root above my head to help pull me up the nearly vertical slope. As I clawed my way out of the tar pits, I could barely stand. I finally was able to find my balance, and as I stood up I noticed that the forest was spinning. The trees danced in circles around me. The trail played tricks on me changing from one direction to another. I closed my eyes desperately trying to make the spinning stop.

I opened my eyes and fell to my knees upon a ground that was still moving around me. "*I have to finish,*" I whispered as I forced myself to stand. The merry-go-round wouldn't stop, and I was not about to get off the ride. The breakfast in my stomach began to rise, but I swallowed it back down. "*I have to finish.*" I began walking, trying to force my legs to run. The swirling of the trees became faster, and blackness began to creep in around the perimeter of my vision, like a thick mud oozing slowly and narrowing my field of vision. The blackness oozed until there was a small hole of light. I was on the verge of a collapse, when suddenly a voice awakened my sleepy mind.

"Hey plebe!"

I looked up to see a blurred image of a man approaching me.

"Hey, are you okay?"

I could tell it was a Marine, just by the sound of his voice—the command and intensity of it.

"Plebe, I'm talking to you!"

"I have to finish," I said as I stumbled toward the man.

"Can you tell me your name?"

"I have to finish"

"Can you tell me what day it is?"

"I have to finish."

"Do you think you need medical attention?"

As incoherent as I was, I managed to maintain my stubbornness.

"Sir, I have to finish." I could not answer any of the Marine's questions. I was beyond being able to comprehend them. All I knew is that I wanted to finish the course.

"Alright you'll finish, just follow me out. Don't fall asleep on me—take a sip of water."

I began to run towards the Marine, who slowly led me back onto the trail.

"Hang in there plebe."

I kept my eyes locked on the blur of a man in front of me. At times, the blackness oozed its way back in, and at these times, the crisp voice of the Marine would penetrate through the thickness. "Don't fall asleep on me. Keep talking to me, plebe."

"I have to finish. I have to."

"You will finish, just follow me. I've got your back."

After what seemed like an eternity, I came out of the woods. My sense of time, like all my other senses, had disappeared. I had no idea how long it had taken me to complete the course. I had been lost apparently for quite a while, and I ended up coming in dead last. As I followed the Marine out into the clearing, my roommate Lily quickly approached me.

"Cath, are you okay? You are as white as a ghost."

I could not answer, I just nodded my head as I was told to drink water. Mr. Montgomery approached me. "Ervin, take a ride back down to the boats. We need to get you to medical immediately."

I still could not answer, I just nodded my head. I was suffering from heat exhaustion and a possible heatstroke. As I rested and took more water, my sleepy mind began to awake. I looked around for the Marine, I wanted to thank him for helping me finish, for guiding me out of the woods, for keeping me from the verge of a collapse. The Marine was gone. I looked everywhere. There were no Marines at all, just a group of plebes with a handful of detailers. Come to think of it, I didn't remember any Marines when we had arrived at the "Endurance Course" that morning.

I stumbled over to my roommate. "Lily, where is that Marine?"

"What Marine, Cath?"

"The one that was with me when I came out of the woods?"

"Cath, I think you need to rest. You must be seeing things."

I looked at her, with confusion.

"Cath, you came out of the woods alone."

"Let's move out 34!" Montgomery yelled. I formed up with the rest of the plebes to follow Montgomery back down to the boats. My pride was already hurt from my last-place finish, and my near collapse. I was not about to *ride* in a vehicle back to the boats. I would tough it out.

The run back had to have been the worst run I remember as a plebe. The pain that I had experienced that day had to have been the worst as well.

That afternoon, as we headed back up on deck, Montgomery asked me how I was doing. I told him "fine," even though I should have gone to medical, but didn't. I required an I.V., cold compresses, and rest. I don't remember much of the rest of that day; all I remember is that Montgomery was impressed with my toughness and fortitude. This contradicted with how I felt. I was embarrassed that I finished last in a group that I had confidently placed myself in. I was in shock that my body had hit a wall. My body had given out on me, something the NAPS "Iron Woman" never thought would happen.

That night when I recited "Man in the Arena," and came to the words "strong man that stumbled," I pictured myself face down on a muddy riverbank. At the time, I had only seen the Endurance Course as a six-mile run through the woods, a physical test of my stamina. Montgomery had seen it as something else, it had been a test of my mind: my spirit. I had endured the course through my mental strength, something that Montgomery held himself personally accountable for. I had proven that I was learning, and therefore that Montgomery's teaching had not been done in vain. The constant yelling and demoralization, the recall of historical dates, and the multiple recitations of "Man in the Arena" had proven their point on a simple wooded trail: that your inner strength, your endurance of spirit could carry you through.

I had inner strength. I had endured, but I also believe that I had help along the way. Like the sunrise during our early morning PEP, someone had motivated me to endure the pain. God had sent me an angel, an angel in camouflage.

CHAPTER 16:
EVERY EIGHT MINUTES

"I LIKE MARINES," Tully said quietly after listening to my story.

"So do I, Tul, they are strong, dependable, and they always take care of their people!"

As I continued to look out across the water at the Endurance Course, I thought of our military men and women who are like our country's angels, watching over us and protecting us, guiding us on our path in life.

Tully and I continued our walk along the unsteady and unevenly spaced rocks. We walked half of the seawall and then decided to run across the grass field to our left. The field was lined with pull-up bars on one side and soccer nets on the ends. It was Farragut Field, named after Admiral David Glasgow Farragut.[74] The field was used by the 150-pound football team, as well as the intramural sports teams.

We continued past 7th Wing when I noticed Tully's pace slowing down.

"How much farther?" Tully asked as we walked past the 5th Wing parking lot.

....

74 *Admiral David Glasgow Farragut:* The "hero of Mobile Bay and the first naval officer to hold the rank of admiral." *Reef Points,* 200. Farragut began his life as a sailor early; he commanded a prize ship captured in the War of 1812 when he was twelve years old. In April 1862, while commander of the West Gulf Blockading Squadron, "Flag Officer" Farragut took the city and port of New Orleans. As a reward, the Union created the new rank of Rear Admiral." Farragut's greatest fame came from the August 5, 1864 Battle of Mobile Bay. The Confederates had placed a large number of "torpedoes" in the waters. The monitor USS Tecumseh struck a torpedo and began to sink, causing the rest of the fleet to back away from the mine-infested waters. At the time, Farragut was watching the battle while lashed to the rigging of his flagship (USS Hartford). Alarmed, Farragut shouted, "What's the trouble?" The USS Brooklyn answered, "Torpedoes!" Farragut shouted back, "Damn the torpedoes! In the end, Farragut's fleet defeated Confederate Admiral Franklin Buchanan and the last open seaport on the Gulf of Mexico fell to the Union. "David G Faragut," *American Battlefield Trust,* https://www.battlefields.org/learn/biographies/david-g-farragut

"Not much farther. I am so proud of how strong you have been! You would make a great plebe!"

Tully smiled as we walked past McDonough Hall, and into the shadows of Chauvenet Hall and Michelson Hall, two of the Academic buildings. Near the building was a bright blue track circling a field of grass and sandpits.

"Tully," I said trying to distract him from his tiredness, "This is Ingram Field, this is where the Navy Track team runs. I looked over to my right at another large grass field that was parallel to the Severn River; a field that had been plowed by cleats, evident by the bald spots in the grass.

"Over there is Dewey Field, this is where the Navy Soccer Team plays." Tully stopped and looked up at me with puppy dog eyes and a whimpering lip.

"Aunt Cathy, could you please carry me?" He stretched his drooping arms out toward me with a dramatic gesture.

"I sure will," I said picking him up, "You have walked a lot today and have not complained at all! I am quite impressed." Tully's body felt warm as I held him in my arms. He placed his damp forehead on my shoulder. He was tired and hot. I opened his lunchbox and pulled out a small water bottle.

"Here drink this," I said as I handed the plastic bottle to Tully. I wasn't sure how long I would last carrying him. Not only was Tully a tall child for his age, but I was wearing a pair of uncomfortable sandals, so the added thirty pounds of weight made my walking a little trickier.

"Thank you," Tully said as he squeezed his arms around my neck.

"You're welcome," I knew that the free ride was much appreciated, and therefore being glad to do it.

As we passed the Academic buildings, I began to think of the many tests I had taken as a plebe, and how I would never want to see another one of those calculus or chemistry tests again. The only tests I ever did well on, were tests that did not take place in any Academic building. Besides the PRT test, there were other tests that, not only did I enjoy, but that I did well on.

"Did you know Tully, that we had to take lots of tests?

"No," Tully replied sleepily.

"Well, we did! We were tested in our schoolwork, like math and science, and we were given other tests that didn't' even have to do with school!"

"What were they?

"One test was called the "PRT"—the Physical Readiness Test. We had to run, do sit-ups, and pull-ups. You had to pass the test with a certain score.

"Did you pass, Aunt Cathy?"

"I did! I did so well that I 'validated' it, which meant that I didn't have to take it again." I smiled as I thought of how I wish I could have *validated* my calculus and chemistry!

"We also had to take plebe tests. Every Friday we were given 'Pro-quizzes,' which tested us on the information we had to learn for that week, stuff like learning about ships and airplanes, how fast they go, how many missiles they can fire."

"Hey Tul, guess what one of my favorite tests was?"

"What?"

"The Fire Team Reaction Course!"

"What was that?"

"I am going to take you there right now! It was a test to see how good of a leader you could be. We had to take turns leading a group of classmates through an obstacle course, and we were graded by our detailers on how well we did. Would you like to go try it?

"Yes!" Tully shouted with excitement.

We crossed the road to a small sidewalk that followed alongside Dorsey Creek, an inlet of water that branched off the Severn. We followed the water to a wooden bridge, which spanned the creek to an area called Hospital Point. I stepped onto the bridge feeling the wood beneath my feet and the sticky saltwater in the air.

We continued to walk along the small footbridge until I stopped at its midpoint. I looked over the right side of the bridge. I leaned over with Tully still in my arms. The water was a flat silvery mirror reflecting all that was around it. A white mist was rising above the reflections, catching sunlight on its way up. The only thing I could hear was the sound of water sloshing up against the side of a hollow hull.

As I looked out in front of me, I noticed a sleek crew boat gliding towards the bridge.

"Look Tully," I said as I pointed to the long thin boat. "That is called a crew boat. The Academy has a Crew Team in which they race against other boats."

We watched as the long paddles sliced through the mirror as if melting the surface. The flat ends of the paddles would disappear then they would resurface pulling apart the liquidy silver. I became mesmerized as I watched the melted silver ripple with each pull of the oar. The reflections that had once been untouched were now distorted. The perfect picture of trees and sky now looked like a Van Gogh painting. We continued to watch the crew boat as it slid through the painting, and then under the bridge on its way back to Hubbard Hall[75].

Tully and I continued to the end of the bridge and stepped onto the grass of Hospital Point, an area composed of Forrest Sherman Field, a cemetery bordering on the left, and a hospital just beyond that. It was also home to the famous Obstacle Course, which every plebe was familiar with.

I became familiar with it from day one. Our detailers had taken us to the course on the night of I-day. I remember doing endless sit-ups and flutter kicks with the smell of wet grass staining my body and sweat stinging my eyes. I also remember having to run the obstacle course but instead of running it traditionally, we had to run it by doing the crab walk.

Around the perimeter of the field were large wooden structures placed about 10 yards apart. The structures were all different shapes and sizes.

"Tully, this is called 'Hospital Point', and this may look like a playground, but it is an obstacle course. As a plebe, you would have to run the course in a certain amount of time."

I walked over to my favorite obstacle, the two 15-foot-high walls that were draped with cargo netting. The walls were about 10-feet-wide and were joined at one end, opening at a 45-degree angle. Cargo netting

75 *Hubbard Hall:* A building located on the Gate 8 side of Dorsey Creek, which houses the crew and baseball teams. It was named after the man who stroked the first Navy crew in 1870.

covered the front of the first wall, and it covered the backside of the second wall. I could smell the pit of cedar wood chips as Tully and I approached the structure.

"Can I try to do the ob-tacle course," Tully said trying his best to pronounce the new word.

"Definitely," I said. I placed Tully down at the base of the obstacle. I grabbed ahold of the brown cargo netting, stabilizing it, and positioned myself behind Tully to spot him on his climb. Tully reached up with two hands and began climbing. I closed my fists around the dry, itchy rope, and instantaneously I could feel it burning the palms of my moist hands. It felt as if I was climbing the rope again. I began to think about the many times that I had climbed up this wall; the times I had climbed it alone, and the times I had climbed it with others by my side.

"Hey Tul, remember I was going to tell you about the 'Fire Team Reaction Course?'"

"Yes!" Tully replied as he began to climb.

"Well, this is one of the obstacles where I was a leader and had to lead a Fire Team through. I will explain it to you and then you and I can be a Fire Team!

"Okay Aunt Cathy, I want to be a Fire Team. Do we get to put out fires?"

I smiled as I thought of Tully's love for firefighters and our countless visits to the local fire stations. With Tully around, a simple couch was often transformed into a firetruck, and our house, a burning building. With a vacuum cleaner hose in his hand, his yellow raincoat and snow boots on, and his taped up plastic red fireman's hat (a gift from the local fire department), Tully would come to the rescue.

"No, Tully, but just like being a firefighter, being on a Fire Team is dangerous and it involves good leadership and teamwork to accomplish the mission.

As Tully continued climbing up the rope, I began my story:

> It was a hot, plebe-summer day, and I was standing right
> here at this obstacle course. I remember Mr. Nash, one of my
> 2nd class, standing with me and a group of my classmates.
> He asked us who wanted to be the leader. We had no idea

what we were doing, and therefore, we had no idea what we would be leading. All we had been told was to go to Hospital Point and wait for further instructions.

Plebe Summer, Training, Day 17

"I will be the one, Sir, I will be the platoon leader," I said as I grabbed a hold of an army-green, metal box. I had recently been defeated on the Endurance Course, and I would *not* be defeated on this course. Like taking the risk of running in the fast group, I was taking a risk of being a platoon leader. However, this time around, not only could I fail myself, but I could fail others. With my inability to memorize "Man in the Arena," I had already failed many of my classmates, but it was teaching me that I had to keep trying, even if it meant failure. I *had to* run in the fast group, and now *I had* to be the Platoon Commander.

The metal box felt like it had been filled with lead. Mr. Nash nodded his head and then placed a flat wooden beam down by my feet. The beam was half a foot wide and nine feet long. I placed the metal box down on the wet grass and re-tucked my white t-shirt into my navy-blue shorts. I squatted down to tie my shoestrings tighter, taking in the familiar smell of mud, grass, and cedar wood chips. My classmates and I had been on this field earlier in the summer to run the obstacle course. I brushed aside slimy blades of grass that were coating my shoes and grabbed a hold of the waterlogged laces. After I tied my shoes, Mr. Nash motioned me away from the other five plebes in my group.

"Okay, here is your scenario, Ervin," Mr. Nash said squinting from the bright morning sun. "Your platoon has been given orders to bring medical supplies to an injured platoon on the other side of this hill. The hill is this wall." I turned my head towards the wooden structure in front of me. I began picturing a green hill, blanketed by lush trees rising from a rolling countryside.

"If y'all do not accomplish this task," Nash continued in his Tennessee drawl, "many could die. You will encounter a few obstacles along the way. First, the entire area surrounding the hill is covered in mines." Mr. Nash briefly stopped and pointed at an area in front of the wall and behind the wall. I looked down at the scattered wood chips and imagined the area covered in a web of tripwires connecting to a series of destructive mines.

"If someone touches any part of this area with their body, they will trigger a mine, and that person will be injured in the explosion. That person will then have to sprint down and back across the field, thus slowing your platoon down as well as taking points off. If any object touches the mines, points will be taken off as well." I looked out across the field, which must have been at least 100 yards long.

Mr. Nash continued, "In addition to safely getting every member of your platoon across, along with the medical supplies, you will have to move quickly. Every eight minutes a squadron of enemy planes, loaded with heavy artillery, will be flying by overhead. Your platoon will be exposed when climbing this hill, allowing you at that moment, to be an easy target. However, there is safe cover on the other side if you can get to it within these eight minutes. If you cannot, then you are dead. Game over.

You, as the Platoon Commander, will be graded on how well you can relay this situation to your platoon, the effectiveness of your plan for this mission, and how properly executed your mission is. Now at this time, do you have any questions, Ervin?"

"No Sir," I said as we both walked over to rejoin the rest of my group. Mr. Nash stopped in front of the group of sleepy-eyed plebes.

"Ervin is y'all's Platoon Commander," he said slowly. Mr. Nash turned and looked at me. "Are you ready?"

"Yes sir," I replied as I motioned my five other squad mates into a huddle.

Mr. Nash looked down at his watch. "Then your time starts… now!"

I looked around and saw all eyes on me. I turned towards one of our most responsible classmates. "Carrington, could you keep track of the time?"

"Sure," he quietly said as he pressed a button on his watch.

"Our eight-minute countdown starts now! Okay, this will have to be quick, so everyone please listen carefully," I said looking around at the unenthusiastic faces.

"The most important thing is to remember that we are a team. Help each other out. Each one of you has different talents, so let's use them! Let's prove that we are the best damn group of plebes at this Academy! Hoo-yah 34!"

"Hoo-yah!" Shouted the waking plebes. A spark of energy was now flowing through my teammates.

I then began to relay the story, knowing that I had to tell it fast, but that I also had to tell it accurately. I also knew that I had to sound confident yet motivating. I was the sparkplug that would have to ignite the rest of the group.

I looked across at Stevens and Damon, two football players, who both possessed a needed quality: strength. Stevens was 6 foot 2 and built like a bear. Damon was a lean and mean 5'11. I turned to the two of them. "Stevens, Damon, you two will be in charge of the beam. This means that I am relying on you with the lifting and placement of the beam. One of you will go first, and the other will go last."

I turned towards Lang and looked into his slanted eyes. "Lang, I need you to carry the medical supplies." He nodded unemotionally and picked up the metal box as if a feather. He curled the box towards his body, while sculpted muscles rippled from underneath his shirtsleeves. Stevens and Damon swiftly grabbed a hold of the beam and walked it over to the edge of the minefield.

"Remember that no part of you or this beam can touch anywhere in these woodchips," I said commandingly. "I want you to place the end of the beam up against the wall so that it rests at a 45-degree angle."

Damon slowly placed his end down upon the grass, as he and Stevens cautiously lowered the other end until it touched the wall. Stevens decided to go across first, stepping upon the inclining beam. The beam began to bend from the middle linebacker's weight. Stevens began to wobble as he placed one foot in front of the other. He looked like a clumsy circus bear trying to walk on the tightrope. His wet rubber soles on his shoes began to slip on the smooth wood.

"Stevens, try crawling. Use your knees," I yelled out, knowing that a lower center of gravity would be better for his balance. Soon, Stevens was shimming up at a slow and shaky pace. He had no problems when he got to the cargo netting, for he used his entire upper body to pull himself up. When he got to the top, he swung a leg over and straddled the six-inch-wide ledge.

The shaky climb of the circus bear seemed to paralyze the rest of the platoon. I needed to restore some confidence, so I decided to go next. I grasped the beam in my hands and inched my way up at a steady pace. Carrington had grabbed a hold of the base of the beam, helping to steady it. I then confidently seized hold of the unsteady cargo netting. The connected squares of twisted rope sagged as I began to climb hand over foot up the wall. I could feel the rope burning in the palms of my hands as I continued to pull myself upwards. The ropes felt like stirrups cutting into the arches of my feet. When I got to the top, I sat upon the ledge next to Stevens.

I looked down to see a mop of straggly short brown hair. I motioned to Summers for her to follow my lead. She grasped the beam, but she had trouble placing her slippery feet upon it. Suddenly, her right foot slid off the beam, dropping only an inch from touching the wood chips.

"Aaaahhh," Summers screamed as she continued to struggle with her lack of coordination. With each move she made up the beam, the platoon became increasingly nervous. Carrington and Lang both clutched the wood to hold it steady.

"Thanks, guys," I said as I observed their teamwork.

Summers not only continued to have problems climbing, but her fear of heights began to make matters even worse. On the cargo netting, she struggled like a helpless fly trapped in a web of an approaching spider. She was either too tired or she was paralyzed with fear, for she suddenly stopped. She was quivering.

"Let's go Summers, you can do it!" I yelled out. Encouraging words exploded from below me. The team began to pull together, realizing that the success of the team depended on each person.

"Summers, you're awesome! You are doing great!" yelled Damon.

As the team's words lifted Summer's spirits, her unsure eyes began to fill with determination. She seized the wobbly rope with confidence, breaking free from the web, and continued to ascend.

"Nice work Summers," I said as I continued to watch her move, "and take your time!"

"Don't look down," Stevens yelled beside me.

When Summers finally made it to the top, I let out the breath that I had been holding. She was a bit shaken up, as her body continued to tremble, but she was smiling.

"Summers, you did great! We can't lose you—we need you and your positive attitude!" I said as I looked down at the rest of the team.

Summers smiled and yelled down to Carrington, "You got it, the netting is shaky," Summers yelled grabbing hold of some of the netting to steady it.

I looked back over the edge to see Carrington already halfway up the cargo net and climbing at the speed of Spiderman. His long arms and legs were sprawled out, moving gracefully upon the ropes. Within minutes, the superhero was sitting beside me, and giving me a report on the approaching enemy aircraft.

"We have five minutes remaining," Carrington said nervously.

"Lang, let's move," I commanded. Lang moved across the beam as steady as a machine, without error or falter. Instead of holding on to the beam, he held on to the metal box, which he pushed up in front of himself. After making it up the beam, he grabbed ahold of the cargo net in his right hand with the medical kit in his left. Before I had a chance to suggest a way to pass up the kit, he began climbing with the use of only his right hand. Not only was Lang strong physically, but he was also very strong-willed. I had no doubts that he would make it to the top.

"You're kicking butt, Lang" I quickly yelled down, "Damon, just give it your best shot," I said as I looked at the remains of my platoon, Damon all alone on the beam. Damon grabbed the cargo net and began weaving his hands and feet in and out of the rope to secure himself.

I scrambled back down the netting to give him a hand. As I scaled down effortlessly, I realized how thankful I was for my childhood, how those countless hours of climbing in trees were paying off now.

I stopped when I was about halfway down. Damon's head was just to the right of my feet. He was in the process of pulling the beam off the ground. With all our strength, which was mostly his, we lifted the beam until it was over our heads. The higher the beam went, the more the beam wobbled and the more my arms hurt. Stevens leaned over from up above and clawed at the end of the wood until he could finally seize it in one quick pull. Carrington helped to pull it up until it was balanced and resting perpendicular on the ledge.

I looked up at Stevens.

"Now we need to place it across to the other side, bridging the gap."

Stevens laid the beam across and with no questions asked, he began crawling over to the other side. Damon and I made it to the top to find Summers on the beam, moving like an inchworm. As if Carrington could read my mind, he held up three fingers for me to see. I nodded my head. "Plenty of time, Summers—you're doing great!"

After Summers made it safely across, Damon and I soon followed. Within one minute, the whole platoon was sitting straddled on the opposite wall.

"Hey guys, you are doing awesome, but I can hear the hum of jets in the distance. We need to move fast," I said as I shot a glance into the sky.

"Don't forget the man beside you, but keep it fast!" I motioned to Damon, who then pulled the beam over from off of the first wall. With the help from Stevens, they began to lower one end towards the grass across from us, extending it over the wood chips. The beam lowered, as weight and gravity assisted in bringing it down quicker. In no time at all, it landed with a thump, inches shy from hitting a mine.

"Let's go," I said as I sat down on the beam with my feet forward, and my hands holding on behind me. I slid down and landed in the wet grass of safety. Stevens barreled down next, followed by Carrington, then Lang, then Summers. Damon had almost made it to the bottom when suddenly he lost his balance and his left leg slipped off the beam. As his foot hit the ground, a cloud of wood dust exploded into the air. The whole platoon froze, as we looked at our injured friend.

Immediately I yelled, "GO, GO, GO!"

"We've got one and a half minutes," Carrington rang out. Damon was fast, and before we knew it, he had taken off in a blur.

"You're running for the touchdown Dee," Stevens yelled out to him. The look of defeat quickly covered the faces around me.

"Hey guys, it's not over yet! You have all done an amazing job and Damon will not let this fine, highly talented team down. We still have time. Never give up. The planes may be close, but they are not here yet!"

"Go Dee," yelled Stevens.

"Give it all you got!" Shouted Summers. Damon's wide-receiver trained legs carried him down the field and back with a few seconds to spare. A proud Damon returned to his relieved platoon. He had made it!

High fives were passed around as Mr. Nash approached our team. "7:58… 59… and… *stop!*" He said as he looked up from his watch. I looked up and imagined the enemy aircraft thundering by with my team now safely out of sight.

"Nice job guys, it was good to see everyone pulling together out there." Mr. Nash remarked as he handed me the score sheet.

"We did great," I added, "I am so proud of each one of you! This was an easy group to lead and therefore made my job a lot easier." I paused and then draped my arms over the arms of Carrington and Summers, who were standing next to me. "5th Law of the Navy guys! Hoo-yah 34!"

The five of us stood together proud of the fact that our group was awarded an "A", but more importantly, proud of who we were and proud of who we were together. As I looked at my teammates around me, the memorized words of the "Fifth Law of the Navy" echoed inside of me,

> *On the strength of one link in the cable,*
> *Dependeth the might of the chain,*
> *Who knows when thou mayest be tested?*
> *So, live that thou bearest the strain!*

Today, this memorized saying came to life for each of us. From now on, these words would not just be spoken, but they would be lived.

We all had been tested today. For Stevens, Damon, and Lang, it was a test of strength; for Carrington, it was a test of responsibility; for Summers, it was a test of courage; and for me, it was a test of leadership.

"The might of the chain" was the success of our platoon. It depended on "the strength of one link," which was the strength of each one of us. Today we were tested, and today each one of us had taken the strain.

I looked at the faces around me. I was glad that they were on my team, and that I had not been alone. Today we had not only performed well at the "Fire Team Reaction Course", but more importantly we had exemplified the meaning of teamwork.

> *For some, it may take a lifetime to figure out how to work as a team.*
> *For others it may take only minutes—say, for example, eight minutes.*

CHAPTER 17:

ST. MICHAEL

"EXCELLENT JOB," I said as I watched Tully shimmy up the cargo rope. "Alright my little monkey, when you get to the top I want to see if you can climb back down." In no time at all, Tully had two feet back on the ground and was ready to take off for the next obstacle. Tully and I ran through the rest of the obstacle course, under the wooden beams, over the wooden beams, up the walls, across the monkey bars. We ran until the heat zapped us of what energy we had left.

As we left Hospital Point and the obstacle course, I thought of my Fire Team, and how by the end of Plebe Summer, like Senior Chief Flora and Major Parrino, and the rest of 34th Company, they had become my family.

As we walked back across the footbridge, I could hear a drumbeat off in the distance.

"I hear something, Tully, coming from across the bridge over there! Let's go check it out!"

"Okay!" Tully replied as he reached for my hand.

We quickly raced across Decatur Road, as we followed the call of the drum. The large basketball arena, Alumni Hall, was on our left as well as a few of the other academic buildings, Mahan and Maury Hall. To our right was a well-groomed field of grass, flanked by a row of trees on our side and by bleachers on the far side. We were closing in on our target as we walked over to the field. Today the field looked like a checkerboard of green and black, patches of grass alternating with perfectly formed groups of midshipmen.

"Tully, this is 'Worden Field'[76], the Parade field. Do you hear the drumbeat? Look—the midshipmen are marching!

"Why?"

"They are practicing for when they will have to march in a parade. *Marching* is called "Drill." All midshipmen must learn how to drill.

"Why?"

"Well, it is another tradition at the Academy that began a long time ago. Ever since 1848 midshipmen have been learning how to drill.[77] The Academy trains midshipmen like any other soldier. A long time ago, powerful armies realized that the best way to move a group of soldiers across a battlefield was in organized groups, boxes of men who move as one single body. In this way, soldiers stayed together and could be commanded by officers. Flags were also used to keep units together, so no one would get lost from their unit."

"Oh my gosh Aunt Cathy, they are carrying guns!" Suddenly drill became a little more exciting.

"That's right Tul, every midshipman is issued a rifle, and must learn how to march with it."

"Can you shoot it?"

"No, not these rifles. They are old and are just used for marching. We did fire rifles but different ones."

....

76 *Worden Field:* Admiral John L. Worden became a U.S. Navy Midshipman in 1834. In February 1862, upon resuming active duty, he was given command of the Revolutionary Ironclad *Monitor* and took her into a historic battle with CSS Virginia on 9 March 1862. Receiving serious eye injuries in the action, he had to relinquish command. However, this battle made him a major war hero in the North. He received the rank of Commodore in 1868 and the next year began five years as Superintendent of the U.S. Naval Academy, during which time he was promoted to Rear Admiral." "Worden, John L.," *Naval History and Heritage Command*, https://www.history.navy.mil/our-collections/photography/us-people/w/worden-john-l.html

77 *Drill:* In 1868, military drill is adopted at the Academy… "instigated by Professor Henry Lockwood, a West Pointer," who is then "hanged in effigy from the school's flagstaff for inventing "Midshipmen P-rades." "A brief History of USNA," Usna.edu, https://www.usna.edu/USNAHistory/History.php
Drill is marching, plain and simple. In ancient times, the most powerful, efficient, and developed empires developed ways of moving troops from one place to another in order to prevent masses of soldiers from getting lost." "The Importance of Drill," *Millitary.com*, https://www.military.com/join-armed-forces/the-importance-of-drill.html

I thought of the M-16 rifle that I had barely qualified on during Plebe Summer. We had *Marksmanship Training* where we learned to fire the machine gun as well as the .45 Caliber pistol.

"Why do they have guns then?"

"Well, in a real battle, guns would be used, and soldiers would have to learn how to hold them while marching. In a parade, the guns are only for show. They want the people watching to see that they are a well-trained group of soldiers who are ready to fight."

"Where is your gun? Can I hold it?"

"I don't have my rifle anymore; it belongs to the Naval Academy."

"Aunt Cathy, they look like robots."

"They do, don't they," I replied as we watched the precise movements controlled by shouted commands.

"Do you see how the midshipmen never move their heads to look around, their eyes are looking forward, this is called "Eyes in the Boat."

We watched as the columns of black marched in complete precision and control. The top half of their bodies were straight and rigid like boards, while the lower half moved in controlled strides. The rifles rested on the left shoulders with the arms bent at the elbow at a 90-degree angle. The butt of the gun was held firmly in the palms of the hand. The rifle moved with the sway of the arms, as if part of the body.

"Hey Tul, did I ever tell you about *Saint Michael*?"

"No," Tully replied moving closer to me.

"I didn't? I am going to have to tell you about him."

"Was he a midshipman?"

"No, Saint Michael was my *rifle*."

Tully looked at me with half a smile, not quite sure whether to believe me or not.

"When we were given our rifles to march with, our detailers told us that we had to name them. Our rifles were considered very special to us and therefore they deserved to be given a name. I decided to name mine after Saint Michael the Archangel, one of the greatest of God's angels. He was an angel that was a soldier and helped to defend the kingdom of heaven for God. He fought against Satan with a sword and a shield."

"Did you march with Saint Michael?"

"Oh yes, not only did I have to march with him, but I had to take him almost everywhere I went. When I went to the bathroom, he had to come. When we lined up in the hallways at the end of the day, he had to come. When Mr. Montgomery was mad, and we had to run up and down the ladderwells, he had to come. At night, I would lock him up to keep him safe. I would keep him clean because he was often inspected as if he was part of my uniform. I even had to memorize a special poem written about him:

This is my rifle. There are many like it, but this is mine.
My rifle is my best friend. It is my life. I must master it as
I master my life. My rifle, without me, is useless. Without
my rifle, I am useless. I must fire my rifle true. I must shoot
straighter than my enemy who is trying to kill me. I must
shoot him before he shoots me. I will...

My rifle and myself know that what counts in this war is not
the rounds we fire, the noise of our burst, nor the smoke we
make. We know that it is the hits that count. We will hit...

My rifle is human, even as I because it is my life. Thus, I
will learn it as a brother. I learn its weaknesses, its strength,
its parts, its accessories, its sights, and its barrel. I will
ever guard it against the ravages of weather and damage. I will
keep my rifle clean and ready, even as I am clean and ready.
We will become a part of each other. We will...

Before God, I swear this creed. My rifle and myself are the
defenders of my country. We are the masters of our enemy.
We are the saviors of my life.

So be it, until victory is America's and there is no enemy, but
Peace![78]

Tully and I moved underneath the shade of one of the oak trees along the parade field. I glanced over at the blocks of midshipmen maneuvering

....

78 *"My Rifle":* The creed of a United States Marine Corps by MGEN W.H. Rupertus, USMC.

their rifles in choreographed movements called *"ordering arms."* All the rifles moved at the same time with precise timing and control.

"St. Michael also helped me to win the Plebe Summer Drill Competition," I said as I continued to watch the rifles perform acrobatics, swinging and spinning from the hands of the midshipmen.

"He did?" Tully replied as he watched along with me.

"Oh yes, he along with 30 other rifles! It was the end of Plebe Summer. We had our second group of detailers trainging us.[79] One of them was Mr. Benevati; he was our Company Commander. He took the place of Mr. Montgomery.

"Where did Montgomery go?"

"It was Mr. Benevati's turn to practice being a leader. Mr. Montgomery did not go anywhere; *he was always around, even when he wasn't there.* Anyways, Mr. Benevati was in charge of teaching drill and with Benevati, something magical happened to the plebes in 34th Company.

As Tully listened and as we continued to watch the drill on the parade field, my story of magic, marching, and St. Michael began to unfold…

Plebe Summer, Training, Day 23

A yell from out in the hallway thundered into my room. "Ervin! Hit a bulkhead—*now!*"

I had heard this phrase so much during the first set of Plebe Summer that my body did not even need to think, it just reacted. I raced out of my room, squared the corner, sounded off, hit the bulkhead, and did an about-face. I waited *at attention* not even caring what exactly I did wrong this time. All I knew was that whatever it was, I would deal with it and do what needed to be done, I had been programmed.

Suddenly, a short man with olive skin, and short curly brown hair, approached me from across the hallway. He stood in front of me with a smirk and a sparkle in his eye. It was Mr. Benevati, our new Company Commander.

"Hey, Ervin…"

79 *Second Set Detailers:* The First Set's job is to "decivilianize" the Plebe. The Second Set's job is to build up the Plebe's confidence and morale. "Waldo News," Plebesummer.com, https://www.plebesummer.com/waldo-news

"Yes, Sir?"

"Disclosed sources have informed me of something about you."

"Yes, Sir?" I replied wondering what Montgomery had said to him. Maybe that I was trouble, or that "Man in the Arena" was my weakness, or just that he hated me?

"I heard that you have a 30-inch vertical jump, which is quite amazing based on the fact that you are only 5′4″. Is this true?"

"Sir, yes Sir," I replied shocked, wondering why he cared about my vertical jump. That was information important to my volleyball coach. Also, how did he know? Was he talking to my volleyball coach? Maybe he had heard about me at the Fire Team Reaction Course last week. I didn't jump, though, to get up that wall.

"Well, I want to see it," continued Mr. Benevati.

"Yes, Sir," I said as I smiled slightly. I couldn't help it—it was unusual that I wasn't getting yelled at. I moved away from the bulkhead and into the center of the hallway. I ran for a few strides and then leaped up into the air hitting a piece of tile from the ceiling.

"*Holy shit, Ervin!*" Benevati jumped into the center of the hallway with the excitement of a little child. "That was awesome."

I stood at attention, wanting to smile, but not daring to break my *military bearing.*

"Okay, Ervin, this is what I want you to do: every time you square a corner here on deck, I want you to jump up and hit the ceiling for me. Okay?"

"Yes, Sir," I replied wondering who this guy was. Was he insane? He didn't yell at me or anything but smiled and actually liked something about me.

"Alright, you may shove off now."

"Aye-Aye, Sir!"

I ran back into my room still wondering what to think of our new Company Commander. One thing was for sure, *he was no Mr. Montgomery.*

The end of plebe summer finally became a reality to the plebes of 34th Company. As Mr. Benevati took command of our ship, it was as if the seas calmed, and our port was in sight. He was a leader who did not need height, a shouting voice, or threats of torture to command our attention—rather he used his magic. His *magic* was taking interest in us and wanting to help us. Before long, we realized that something special was going to happen with Mr. Benevati at the helm—and it did.

I was standing in my room looking over my P.O.D[80] and noticed that Company Commander Time was soon approaching at 1830.

"Hey Lily, Mr. Benevati said BDU's and rifles for Company Commander Time today, right?"

"Yeah," Lily replied as she went to her locker to unlock her rifle.

"Do you think we are drilling?"

"God, I hope not!"

"Well, with Mr. Benevati, I am sure it will be cool!" I replied as I grabbed my camouflaged outfit from my locker and quickly got dressed.

At 1830 exactly, the 34th Company plebes were lined up on Turf Field. We stood at *parade rest*, with the butt of our rifles on the ground and the nose of the rifle leaned forward with our right hand. We were dressed in our BDU's with a white "watch belt" securely fastened around our waist. We waited, resting in the cool breezes from the water behind us. The sun was getting tired and was lowering itself on the horizon, leaving behind a swirl of colors that transformed Bancroft from grey to soft purple. The tips of our rifles glistened with the last pieces of the sun. I was relaxed—it was an unusual feeling.

I looked across the field and saw Mr. Benevati quickly approaching. He held in one hand, a sword, and in the other, a book. As he got closer, I noticed a look of determination.

"Alright, good job in getting formed up, you guys look good." Mr. Benevati spoke as he opened his book.

"As you know, this is Company Commander Time, *my time*, and I have decided that with my precious time, I am going to teach you how to drill. This is not a chance for me to harass you, quiz you on your rates, or just beat the crap out of you. I want to turn you into the finest group of marching plebes that this Academy has ever seen. Is this understood?"

"Sir, Yes Sir," we all replied in unison.

"That didn't sound too convincing," Mr. Benevati said getting closer to us.

---

80 *P.O.D*: "Plan of the Day." A plebe's life was planned out down to the minute, and the P.O.D. was a helpful agenda that listed when, where, and what we should be doing throughout the day.

"Sir, yes Sir!" We yelled as loud as we could.

"Good, because ya see, this is a team effort, and if I am out here busting my butt, learning what I have to learn,..." Benevati opened up the book he had been holding on to. "Then I expect the same from you. We can do this. We *will* become the finest marching machine! Hooyah 34!"

"Hooyah, Sir!" We yelled back, motivated by the man in front of us. And that was just it, this man brought to us a new style of leading and it motivated each one of us. We saw how determined he was to learn and teach us. We saw how important this was to him, and after that first session with Mr. Benevati, it had become important to us.

34th Company marching

For the first time, we looked forward to Company Commander Time. We drilled with a backdrop of the Severn River, wrapped in cool breezes and the rays of the setting sun. The environment relaxed us, and the sound of one man's voice inspired us. We learned how to step with precision, how to move and turn as one. We learned the different "manual of arms," and soon our 10-pound rifles became an extension of our bodies. We moved them around our bodies, effortlessly. We each became a mirror to the person in front or behind us, our every move was the same. We were becoming one. I remember leaving the field, as Mr. Benevati would stay behind. I will never forget the image of him standing on the field, a silhouette in the sunset with his book and sword in hand, practicing alone the steps, the maneuvers that he needed to master.

As Plebe Summer marched on, so did we. We practiced tirelessly, with Mr. Benevati at the helm. Like the tide along the sea-wall rocks, we never ceased and within a matter of weeks, we had been transformed. We were an image of control, discipline, and perfection. Not only did we want Mr. Benevati to be proud of us, but we wanted all of 34th Company to be proud. For the whole first half of Plebe Summer, we had felt like failures. Drill was a chance to prove that we were not. If we won the competition, we could no longer be considered failures.

The day of Plebe Summer Platoon Drill Competition had arrived. Nineteen platoons would be competing for the title. As we took the field, we immediately formed up as was instructed by the Marine Corps Major that would be doing the grading. She did a thorough uniform inspection on each one of us before any marching even began. We then performed our routine, as had been practiced and perfected. Our bodies were aligned and our steps were together. Our rifles moved effortlessly around our bodies, with precisely calculated movements. We did what we had been taught as we followed Mr. Benevati's commands. We left the field that day unsure of what the outcome would be. All we knew is that we were proud of who we had become and the fact that in Mr. Benevati's eyes, we *were* the "finest marching machine."

That night, as I locked up my rifle before turning out the lights, I thought of those soldiers, whose rifles would never be used for drill, but rather for *another purpose.* Like modern-day St. Michaels, they would be defending our kingdom, with a creed that would be spoken across a foreign land: "My rifle and myself are the defenders of my country. So be it until victory is America's and there is no enemy, but Peace!" I then thought about what St. Michael had become to me. When I looked at him now, I did not think of him as a 10-pound burden that had caused me so much pain, rather he was a 10-pound extension of me. Drill was a manifestation of what we had been taught during Plebe Summer. It was core values of the military: discipline, attention to detail, the will to fight, unity, and pride…

Now every time that I held St. Michael in my arms, I would be reminded of this. I would also be reminded of how it felt to be part of the winning platoon of the 1994 Plebe Summer Platoon Drill Competition.

CHAPTER 18:
THE TARGET

THE SUNLIGHT GLISTENED off the tips of the rifles, as Tully and I continued to watch the units of midshipmen march across the parade field. They were now passing the stands for the "*pass and review*," where a salute was bestowed upon the imaginary Brass[81] that would one day be watching the parade. Flags were titled forward, Company Commanders saluted, and the units snapped their heads to the right at the command of "eyes right." Soon they would be marching off the parade field, and onto Decatur road.

"Quick, Tull, come on," I said as I motioned for him to follow. We ran further up the sidewalk until we came to the end of Decatur road. We crossed Maryland Avenue, the street perpendicular to Decatur, and onto a patch of grass underneath a tree. We were now directly facing the approaching column of black.

"Oh, my gosh," Tully exclaimed as a tidal wave of black was heading our way.

The impressive sight of hundreds of uniformed midshipmen marching in unison was a little intimidating at first. Tully quickly hid behind my legs as the midshipmen stepped closer. Suddenly a wall of black was a few feet in front of us. The midshipman on the left corner of the first row was holding up a gold flag with a navy blue #1. In front of him was a midshipman with a sword and gold stripes circling the cuff of his sleeve.

"That is the Company Commander," I said pointing to the mid. "Look at the flag. This is 1st Company!"

As the Company Commander approached the intersection of the two roads, he immediately held his sword straight above his head and yelled, "Company... left turn... *march!*"

81 *Brass:* Term used to refer to officers

His row made an abrupt 90-degree turn to his left. The columns followed like a set of dominoes, each person pivoting to the left upon the same spot as the person in front of them had done. First company had broken away from the black column and was now marching down to the right of us and over to Stribling Walk. Soon to follow was 2nd Company. Tully continued to peek around from behind me as we watched another block of midshipmen break off to the right. After 4th Company, Tully realized that the army of marching midshipmen was harmless. He snapped back to his old self and in no time at all, he was standing out in the open saluting each company as they pivoted by us. I stood there quietly as we watched the companies separate. Some broke off to the right, towards Stribling walk, and others broke off to the left, towards the Chapel. The direction of their path depended on the location of their company in Bancroft Hall.

"Tully, look at how straight they are lined up and how they are all marching in step. Do you see the midshipman that walks alongside the group?" I pointed to the midshipman that was marching beside his company.

"Listen to him as he gets closer."

Tully and I watched as 5th Company approached us. Soon we were able to hear, "Left, Left, Left-Right-Left,"

"That is called 'Cadence'," I said to Tully. "One of the midshipmen will call the cadence for the rest of his company. When you hear 'left' you step with your left foot, when you hear 'right' you step with your right foot. This helps everyone to stay in step when they are marching."

As we watched the companies march by, I noticed how each company walked alike, pivoted alike, and shouted out the same commands. 1st Company could have been 30th Company. As I looked down Decatur Road, it reminded me of one of those rooms in a *funhouse,* where the mirrors created the optical illusion that the room extended on forever. The marching column stretched back as far as the eye could see and each one of the mids looked identical to the other. It was only until the midshipmen were right in front of us that you could make out any differences.

"Tully what was the number on the flag that just passed us." I had begun daydreaming as 5th Company had passed by, and now I had no idea how long we had been standing there for.

"Five-teen," Tully said as he continued to focus on the marching midshipmen. I smiled at Tully, fifteen was always that one number that was hard for him to remember.

Tully seemed content in watching the midshipmen and somehow I knew that he would want to watch the entire brigade go past. We both sat down on the soft grass under the shade of an oak tree. I could feel the dampness of the ground through my thin shorts and the smooth blades of grass in between my toes. The afternoon sun was cooling down, and a gentle breeze shook the leaves like the crinkling of tissue paper. The smell of cut grass and sweet flowers filled the air as Tully and I relaxed to the rhythm of polished footsteps. The flags of each company waved at us as they passed, and I watched as the sea of black continued to march by us, an endless tide of perfection and discipline.

As I watched the midshipmen walk by I thought of how I had marched as a Platoon Drill champion; I had been molded to fit in with the rest of the 34th Company plebes. The blending in, the staying in step, the being noticed as one unit, not as one person. I seemed to have no problem with it on the parade field. Off the parade field, however, was a different story. Back on deck in 34th Company, I seemed to stand out too much. Whether it was the repeated failure with "Man in the Arena," the twelve kills I scored during sailing lessons, or the constant smile upon my face, I was not doing a good job of blending in. I was being too different, which is a positive trait, ordinarily. However, at the Academy, where you are being molded into the person they want, *individuality* is not a good trait to have. The goal of Plebe Summer was to *sweep away* our identities, to replace them with the Academy's, to transform us from who we were to who they wanted us to be. The goal was not to stand out.

By the end of Plebe Summer, I had become a target. Not only was I on Montgomery's radar screen, but I would soon show up on radar screens throughout 34th Company. In only 8 days, the rest of the Brigade of midshipmen would be returning from Summer Break. I needed to make a transformation fast, but instead, an incident took place during Parents Weekend, in which I made matters even worse.

End of Plebe Summer: Parents Weekend,
Plebe Summer, Training, Day 45

It was a Sunday night, and I was feeling sick. I was dreading the upcoming week as thoughts of it continued to churn in my stomach. I had just had my first weekend away from the Academy. "Parents Weekend." It was a weekend that marked the end of Plebe Summer and the beginning of the Academic Year. The heat of Plebe Summer had cooled off and Parent's Weekend was our first taste of freedom. The taste was no longer in my mouth, in fact now looking back on it, I would have rather not have tasted it at all. If you never taste chocolate cake, then you have no idea what you are missing.

Mom and Dad at Parent's Weekend

I was slumped over at my desk, weak from exhaustion. My right hand was cramping. I put down the pen and stretched my hand for some relief. My palms were sweating. I looked down at my tired writing, jumbled upon the pages. I flipped back through the hand-sized notepad, counting the paragraphs I had been writing.

Ten—only ten. You have got to be kidding me, I thought as I began to recount. *"Eight, nine, ten... damn it... just ten. It feels like I have written at least 30.* I sighed with frustration, as well as tiredness, and closed my eyes.

This is going to take me forever, I thought trying to relax. I had been given an assignment a few days ago by Mr. Montgomery; I was to write the 119-word passage "Man in the Arena" 340 times (symbolic of 34th Company). The assignment was a punishment for all the times that I had been asked to recite the passage and failed. I could understand why Montgomery was so mad at me. He asked me almost every single day to recite the passage, and every time I failed. I was trying my hardest, but I would get nervous, my mind would go blank, and then the yelling and screaming would begin.

I opened my eyes and picked up my pen and continued to write.

"It is not the critic who counts, not the one who points out how the strong man stumbled..." I immediately stopped at the word "stumbled" and suddenly realized I was forgetting something. I looked at the clock, which read 5 minutes to 7:00. I had a meeting with Mr. Wyatt at 1900 hours.

I was in trouble and had taken quite a "stumble" as a plebe. I opened the top drawer to my desk and fumbled through some papers until I found the one I was looking for. I reread the letter for one last time:

To: Midn. 2/C Wyatt
From: Midn. 4/C Ervin
Subject: Uniform Regulations

This past Saturday I violated one of the Naval Academy's uniform regulations. I drove back on base in Navy Pep Gear instead of being in Summer Whites. I should not have done this for many reasons. First of all, I am breaking a rule, which we are all instructed to uphold. I was deliberately defying authority. I knew it was wrong, yet I still went ahead and did it. Secondly, I was only thinking of myself. All of my other classmates took the strain and wore their Summer Whites, however, I did not. It was not fair to them, nor was it right to let them down. Lastly, I was setting a bad example for my classmates in 34. If I want to become a good leader, I should set the standards that we must live up to and abide by them. Hopefully, everyone will learn from the mistake, which I made. It was stupid, thoughtless, and unbecoming of a plebe. I apologize for my actions.

Very Respectfully,
Midn. 4/C Ervin

I got up from my desk and pulled my white tube socks up until they were stretched over my calves. I tucked my blue-rimmed t-shirt into my shorts and gathered half of my chin-length hair clipping it back with a barrette. I picked up the letter, and I walked out of my room.

"Good luck Roomie," I heard Lily say as I left my room in a rush. I walked through the hallway quickly, hoping to avoid any upperclassmen. Luckily, the hallway was empty with no signs of the enemy. However, I knew that I was heading straight into the bunker of one, Mr. Wyatt, to receive my punishment, and no doubt a lecture, from Mr. Wyatt.

Mr. Wyatt was the Second-Class assigned to training me. I was a reflection of him. When I did well with all of my plebe duties, Wyatt looked good; when I messed up, as in the case at hand, Wyatt looked bad.

I approached the closed door of Mr. Wyatt's room in the back shaft, and knocked three times, "Sir, midshipmen Fourth Class Ervin reporting as ordered Sir."

I took one last deep breath.

"Come aboard Ervin."

I opened the door and walked in. Wyatt was sitting at his desk across from his roommate, Mr. Ross. Ross got up from his chair and began to gather his books.

"Thanks, man," Wyatt said to Ross.

"No problem, I just wish I could stay and witness the *training session,* Ross said with a laugh. "Man, it sucks to be you, doesn't it Ervin? Ross said as he left the room.

"Have a seat Ervin," Wyatt said closing his books on the desk. I immediately sat down and handed Wyatt my letter. As he read the letter, my eyes left the boat and began sailing around the room. It was a typical room, except you could tell that it belonged to upperclassmen. For one thing, it would not pass inspection; clothes were hanging off chairs, cowboy boots were scattered about the floor, and the racks were poorly made. Also, it contained items that were forbidden in a plebes room; I noticed a CD player, a cappuccino maker, and a closet full of civilian clothes.

"Ervin, what in the *hell* were you thinking?" Wyatt said as he placed the letter down on the desk.

"Sir, I don't know Sir," I replied as my eyes returned to the boat.

"You should know better than this. You're a *Napster!*"

"Yes Sir, but I had had a volleyball game that afternoon and instead of going back up on deck to get my uniform I just left right after the game—"

Wyatt interrupted, "Don't give me any excuses, Ervin. You messed up. I mean *come on*, it was your first weekend-liberty after Plebe Summer, and you come waltzing back on the Yard without your uniform on? You know the uniform regulations! All plebes have to be in uniform within a 30-mile radius of the Academy!" Wyatt's voice began to shake. If I wasn't careful, Wyatt's Wyoming cowboy side would be set loose.

"It's almost like you purposely did it to defy us, which makes me want to bring up another point." Wyatt paused trying to rope in his composure. "Many of your upperclassmen think you have an attitude, a *Napster attitude*. They feel that you think this is all a game because *you have been through this before*, and that you are not *intimidated by it*. Well, Ervin, it *should* and *must* be taken seriously. You are giving everyone in 34 the perception that you don't care."

I stared at Wyatt in complete shock. I could not believe what I was hearing. I was hurt, hurt in the fact that I did not want to be thought of like this. It was not who I was. As a Napster, I felt as if I had come to the Academy a step ahead of many of the others. I came more confident, figuring life as a plebe would be easier because I was a Napster. However, I *never* felt like I was *better or beyond* all of this.

"So, what do you have to say, Ervin?" Wyatt sounded like a cowboy after a long, hard ride.

I could hardly speak. I had no idea what to say and I was trying to hold back tears.

"Ervin, I didn't say that *I* perceived you as this, did I?" His voice softened with compassion.

"No Sir," I replied as my throat tightened, a noose of emotions making it difficult to breathe.

"Ervin, what I believe we have here is a 'perception problem'. The upperclassmen have a certain *perception* of you, and it is your *problem* to deal with it. I know the type of person you are; I know that you care; I know that you give 110% day in and day out. I have seen it, Ervin. You score *A*'s on your Pro-Topic quizzes every Friday; you validated the PRT;[82] you have been passing your room and uniform inspections, and you are playing varsity volleyball. You are doing what you are supposed to be doing and doing it very well. For some reason though, you are being perceived differently. I want you to think about why this is happening and start analyzing every action you take. Right now, can you think of anything, *besides the uniform screw-up,* that you have done that could have given someone the wrong impression of you?" Wyatt stopped and looked at me intently.

"Yes Sir. I still cannot recite 'Man in the Arena' without messing it up. I have some type of mental block and it has become like a joke in the company."

"It has been hurting you, Ervin. It has made you stand out among your classmates, and you have become the main *target* for Montgomery!"

"Sir, Yes, Sir," I replied as I pictured a large red bullseye on my back.

"Well, that is something you will have to figure out on your own. Maybe you need to try to *understand* the words, instead of just memorizing them. Besides your battles with Montgomery, what else do you think is the problem?

"Well Sir, I know that I smile a lot," I answered smiling. "In fact, at the Prep School, my XO, Major Parrino, nicknamed me 'Sunshine'. I was the only one that could make him smile. Once, the Major had said to me, 'Ervin, you're the only person I know that is smiling while you're being dropped for pushups.' It probably doesn't look good that I'm always smiling, but that's just the way I am."

....

82 *PRT:* "Physical Readiness Test." It is a test that all midshipmen must pass in order to graduate from the Academy. The test includes a 2.5-mile run, sit-ups, pushups, and pull-ups.

"I one-hundred-percent agree, Ervin, I think it would be a good idea to stop smiling. You need to appear more serious, so you will be taken seriously. You don't want anyone to think that you're having a good time here. That's *not* what being a plebe is all about."

"Also Sir, it probably isn't a good idea for me to yell out, *'we want more!'* after we have been dropped for pushups."

Wyatt tried to hold back another smile. "Yes, I agree Ervin. That's the *Napster attitude* I was talking about. It sounds like you think that you've got this plebe stuff down and that it's all too easy for you." Wyatt's southern drawl rolled as a small smile cracked through.

"It's not that Sir, it's just that I'm motivated, and I try to get everyone else motivated."

"What about the time, when you and Sinclair knocked over all those sailboats during Plebe Summer? Were you motivated then too? Because your classmates didn't seem too happy."

"No, Sir I was just trying to lighten things up—you know release some built-up stress."

"Yeah, well, do you see what I'm getting at here, Ervin? You have got to look at all of this from an upperclassman's point of view. The way you have been carrying yourself is not a true reflection of who you are, and to make it even worse you came here already marked."

"Marked Sir? I don't understand?"

"You're a *Napster*, Ervin."

"Yes Sir, and proud of it!" I began to picture some of the two hundred close friends of mine that I came to the Academy with. We were "Napsters", individuals who had spent the previous year at the Naval Academy Preparatory School in Newport Rhode Island. Most of us, for example, Kala, Abby, and I came to NAPS directly after high school. Others came straight from the fleet, with sea legs and stripes upon their sleeves, or from the Corps where they had earned the right to wear the "globe and anchor." There was even a SEAL who swam in from the shores of California.

The reasons why we came to NAPS varied like the states in which we came from. The majority, like in my case, were unable to get a direct appointment to the Academy by a Congressman or Senator. After the completion of a year at NAPS with a "C" average or better, the

Secretary of the Navy granted an appointment to the Naval Academy, the Coast Guard Academy, or the Merchant Marine Academy. Many of the Napsters were athletes who had been recruited by coaches at the Academy, so NAPS was not only a way in for those needing academic strengthening but also a way in for the athletes.

The New England coast had salted us and the seafaring town of Newport had been our birthplace. It had transformed us. It had made us who we were. We were given strength as strong as the wind that had blown us back and forth to class. We acquired determination as lasting as the dark blue ocean which cradled the island. We learned to be proud, to stand tall as the cliffs were, the ones that jutted out overlooking the beaches. Newport breathed a new life into us, one that many of us had never experienced before. I come to the Academy prepared, a step ahead of the other civilians.

NAPS was like a miniature Academy. We were trained morally, mentally, and physically. We took academic classes, we stood watch, we cleaned, we marched, and we even had a small version of Plebe Summer, called Indoc. For a year we had been playing for the Navy's farm team and now we were moving up to the Majors. We were stepping into a bigger stadium; a stadium filled with greater expectations, greater prestige, and greater glory. The coaches were going to expect more out of us and our stats would be scrutinized. We knew what the Academy was all about, it was time to either step up to the plate or pack our bags. Not only did I come with the experience of a year of minor league, but I came with my entire team.

"I was a Napster once too Ervin," Wyatt continued. "Napsters are typically stereotyped as cocky and self-centered. Some prove that they are not the stereotype, in your case Ervin you are *reinforcing* the stereotype."

"First of all, Sir, I never would describe a Napster like that, at least not the ones I know, and especially not me! I am *not* cocky, and I am *definitely not* self-centered. I'm a team player; I mean you saw me at the Fire Team Reaction Course—I always scored *A*'s for my team. I help my classmates out; I have never stabbed a classmate in the back."

"I *know* Ervin," Wyatt said cutting me off, "As I said before, we have *a perception problem* here."

"Sir, what am I to do, or am I marked for life, Sir?"

"What *we* are going to do?"

"*We,* Sir?"

"Yes, Ervin, I plan on helping you through this. *We* are going to have to work very hard to make everyone see the real Ervin, and you know how it is when someone has been stereotyped—it is very difficult to change minds but with determination and hard work we can do it."

"I am determined Sir; I don't want to be perceived like this. It's kind of like in volleyball when someone questions my ability because of my small size, it makes me even more determined to beat them."

"This will not be any volleyball game, Ervin. This is going to be difficult. You are going to have to go beyond your typical plebe duties. Appearance-wise, first and foremost, no smiling. Also, your uniform should always be prepared for an inspection. In fact, it may be a good idea for you to iron your shirts Marine Corps style."

"Sir, the three creases down the back of the shirt?"

"Yes, if you are unsure of how to do it, you can stop by my room and I will show you. Also, Ervin, I think that it may be a good idea for me to give you a room inspection every week besides the random Company Room Inspections."

"Every *week,* Sir?"

"Yes. We are going above and beyond here, remember? Your room-mate, Sinclair, will not be held accountable for any of this, okay? She may help you out, but she is not under scrutiny as well. Let's see, what else? Oh, what about that essay that you have been assigned as part of your punishment for last Saturday?"

"Sir, I have to do a ten-minute report on the 'Uniform Regulations of midshipmen' on Friday to my squad."

"Okay, you better make sure that you do a good job. Also, what is your Pro-Topic for this week?"

"For this week, Sir, it's the 'Missions of the U.S. Navy,' for our Professional Awareness; 'Relationships with Juniors' for our Etiquette; and the 'LCAC' for our Pro-Platform."

"Okay, now besides knowing the Mission of the Navy, I want you to learn the Marine Corps mission as well; besides learning about the Landing Craft Air Cushion (LCAC) I want you to learn about the other landing crafts used in amphibious operations. For everything that you will be required to know out of that Pro-Book, Ervin, you will know *twice the amount*. Is this understood?"

"Sir, Yes, Sir," I could feel the weight of the load that had been placed on my back. "What about the 'Etiquette,' Sir, you forgot to mention about the Etiquette?"

"No, I didn't forget it. Besides knowing relationships with Juniors, you will be working on your relationships with Seniors. *First-hand experience*, right Ervin?" Wyatt said smiling.

"Yes, Sir."

"I am going to inform Mr. Pretorius on what we have discussed. I am sure he will agree with me on our plan of action. As your squad leader, Pretorius has been concerned with you as well and is holding me responsible for you."

I realized that Mr. Wyatt was carrying a pack as well. It might not have been as heavy as mine, but he was bearing a load as well.

"Okay, so do you have any questions, Ervin, I know that this is a lot to take in all at once."

"Yes Sir, I want to know how I go about getting the extra information, not included in the Pro-books, that I am going to need to know?"

"Good question. I would recommend going to Preble Hall.[83] Preble Hall is not only the museum but on the top floor, there is a small library containing all types of military publications. I think this would be an excellent source for you."

"Yes Sir, oh and Sir, thank you. Thank you for going *above and beyond* your duties as my 2nd class."

"You're welcome, just don't think that we're friends now or something, okay? Why don't you shove off from here and get back to your books."

....

83 *Preble Hall:* Named after Edward Preble who began his naval career during the American Revolution as a midshipman in the Massachusetts State Navy aboard the frigate, *Protector.* As a 1st Lieutenant of the Massachusetts State sloop *Winthrop,* he distinguished himself by his daring capture of the Loyalist privateer Merriam under the guns of Fort George at Castine, Maine. During the outbreak of the undeclared naval war with France (1798–1801), Preble was commissioned in the newly established Federal Navy. As captain of the frigate *Essex,* he provided valuable service in protecting U.S. merchantmen from French privateers, and he extended the U.S. Navy's presence beyond the Cape of Good Hope—for the first time in a convoy mission that showed the flag as far east as Jakarta, Indonesia. "Edward Preble, *Britannica,* https://www.britannica.com/biography/Edward-Preble

I got up from the chair, pushed it back under the desk, and stood at attention.

"Sir permission to shove off?"

"Shove off, Ervin."

As I turned to leave the room, Wyatt quietly said, "I know you're in a position where you have to change for someone, your upper-class. You have to act like the plebe they want you to be, but ultimately, make the change for *yourself, become the better plebe for yourself.* You will make yourself proud and take the credit, for you will be the one that will have to fight your way out of all of this."

As I walked through the quiet hallway, I thought of Mr. Wyatt's words, and I thought of "Man in the Arena." The credit will belong to *me*—the one who is *actually in the arena*—it will not belong to those *critics or the ones who point out how I have stumbled.* Mr. Wyatt had motivated me to erase this mark, but I am the one that has to do it. It will be hard for me, and even harder for my upperclassmen. Will they be able to forget about my past mistakes? Will they see my present accomplishments? Would they be able to see past the *mark*? I was unsure if they would be able to, but I knew that I had to try. I was determined to erase the mark—not for them, but for me.

After my sit-down with Mr. Wyatt, plebe life changed dramatically, and by the next day, I felt the weight of the challenge upon me. Wyatt's mission to fix my "perception problem" hit hard and with no mercy. I was held to a standard above the rest of my classmates. Everything my classmates did, I had to do better.

My day began at four in the morning. To avoid being caught with lights on before 5 am, I would huddle in my shower with the curtain closed and my flashlight in hand. I had so much extra information to learn and memorize that I had to go to extreme measures to do it. The shower became my foxhole, where I would hide and prepare myself for the coming attacks. The extra studying was supplemented with frequent trips to Preble Hall, which provided me with books, slides, and notes on the various topics that were assigned to me each week. Every Friday, I was required to give a 10-minute presentation to my upperclassmen on a topic that I had thoroughly researched during the week. I would stand alone in the Upper-class Lounge in front of the enemy, who would relentlessly fire questions—testing me, judging me, and marking my progress. This along with the frequent room and uniform inspections ate away at my mind until I was at a point of complete mental exhaustion.

At times I lost sight of my mission, and anger would seep in under my perfectly poised skin. I knew I had a *perception problem*, but it still felt like I was being punished for being me. The sight of Mr. Wyatt even began to make me sick, for he was the force and face behind my "changing." He involved himself in every aspect of my plebe life. Every move I made, every word uttered from my mouth, every expression on my face was watched carefully and criticized. My academic grades began to suffer, and my focus altered on the volleyball court. My life was revolving around this mission to change. The change was painful, and I would cry myself to sleep at night or over the phone with my parents. I experienced the darkening of my spirit, where I felt broken and the desire to give up. Macdonough nor the Chapel couldn't even help to restore my spirit.

> *I was finding out the hard way that in the Navy, those who stand out become targets, and targets are what get fired at. A target is eventually destroyed—unless it is able to change.*

CHAPTER 19:

G.I. JOE

"HEY TULLY, wait up!"

Like a bullet released from the barrel of a gun, my nephew shot from my side and was heading towards a target. The small boy, dressed from head to toe in camouflage, was easy to spot among the sea of black uniforms. The sea of midshipmen were heading back to the Port of Bancroft, and I was heading to wherever my nephew decided to aim his scope. As I followed Tully, I thought of the target that had been on my back and the fact that I wore it for my entire Plebe Year. The target never changed, however, *I did*. I had a *real* Plebe Year because of what Mr. Wyatt did for me, and I am proud of who I became and what I had overcome.

Tully and I firing cannons at Macedonian Monument

Tully had abruptly stopped at the Macedonian Monument. I walked towards the monument, which commemorated Stephen Decatur's victory over the H.M.S. Macedonian, a British frigate, during the War of 1812. At the top of the square stone base, I recognized the man staring down at us. It was Alexander the Great. It was the actual figurehead that had been captured from the Macedonian. The wooden bust depicted the strength and steely determination of Macedonia's greatest king.

Tully's eyes were wide with excitement as he approached the target he had been aiming for. His focus had not been on the ancient Greek king, but rather on the four metal cannons at the base of the monument (originals also captured from the Macedonian herself).

Tully grabbed ahold of one of the cannons and pretended to aim the immovable piece of metal at the innocent tourists walking by. Within a matter of seconds, a full-fledged battle erupted. I helped load the cannonballs as Captain Tully shouted out the orders and aimed the cannon. Together we destroyed a fleet of enemy British ships as well as the unlucky tourists who were caught in the crossfire.

"Looks like we won that battle, and like Decatur, I have another great warrior I want you to learn about!" I quickly grabbed Tully's hand and walked him down Stribling Walk.

At the end of the brick walkway, we stopped in front of a much larger bust. It was a bronze bust of a Native American. I looked up at the ten-foot-tall Delaware chief whose poised body had been tarnished by the weather. His lifted head seemed to embody the strength and courage of all those who had been in battle, and his eyes seemed to mirror the fighting spirit that lies within every man.

"It's an Indian," Tully said as he looked up at the immense statue.

"This is 'Tecumseh'![84] He is good luck for midshipmen."

....

84 *Tecumseh:* The original wooden image was sent to the Naval Academy in 1866 after being salvaged from the wreck of the old ship of the line "Delaware," which had been sunk at Norfolk during the Civil War to prevent her from falling into Confederate hands. The builders of the "Delaware" intended the figurehead to portray Tamanend, the great chief of the Delawares, a lover of peace and friend of William Penn. But to the midshipmen of the period, there was nothing in the name of Tamanend to strike the imagination. The effigy was also known by various other names—Powhatan, King Phillip, and finally Tecumseh—a great warrior and thus heroic and appropriate to the midshipmen. Tecumseh has become not only the "God of 2.0"—the passing grade point average at the academy—but also the idol to whom loyal midshipmen give prayers and sacrificial offerings of pennies. Midshipmen offer a left-handed salute in tribute to Tecumseh, and they toss pennies his way for good luck in exams and athletic contests. "Tecumseh," *Usna.edu*, https://www.usna.edu/PAO/faq_pages/Tecumseh.php

"Why is he good luck?" Tully asked as he circled the base of the statue.

"Well, he is supposed to bring midshipmen good luck on their school tests. Midshipmen throw pennies to Tecumseh before they take their tests, wishing for good luck, kind of like a wishing well."

Tecumseh was considered the "god of 2.0", so in keeping with Academy tradition, I had tossed my share of pennies requesting good luck on my exams throughout the year. (For me, however, it never seemed to help!) The U.S.S Delaware had brought Tecumseh to the Academy, and ever since then, the bronze warrior has been showered with pennies and adorned with paint. The war paint is a request for good luck before a football game.

"Can I throw a penny," Tully asked as he stared up into the face of the chief.

"Sure," I said as I handed Tully a penny. *Here is one more penny, Tecumseh*, I thought as I watched Tully toss a shiny coin at the base of the statue,, *except this time I'm not asking for help on any exams."*

As I looked up at the stoic figure, I made one last request to the Delaware chief. *May you always bring luck to my nephew if he should one day decide to pass by you as a midshipman.*

Soon, Tully and I found ourselves in the center of an open courtyard, "Tecumseh Court," named after the legendary Native American. We were now standing face to face with the massive stone structure that we had never really lost sight of on our travels around the Yard, the impressive Bancroft Hall.

I looked out across the open courtyard that surrounded "T-court." The courtyard appeared so much larger when standing alone. I looked out into the emptiness and remembered standing there with the entire Brigade of Midshipmen, every day at noon. In keeping with the tradition and the pageantry of the Academy, each day the entire Brigade of Midshipmen publicly performed "Noon Meal Formation." From a tourist's point of view, it was quite a spectacular sight to see. Flags were held high, the Navy band played, swords were raised, and then all thirty-six companies of midshipmen marched simultaneously into Bancroft Hall. The glamour and discipline of the Academy were exposed to the public for a momentary glimpse, leaving everyone with a lasting impression.

As I looked out over the courtyard, I could still hear the slow beat of the drum, the pied piper who was always there to lead us back into Bancroft.

"Come on Tully," I said, as he stood motionless staring into the face of Bancroft.

"It's huge isn't it?" I had to pull on Tully to break him out of his trance. We crossed the sand-colored tiled courtyard towards the main entrance, walking slowly to the step of the drumbeat echoing in my head. We walked up the large steps leading into the entrance and stepped through a smaller door on the left.

We were now standing in the middle of a marbleized grand foyer, the "Rotunda." Mammoth pillars of marble circled the foyer as winding staircases wrapped around from both sides.

I pointed to a large marble staircase in front of us. "Let's go up here, Tully, there is something I would like to show you." Tully ran up the steps ahead of me and into a large rectangular room. The backside of the room was filled with large windows and a mounted flag. The outside light had been fading, so the room was lit from the soft glow of wall mounted torch-like lights and hanging chandeliers. I stepped onto the polished wooden floor and quietly walked to the back of the room. More white pillars outlined the perimeter of the room, and more rounded doorways marked the entrances and exits. I walked over to Tully who was standing under the large flag and peering into a glass case the size of a table. I looked down into the glass casing and noticed the rows of names illuminated by a light underneath.

"What is this," Tully asked as he looked in with his small chin pressing on the glass top.

"This is a special memorial to all midshipmen who have died while defending their country. It is to honor all those graduates who have given their lives throughout the wars in the United States' history."

I looked down into the memorial and began reading the different names. As the names shined through the glass case, I knew that each name held a story, and in each story, there was a hero. As the golden light shined through the simple shrine, so did courage, honor, and commitment. As I stood in the darkened, hallowed hall, bathed in a golden light, I knew I was in the presence of sacredness.

There was a navy-blue cloth banner mounted on the wall in front of us, which read, "Don't Give Up the Ship."

"See this Tully," I said pointing to the tattered and faded words.

"This is a famous quote by by Captain James Lawrence. He was killed in a battle with a British frigate during the War of 1812. These were the last words he spoke before he died." The silence in the Hall and of Tully, mirrored the silence of death. "Tully, Captain Lawrence was telling his crew to never give up… to fight for your ship… to fight for your country." Tully nodded his head as he stared at the simple words sewn into the famous flag.[85]

Tully and I lowered our heads as we stared back into the glass case.

I whispered a prayer as we continued to walk around the somber room. I began to think of the very first time I had stepped into Memorial Hall. Mr. Montgomery had taken all the 34th Company plebes into the sacred room the week after Parent's Weekend. A visit to Memorial Hall was not a "mandatory function" for the 4th class, but it was considered *mandatory* by Montgomery. Not only was it for educational purposes, but Mr. Montgomery also wanted to re-focus us, especially after our brief visit to the outside world. Memorial Hall would remind us of *where* we were and *who* we were.

Mr. Montgomery was well educated in history and was constantly testing us on military history *he thought* we should know. Besides the usual "Ervin! 'Man in the Arena'—*go!*" echoing down 34th Company hallways, you would often hear *"When was D-Day?"* or *"Who was the Commander of the Allied Forces during World War I?"* or *"What happened on December 7, 1941?"* Many of us had dreaded the trip to the Memorial Hall because we knew that it would later bring about harder and heavier attacks from our *history buff*.

....

85 *The Captain Lawrence Flag,* aka Commodore Perry Flag: The legend it bears is based on what are alleged to be final words repeated by Captain James Lawrence after his severe injury at the hands of British frigate gunfire while aboard the *USS Chesapeake* battling the *HMS Shannon* on June 1, 1813. Commodore Perry learned of Captain Lawrence's death and was distraught. He commanded that a brig be named Lawrence in honor of his dead friend. The ship now needed a battle flag, and the parting words of Captain Lawrence were seen as ideal. Seamstress Margaret Foster Steuart was charged with creating the flag, which would fly from the Lawrence in battle. The original flag can be seen in the United States Naval Academy Museum. "Don't Give Up the Ship," Ammo.com. https://ammo.com/articles/commodore-perry-flag-dont-give-up-the-ship-american-bravery

I will never forget that one afternoon in Memorial Hall, as golden rays of the August sun stretched across the floor, and the words of Montgomery echoed in the silence. *"Take out your notepads,"* Mr. Montgomery whispered.

I quickly pulled out my notebook and began taking notes on the stories that would stay with me for the rest of my life.

Now, as I walked through the Hall with Tully, the words of my former upperclassman, still echoed among the pillars of marble.

"You will always be a part of the Naval Academy, Cath—you should be proud of that. You are an alumna, so come back to the Academy, hold your head up high, and walk proudly through Memorial Hall."

I lifted my head, and I walked proudly as I stepped reverently across the room. I *had* come back, and I *would continue to*. The Naval Academy was a part of me, and I would *never* forget that.

"Aunt Cathy, come look at this!" Tully's voice cut through the stillness of the room.

I glanced around the room looking for my small soldier, but he was nowhere to be found.

"Tully," I whispered loudly, "Where are you?"

"Over here Aunt Cathy,"

I suddenly saw a flash of his rosy cheeks and red lips peering out around one of the corners of the room. There was impatience in his voice, so I quickly ran over to where he was. I found him standing in a small rectangular alcove, staring into a mounted glass casing the size of a large fish tank.

"Look at what I found!" Tully exclaimed with excitement.

"Wow Tully, do you know what this is?" I said as I moved closer to the glass diorama.

"It's a GI-Joe man!" Tully smiled with pride at his newly founded discovery.

"Well, it does look like GI-Joe but it is supposed to be *Colonial Ripley*. This is a little replica or a model, that explains the story of this very special man. He is a Marine who fought in the Vietnam War."

"Why is he hanging off the bridge like that," Tully asked pointing to the small plastic figurine. The figurine was dressed in fatigues and true to Tully's observations, had the size and look of that of a GI-Joe figure.

"He is doing something so brave and that saved the lives of many people."

As Tully looked into the diorama with great attention, I quietly said, "Would you like to hear the story?"

Tully moved closer to the display until his small button nose was breathing vapor on to the glass.

"Yes, Aunt Cathy!"

As I looked into the small display box, I quietly began to tell the story that I had once been told—told by Mr. Montgomery—a story that had been etched in my notepad and upon my heart. A story that has been described as "one of the most extraordinary acts of individual heroism of the Vietnam War or of any war."

*   *   *

It was Easter Sunday, 1972. It was a typical day in the jungles of North Vietnam, hot and humid with a chance of scattered gunfire. However, an extraordinary man was running amidst the gunfire, a man that would change this typical day and the course of history.

From the cover of dense jungle, two American G.I.s dashed out into the open and across a bullet-infested terrain. Within a matter of minutes, they had managed to dodge North Vietnamese gunfire and make it to relative safety. The two men, Colonial Ripley and Major Smock, both of the United States Marine Corps, crouched with beating hearts into the shadows of the Dong Ha bridge. The waters of the Cua Viet River rumbled by, echoing the rumbling gunfire from the North.

Suddenly, the two officers noticed that they were not alone underneath the bridge; they looked over to see five ARVN[86] engineers huddling in the shadows. Ripley and Smock were there to assist the engineers. They had just received orders to destroy the concrete and iron bridge. At that moment, two North Vietnamese Army (NVA) divisions consisting of over two hundred tanks and thousands of soldiers were

<hr>

86   ARVN: The Army of the Republic of Vietnam (ARVN) were the ground forces of the South Vietnamese military, trained by and closely affiliated with the United States. The ARVN suffered 1,394,000 casualties during the Vietnam War. "ARVN," *Wikipedia*, https://en.wikipedia.org/wiki/Army_of_the_Republic_of_Vietnam

attempting to cross the bridge. Their goal was to capture the capital of Quang Tri as well as the capital of Hue.

With no time to spare, the two Marines looked over the work that had already been laid down by the engineers. The engineers were nervously waiting for the orders to detonate. Ripley quickly noticed that the five-hundred pounds of TNT and plastic explosives had been improperly placed beside the bridge. Ripley determined that with the emplacement of the explosives, only one span of the bridge would be destroyed and would therefore leave the bridge functional. Ripley knew that the explosives would need to be reset so the bridge could be properly destroyed.

Like a storm brewing in the distance, the slow-moving group of NVA tanks was approaching, bringing with them a high-pressure system and a rain of fire. If the tanks were to cross the bridge, there would be an inevitable storm. American battle lines would be lost and Vietnamese control would be gained.

Operating on little sleep, malnourishment, and complete exhaustion, Colonial Ripley relied on his energy reserve: *his sense of duty*. Not only would he have to contend with enemy gunfire, approaching tanks, and exhaustion, but also all five of the NVA engineers suddenly disappeared.

Despite the lack of manpower, Ripley and Smock were not without explosives. As they looked around the muddy banks of the river, they counted thirty boxes full of explosives, enough to level the bridge if done properly. Fortunately, Ripley had fought alongside this bridge five years ago and had the opportunity to examine it during the many times he had crossed it. He decided that he would take on the responsibility of the placement of the demolitions.

Before the explosives could be placed, Ripley had to scale an *anti-sapper fence*, a high chain-linked fence topped with razor-sharp barbs used to keep *sappers*, mine-laying engineers, away. As he scrambled up the fence, the metal razors sliced into his legs and back. This, however, was the least of his concerns, for he was now exposed to the enemy infantrymen on the north bank of the river.

Smock's job was equally as dangerous. He had to repeatedly climb the fence to hand over the boxes of TNT to Ripley on the other side. Sounds of gunfire ricocheted around Smock as he held his breath clinging onto the iron deathtrap.

Ripley quickly placed two fifteen-pound C-4 satchels over his shoulders, adding to the burden of the extra gear he was already wearing. He had left on full canteens, his field webbing, and his CAR-15 rifle with a full magazine. With the weight of the gear and the task at hand, Ripley grabbed a hold of one of the "I" beams of the bridge. He maneuvered hand over hand, the river rushing below him and adrenaline rushing within him. Every ounce of his body ached with pain as he fought to hold on to the metal beam. When he reached half-way across the bridge, weight and gravity pulled stronger upon his dangling body, and he knew that the more he hung, the harder it would be to hold on. Ripley began to swing his body back and forth until he was able to hook his heels up onto the beam. He then pulled his tired body up onto the bridge.

Ripley noticed that the separation between the beams on the bridge was the same width as the boxes of explosives. With Smock feeding the boxes to him over the fence, Ripley would end up placing all 30 boxes in a staggered alignment across the beams of the bridge. This difficult task involved continuous hand-over-hand walking, swinging, and balancing, requiring strength and agility equal to that of a "high-wire act in a circus"[87] As if that wasn't enough to contend with, a damaged NVA T-54 tank was on the bank of the river firing off 100MM rounds at Ripley.[88] Luckily the main gun on the tank was unable to rotate and had too low of an angle of fire to hit Ripley. According to Ripley, however,

> *Successful or not, a 100MM round slamming into a steel*
> *stringer beside you pumps up your adrenalin, cleans out*
> *your ears, and motivates you to a greater speed of efficiency.*

Luckily, the enemy on the North bank did not understand what was going on and therefore did not concentrate their fire on Ripley, but instead watched with amusement at the American's strange behavior on the bridge. They also had been kept busy, firing on the 3rd Battalion Marines who were relentless in diverting attention away from the bridge.

....

87   *USNA Naval Leadership Reading 2*, 10–18

88   Ripley attributed his success to the help of God and his mother. When his energy was about to give out he began a rhythmic chant, "Jesus, Mary, Get me there." "John Ripley USMC," *Militarywikia.org*, https://military.wikia.org/wiki/John_Ripley_(USMC)

After two hours of scaling the fence, dodging enemy fire, packing explosives, hand walking back and forth, swinging under beams, and setting the charges. Ripley was ready to detonate. Without any standard tools for preparing demolitions, Ripley used his arm length to measure the fuses, and his mouth to crimp the detonating cap to the fuses. At the last minute, with the fuses lit, Ripley noticed a box of electric detonators that he had overlooked. Ripley went back out to the bridge and placed the caps along with the burning fuses as a backup.

At this time, Smock had noticed a small railroad bridge with a 10 to 20-foot span missing. He realized that with the Dong Ha bridge blown up, NVA engineers could think of repairing the railroad bridge to use to get across the river. With Ripley's guidance, Smock quickly placed explosives at the railroad bridge while Ripley ran another wire to the detonator to blow both bridges up simultaneously.

Smock later said of Ripley's actions at the bridge,

> *I was convinced that there were sufficient demolitions present to destroy all of Dong Ha, let alone a silly damn bridge, but I acquired the company of a "dumb mom, ranger school-trained Marine."*[89] *Not only were we going to destroy the bridge, but we were going to do it by the numbers, in accordance with ranger school doctrine.*

Smock had been right, and after ten failed detonation attempts, Ripley and Smock were finally thrown against the ground from the impact of the much-welcomed explosion. As they laid upon the ground, portions of the bridge sailed through the sky overhead, and a large ball of burning fire erupted over the River. At 1630, Ripley reported, *"The Dong Ha Bridge has been destroyed."*[90]

The destruction of the Dong Ha bridge brought the NVA's armored movement to a halt, changing the whole course of the war. New American battle lines were stabilized which allowed for the continued bombing in North Vietnam and the ultimate release of POWs in Hanoi.

....

89 *USNA Naval Leadership Reading 2*, 10–21

90 *USNA Naval Leadership Reading 2*, 10–22

Colonel Ripley would return from Vietnam with six valorous and fourteen personal decorations pinned upon his chest. For his heroic actions at the Dong Ha Bridge, he had earned the right to wear: the Navy Cross, the Silver Star, two awards of the Bronze Star with Combat "V", two awards of the Legion of Merit, the Purple Heart, the Navy Commendation Medal, the Defense Meritorious Service Medal, the Presidential Unit Citation, the Navy Unit Citation, the Vietnamese Distinguished Service Order, the Combat Action Ribbon, and the Cross of Gallantry with Gold Star.

From the shores of the Cua Viet River to the Halls of the Naval Academy, this act of heroism would go beyond written citations and pinned medals, and is considered one of the greatest examples of concentration under fire in the annals of U.S. military history. Colonel Ripley's actions that day at the Dong Ha Bridge was selected as the single act to memorialize all Naval Academy graduates during the Vietnam War, and thus, he is the only Marine of the Vietnam war commemorated in the hallowed halls of Memorial.

It was Easter Sunday, 1972, when a man rose out of the jungles of Vietnam and into the eternal gratitude of a country. Symbolic of this religious holiday, Colonel John Walter Ripley had risen from a simple man to an eternal hero.

CHAPTER 20:

CURAHEE

TULLY AND I walked out of Memorial Hall with the image of Colonial Ripley and the bridge, suspended in our minds. It had been good to be back in Memorial Hall even though I was still having random feelings of anxiety. These feelings continued to come and go as we traveled around the Yard. At times, pride and excitement would override them, but they were there... hiding in the shadows of my spirit. *What was I still afraid of? I was no longer a plebe, I had no academic test to take, and Mr. Montgomery was off on some ship in the middle of some ocean. Why was I not at peace?*

The afternoon sun was lowering as we walked out of Bancroft. Tully and I stood for a moment on the steps, like Kings standing before a kingdom. The powerful feeling of Bancroft was harnessed as you stood upon the top steps. There was a sense of command and control in the towering building and of the green landscape that sprawled below. It was all quiet in the kingdom, except for the flapping of a seagull doing a fly-by. Two large cannons were flanking us on the left and right. They were mounted proudly on the steps, like knights guarding the entrance to the castle. Tully immediately stopped, noticing the cannons, and as with all the other cannons on the yard, climbed one of them and began firing off a few rounds of the invisible cannonballs, safeguarding his kingdom. As Tully continued to fire, I slowly walked down the steps and stopped in front of a large bell.[91] The bell was green with patina, like all the other copper on the Yard, and hung beneath a wooden frame mounted on a granite block upon the ground. Directly across from the bell was a similar one, however, it hung under the cover of what looked like a small Japanese rooftop. Tully quickly noticed my interest and soon joined me beside the large bell.

"Can I ring the bell," Tully asked as he approached the sleeping bell.

"I wish we could," I replied, "But we have to beat Army first!"

"What, Aunt Cathy?"

This bell, Tully, is a victory bell, as is that one over there," I pointed to the Japanese bell. "They are rung when Navy beats Army in a sports game. Each player, the coaches, the Superintendent, and the Commandant, will each get to ring the bell for victory!

"Hey, let's look at the Japanese one over here."

"Did you get to ring the bell, Aunt Cathy?"

"My volleyball team did when we beat Army!"

Tully continued to look at the bells, as I continued to look around me. I realized that this was the first time that I had stood *alone* in Tecumseh court (besides Tully by my side). The sand-colored tiles spread out around me like a barren desert. No polished shoes were marching upon these sands, no rows of classmates lined in perfect formations. There were no voices shouting commands, no bells ringing—only a squaw from the seagull above, echoing upon an empty land. As if just a monument, like the sleeping bells, Bancroft stood still and lifeless. I felt an emptiness, for at that moment as I stood still and alone in the shadows of Bancroft, I knew that I would never again experience what I had once felt here. I had felt a classmate to my left, to my right, in front of me, and

....

91   The Academy's "Victory Bells" flank the steps of Bancroft Hall, the home of the Brigade of Midshipmen. On the left is the Japanese Bell, a replica of the bell presented to Commodore Matthew C. Perry in 1854 (the original was returned in 1987 at the request of the Governor of Okinawa). To the right is the Enterprise Bell which was brought to the Academy in 1950 from Fleet Admiral "Bull" Halsey's flagship USS Enterprise, the most decorated flagship in World War II. Each time Navy defeats Army in Varsity Football, the Enterprise Bell is rung from the time the results are known until the team returns. During the team's reception, the Navy score is rung on the Japanese Bell by the team Captain(s), Coach, Superintendent, and Commandant, followed by each team member ringing the bell once. EOA Staff, "History and Traditions of the Army Navy Game," *Eye on Annapolis*, https://www.eyeonannapolis.net/2019/12/army-navy-football-the-history-and-traditions-2/

in back of me. I stood with an enemy who lined me up, chewed me up, and spit me out. *But I did not stand alone.* I marched into the hallowed halls of Bancroft, and I marched out, but *I did not march alone.* I heard the ring of the bell and I cheered for our team, *but I did not cheer alone.* As I looked out across the empty Court, I noticed movement ahead of me. An American flag was dancing with the wind. As it moved, so did my thoughts. As I watched the roll of the stripes and the wave of the stars, I began to forget about how alone I had been feeling. As I looked at the flag, I was no longer alone for I saw the faces of my classmates, my upperclassmen, and my officers who were somewhere sacrificing for me and my nephew beside me. The wind whispered the word *Currahee* into my memory—one simple word which would remind me of all of this...

Plebe Summer, Training, Day 49
Last Day of Training Days

I was standing at attention against the bulkhead, shoulder to shoulder with the rest of the 34th Company plebes. It was the last day of our Plebe Summer Training Days. As of tomorrow, we would be officially moving into the Academic Year. The August heat may have been sailing away from the harbor, but there was no cooling down in Bancroft. We still had 10 months until we "climbed Herndon," the official end of being a plebe, and with the return of the rest of the Brigade in four days, things would only get hotter.

We had just returned from lunch, and according to our Plebe Summer Training Manual, it was "E-9 Time," which was time for a "motivational brief given by a Senior Enlisted Advisors."[92]

A small, silver-haired woman in uniform walked down the center of the P-way, with a folded American flag cradled in her arms as if holding a newborn infant.

....

92 *Plebe Summer Training Manual*, 10.

"I am Master Chief Marralas, and I have a question for all of you today." The Master Chief[93] stopped in the middle of the hallway and paused. "Why are you here?"

The hallway was silent.

"Why are you here?" The Master Chief asked again approaching the nearest plebe.

"To become a Naval or Marine Corps officer," replied the plebe with confidence and resolve.

"Midshipman 4th Class Davis is correct," continued the Master Chief, "But why else? The Master Chief walked down the hallway, looking to pick out her next target.

"What about you, Jimenez, why are you here?"

"To serve my country, Master Chief!"

"That is also correct. Every one of you has been given a job unlike any other job in the world. You will be trained hard, you will practice relentlessly, and as Jimenez said, you will *serve your country*. Like any other job, you will sacrifice your time and your energy. But my friends, with this job comes the *greatest of all sacrifices…*"

The Master Chief paused and stepped back into the middle of the hallway.

"I want each one of you to turn and face the person to the left of you."

Immediately and at the same time, we all did a left face. I was facing 4th Class Andrew Mason, who lived next door to me.

"Now" continued the Master Chief, "I want you to look into their eyes."

I stared at Andrew, noticing his bright blue eyes staring straight back at me. We both stared at each other, as I thought of how for the past five weeks, I never really had a chance to stop and notice the color of his eyes.

....

93   *Master Chief Petty Officer:* A Senior Noncommissioned officer and is one of the highest ranks available to enlisted members of the United States Navy and is rated at the maximum enlisted DoD paygrade of E-9. Less than 1% of the Navy's personnel make it to the rank of Master Chief, and those who do are considered to be among the best and the brightest in their respective specialties. "E-9 Master Chief Petty Officer—Senior Noncommissioned Officer—U.S. Navy Ranks," *Military-Ranks.org*, https://www.military-ranks.org/navy/master-chief-petty-officer

"As you look at this person next to you, I want you to tell them that you will give your life for them."

There was silence as the gravity of Master Chief's words fell upon us.

I continued to look into Andrew's blue eyes and said, "Andrew, I will give my life for you."

He in return said, "And Ervin, I will give my life for you."

A watery glaze coated Andrew's eyes and mine as I began to feel the words of our sacrifice.

I didn't know much about 4th Class Andrew Mason. He was just the chill guy who lived next door to me. He was quiet and a good plebe, was one of my 12 kills. I didn't know where he grew up, I didn't know his family or is religion. I didn't need to know—all I knew was that I would give my life for him.

We all continued to stare at one another until Master Chief motioned for all of us to join her in the center of the hallway. She carefully began to unfurl the flag, directing us to each take hold around the outer edges. The flag spanned across half of the hallway, held by each one of our hands.

The Master Chief spoke silently, "You are here… to give your life… for *this*." She nodded at the flag. "For the people of our country. You like, others before you have accepted a job in which the ultimate sacrifice is your life. Are you willing to do that? Be prepared to stand alone, for others may not understand your job. Others may only see the politics, the news coverage, or the face of war, but you will see the courage, the sacrifice, the lives you are defending, and the freedom you are safe-guarding. You will stand alone, but you will stand alone together. The motto of the 506th Regiment of the 101st Airborne is 'Currahee!' which is Cherokee for "We Stand Alone Together."

So, as you continue through the Academic Year, never lose sight of why you are here. Never lose sight of that man beside you, for one day you may be called to give your life for him or her."

We continued to stand in silence, together holding the flag, together a company of plebes, together a military of men and women.

Master Chief lifted her head with pride and her voice with command,

"Currahee, 34th Company—CURRAHEE!"

CHAPTER 21:

LATE LIGHTS

AS I STARED at the flag dancing in the wind, I was forever grateful for having the opportunity to experience what it felt like to have someone stand beside you and knowing that they would lay down their life for you, as you would for them. I had felt this wherever I was at the Academy, as I stood in 34th Company hallway or upon the sand-colored tiles of Tecumseh court.

I glanced away from the stars and stripes and looked over at my nephew. "How are you feeling Tully?" I asked as I noticed Tully sitting next to the Japanese bell. He looked as if he had stepped into a Bruce Lee movie as the bell's oriental rooftop framed his resting body. I was expecting to hear his words not match up with the movement of his lips… but they did.

"Good… but I want to go back and play on that airplane again," Tully said as he stood up.

"Okay… but that is *all the way* back near the visitor center."

"I know… let's go, Aunt Cathy!"

I grabbed Tully's hand wishing I had his endless energy.

"Before we go, I want to point another special place out to you. Do you see those brown buildings over there?" I pointed to the pair of rectangular buildings across and to the left of T-Court. Not only were the buildings unattractive, but their modern design seemed to clash with the older, Beaux-Arts style[94] structures, such as Bancroft Hall and the Chapel.

....

94 *Beaux-Arts*: Grandiose, ornate, and theatrical, Beaux-Arts buildings are based on the symmetry and proportions of Roman and Greek classicism but combined with more flamboyant French and Italian Renaissance and Baroque influences. Beaux-Arts, which is sometimes called Academic Classicism, American Renaissance, or Beaux-Arts Classicism, became a favorite architectural style for government and institutional buildings such as art museums, train stations, libraries, university campuses, and court houses in Europe and the United States. "Summary of Beaux-Art Style" *The Art Story*, https://www.theartstory.org/movement/beaux-arts-architecture/

"Yes," Tully replied lifting his head.

"Those buildings are Chauvenet and Michelson Hall[95]... Guess what we did in there?"

"What?"

"We did math and science!" I said with pretend enthusiasm.

"Oh," Tully said lowering his head back down. I had mentioned the dreaded word among all children... "math." I had dashed his hopes and filled his head with numbers instead of swashbuckling pirates and naval battles.

"Did you know, that as a midshipman you have to learn, not only how to be a plebe and a naval officer, but you have to go to school and do math, science, reading and writing!"

"Oh," Tully whispered. Tully would soon be falling to sleep if I kept this up.

"Did I tell you that your Aunt Cathy was *not a very good student*?"

"No," Tully replied with a smile, his curiosity wakening.

"Well, I had a difficult time. I had to work very very hard, and I realized how important school was."

"When did you go to school?" Tully asked.

"That is a great question, Tul, a lot of people think that being a midshipman is all about marching, wearing a uniform, and sailing on boats. Actually, most of your day is spent learning, studying, and taking tests! It is like college with a twist." (A twist that tied you into one big knot of stress; a twist that spun you around relentlessly, until you were dizzy with exhaustion; a twist that was unforgiving and never unwound... but one, nevertheless, that would strengthen you, bend

95 The School of Mathematics and Science of the U.S. Naval Academy is located in the twin buildings Michelson and Chauvenet, which overlook the Severn River near its mouth on the Chesapeake Bay. Albert Michelson was a midshipman and later an officer instructor at USNA. Michelson's early experiments on the speed of light were conducted along the edge of the Severn River just outside the building that now bears his name. The Nobel Prize in Physics was awarded to Albert Michelson in 1907 for his "optical precision instruments and the spectroscopic and metrological investigations carried out with their aid." Michelson was the first American Scientist awarded the Nobel Prize. William Chauvenet was one of America's premier mathematicians in the mid-1800's. He was a founder and one of the first faculty members of the Naval Academy. "History," *USNA.edu*, https://www.usna.edu/MathDept/about/index.php

you, mold you, tie you together to your classmates with the strongest of bonds.)

"Tully, this is one of the best schools in the whole world. I learned so much. Any school is important. It fills you up with knowledge. It makes your mind strong so you can use it to do good things. It's as if you are a mountain climber... school is what gives you the ropes and teaches you how to climb so that one day you can make it to the tops of mountains!"

As Tully and I walked through the shadows of the academic buildings, and as the darkness of academic memories emerged from the depths of my mind... I began to explain to Tully a typical day in the life of a plebe during the Academic Year. Up until now, I had been focusing on the stories of Plebe Summer. I needed to show him that it was not all about pirates and battles, marching and memorizing, yelling and chopping, but that there was actually studying and Academic learning going on.

Academic Year, October

I was standing in front of Midshipman 1/C Sullivan's door.

I knocked three times and spoke loudly, "Sir, Midshipman Ervin requesting permission to come aboard."

A muffled reply came back.

"Come aboard Ervin,"

I approached the round-faced upperclassman sitting at his desk. I handed him a small piece of paper that he quickly snatched from my hand.

"Not again, Ervin!" he replied with aggravation. He forcefully scribbled on the paper and handed it back to me.

"Thank you, Sir."

"Just get yourself straightened away, Ervin!"

"Yes, Sir. Sir, Permission to shove off?"

"Permission granted... and hit those books!"

"Sir, Yes Sir,"

"Hit them *hard!*"

"Sir, Yes Sir."

I left my squad leader's room and immediately headed back to mine. As I walked through the hallway, I looked down at the piece of paper. It read:

To: Midn. 1/C Sullivan
From: Midn 4/C Ervin
10/12/94

Sir,

I respectfully request late lights to study for my chemistry test and math test.

At the bottom of the paper in thick black pen, Mr. Sullivan had written, "Indefinitely!" I had been requesting late-lights now for the past month, and to Mr. Sullivan's aggravation (due to my frequent visits to his room every night) he had given me a late-lights pass good for the rest of the year. "Late-lights" was given to those plebes who were struggling academically. It allowed them to keep their lights on past 2300, which was mandatory lights out for plebes. I had been averaging a 1.8 grade-point average and thus had easily qualified for late lights.

I taped the late-lights pass to my door, warding off any upperclassmen that would act like killer moths drawn to the light of my room. I sat down at my desk and stared at my pile of books. With a sigh of exhaustion, I opened my planner to find my assignments. Taped to the inside cover, was my daily schedule. I stared at the schedule wondering how I managed to fit 16 academic credits, varsity volleyball, and life as a plebe all in one day. As a plebe, an important lesson you learned from day one was that time was precious and there was never enough of it. You were given an unreasonable number of things to accomplish in a 17.5-hour day, so you learned to prioritize and to make good use of each minute of the day. I looked over my schedule mentally preparing myself for the next day:

0530: Earliest Rising Time for Fourth Class

This was the case unless you were Midn. 4th Class Ervin. For most of the Academic Year I was in the process of fixing my "perception problem." One way to fix it, *according to Mr. Wyatt*, was "to go above and beyond the duty of a plebe." The only way I could fit in extra study time was to wake up at 0400. Not only was it a challenge to stay awake at that hour, but also it was a challenge to not get caught. Having lights on before 0530 was not permitted, but a plebe has to do what a plebe has to do. So, while all the other plebes were tucked peacefully in their racks, I was huddled in my shower, sitting on a cold tiled floor, with a flashlight in hand and rates in the other. A towel was stuffed under the door to my room for added precaution, and my roommate was sworn to secrecy. I spent the rest of Plebe Year starting my day this way... in a secret bunker preparing myself for the next battle.

0600: Physical or Professional Training

During Plebe Summer we had mandatory PEP (Physical Exercise Program) in the mornings, but during the Academic Year, there was time set aside in the morning for training. Usually, this was the time when we squared away our rooms, got dressed, and read the newspaper. Every day we were required to read three articles from the newspaper, one from the sports section and two from the front page. We needed to know them with "conversational knowledge" so that we could talk about what we had read at breakfast or lunch that day. We had perfected the art of saving time and learned to do multiple tasks all at once. It was not unusual to see a plebe shining a pair of shoes while reading the newspaper in one hand and studying from *Reef Points* in the other.

0630: Reveille for Upperclassmen

A few of our upperclassmen were up at this time, others would wait for a more personal alarm clock... the ringing of plebe voices as chow calls were being shouted down the hallways.

0630-0700: Fourth Class Instruction Period

For those upperclassmen that were awake, this was a time to squeeze in a "come around" in which they would *come around* to your room and rate you (quiz you) on professional knowledge, give you a heads up on something important, or just remind you that they were there...

always there... always watching. This was also the time for the dreaded chow calls, which would occur at 10 minutes and 5 minutes to the hour.

0700: Morning Meal Formation

The entire brigade formed up with their companies either inside of Bancroft or outside at assigned locations, according to the weather.

0710: Breakfast

The first meal of the day, usually the one in which you had the best chance of actually eating. This meal was light on the rates but heavy on the anxiety, knowing that you had a whole day ahead of you.

0755–0845: 1st Period

Government/World History: The first Academic Class of the day. Now, this was a class I enjoyed. No numbers, no labs... just real names and real events. My problem, though, was staying awake. In this class, I felt like a ship in port. I had after a rough night on a turbulent sea. I was anchored by the weight of my tiredness, unable to listen and concentrate. I would often stand up in the back of the class, fighting to stay awake... but I never seemed to be able to set sail no matter how hard I tried.

0855–0945: 2nd Period

Calculus: In this class, just opening my book was a dreaded task. Strange numbers would fly out at me as vectors shot off the page. The blackboard was always chalked with a problem that was as long and as wide as the blackboard itself; my teacher, a large man with a mustache, standing in front, speaking a foreign language that I could never seem to translate. In calculus, I was like a ship sinking. I kept filling up with material I couldn't comprehend... sinking deeper and deeper until I was at depths where there was no type of understanding at all.

0955–1045: 3rd Period

On certain days, 3rd period was a free period. It was intended to be used for studying; I, however, used it for sleeping. I would sneak into my volleyball locker room, spread a sleeping bag across the floor, and catch up on what I was always missing.

1055–1145: 4th Period

English: A typical English class that was filled with reading, writing, and discussion. It was my last class before Noon meal, so I was often distracted by the battle that laid ahead. I was more worried about what I had read in the newspaper that morning rather than what I had read in the novel we were assigned. Reef points and rates took precedent over grammar and essays. I had to lay out an offensive attack for the toughest battle of the day. In English, I was like a ship being prepared for battle. My armament was loaded on board, cannons were put into place, and my sails were unfurled. Literature, however, was not onboard; It would not help me win the war and it was a mental barrier that was always in my way during the last big push towards the enemy.

1155–1205: 4th Class Instruction Period

This "Instruction Period" was a nice way to say "chow calls." At 10 minutes and 5 minutes to the hour, chow calls were sounded off on decks throughout Bancroft. I guess the "instruction" part of it was being yelled at if you failed to deliver the chow call properly.

1205: Noon Meal Formation

One of the most dreaded times of the day for a plebe. For those tourists on the outside, Noon Meal was the highlight of a trip to the Academy. Pomp and pageantry, uniforms, and marching band; a show put on by the best and brightest in the country. The entire Naval Academy Brigade would form up in ranks on T-court with flags and swords held high. For a plebe, however, Noon Meal formation was not something you got excited about… it was a death march that occurred every day.

1205–1240: Noon Meal

Noon Meal was where you had better be *squared away* or you would pay… where all of your rates, such as pro-knowledge, newspaper articles, and *Reef Points* better had been swallowed, understood, and ready to be spit back out. It was a time where food was consumed by the upperclassmen and yelling was consumed by the plebes. Lunch began with the entire brigade standing in prayer. From the center of King Hall, the Chaplin would bless the food, the Brigade Commander would speak, and then we would all be seated at large wooden tables. Firsties (seniors) sat at the head, second class (juniors) and youngsters (sophomores) filled in on one side, and plebes sat on the other. The "hot seat" was the worst place for a plebe to sit, for it was to the immediate right of a Firstie. If you were in the hot seat, you were the one under fire. Most of the rates, yelling, and verbal beating was dished out to you. You were given a lot to digest. Your plate was always full, yet you would never have a chance to eat.

1240–1320: Company Training, Company Commander Time

I don't remember what actually should have gone on at this time, all I remember is that on every Friday at this time I served my punishment for the mistakes that I had made. I was required to give a "Pro-Report" to my upperclassmen at this time. They would all gather in the wardroom to listen to my 10-minute presentations on various topics. I felt like a prisoner of war, surrounded by the enemy, put on the spot, and interrogated. I remember speaking about the SH-60B Seahawk, a search and rescue helicopter, about the LCACs, amphibious landing craft. I remember using slides, diagrams, and pictures to enhance the report. I remember being fired at with corrections and bombarded with questions from an angry and never-accepting audience. I was a shy girl who had been petrified of public speaking in high school, and this was my hell. "TGIF" had absolutely no meaning for me.

1330–1420: 5th Period

Chemistry: Science had always been my favorite subject until I met chemistry. Chemistry was good friends with math and therefore I felt like I was being double-teamed. In Chemistry class, I felt like I was a ship caught in a fog out at sea. Not only was I wearing fogged up lab-goggles, but also I felt like I could never quite see the whole picture. I would do the labs, but when it came to the lab reports, I could not see clearly what I was hypothesizing, and what I was concluding… and then of course math always snuck in to complicate matters even more.

1430–1520: 6th Period

Naval Leadership: This was my favorite class. I enjoyed the readings we were responsible for and the discussions we had. We would read about a famous military leader like Admiral Stockdale and then discuss the qualities of a good leader and how to incorporate them into our lives. I felt like a flagship, where I learned to lead. I felt the importance of my job as a Naval officer, and I wanted to be like one of the leaders we read about. The winds of the military blew strong in this class and I harnessed those winds and set sail.

1530–1700: Sports/ Drill

This was my favorite time of the day, where I was able to sweat out all my frustrations and problems of the day. I was able to forget about classes and forget about being a plebe. Varsity volleyball saved me from being swallowed by the raging seas of the day; it gave me something to look forward to. Those who participated in sports were exempt from the mandatory drill. This often caused mixed feelings within the company; some were proud of you for being on a sports team, but then others were upset at you because you got out of drill. We still had to march in the parades and to the home football games, yet did any of the non-athletes have to sweat through one of our grueling practices? No. End of story.

1700–1900: Evening Meal

I never liked evening meal because I had to go after practice, which was at 1900, unlike the rest of my company who went at 1700. For all varsity teams, you were required to eat with your team at "team-tables." At team-tables plebes had *carry-on*, in which we did not have to act like a plebe, and our upper-class teammates treated us like one of them. I always felt that this was wrong, that it was unfair to my classmates who did not play a varsity sport. I remember one night in particular when I was coming back from team-tables with one of my teammates, Jennifer, who was a Firstie. It was 1930 hours, and chopping was still mandatory for plebes (after 2000 hours chopping ceased throughout Bancroft). As Jennifer and I approached the 8th Wing staircase, I began to run up the stairs. Jennifer yelled at me to stop. She said that I didn't have to chop because I was with her. I turned toward her and said, "No thank you, Ma'am" and continued chopping. After that incident, Jennifer never spoke to me again.

2000–2300: Mandatory Study Hours

After a full day of being a plebe, going to classes, and varsity sports... your day was only half over. Now the academics would begin... homework, projects, and studying. At this time, there was an eerie silence throughout the hallways that almost made you believe that you were at a *normal* university.

2300: Mandatory Lights Out for Plebes

The greatest part of a plebe's day. It was more than the chance to sleep, it was the chance to escape the holds of the upperclassmen, to experience freedom... even if it was a dark and unconscious freedom. Lights were turned off and another day was put to rest. My lights, however, were usually on.

> With late-lights and my early rising at 4... I was lucky to get in three hours of sleep. I was a ship in port... but without enough time to tie my bowlines. With what time I had, I prepared myself as best I could for the next battle... a battle that would leave me with more knowledge, more experience, and more strength... a battle on an ocean that was unlike any other.

CHAPTER 22:
BEAT ARMY

TULLY AND I LEFT the shadows of the Academic buildings and the shadows of a day in the life of a plebe. We headed into the afternoon light on Bancroft's south side. The sun was continuing to lower as we continued back to the east side of the yard. The air was cooler, and the wind was blowing stronger off of the bay.

"Hey, Tul, are you tired, do you want to go home?"

"No! Aunt Cathy, I like it here. It's fun!"

"It is fun at the Academy, and it is even more fun with you, Tully!"

I began to think about the Academy as being "fun." Ask any plebe going through Plebe Year, and "fun" is not the first word that would come to mind.

Tully and I continued past Dahlgren Hall and once again we were back at the 8th Wing of Bancroft Hall.

"As you know, Tully, at times it isn't fun at the Academy. There were times when I wanted to leave, days when I cried and wanted to go home. However, there were also good times too, days when I laughed and wanted to stay… those days *were* the fun! I will never forget "Beat Army Week." It was the week before the big Army-Navy Football game, and it was a tradition to have *fun* during this special week. We had special meals at lunch, we had a big pep rally with a bonfire, and the best part of it… was that you could get back at your upperclassmen if you wanted to. You could *play tricks on them* if you could get away with it!"

"Did *you* play any tricks, Aunt Cathy?" Tully asked, stopping for a moment.

"Now what do you think?" I asked, glancing down at Tully with a mischievous smile.

"Yes!" Tully said laughing.

"Of course I did! Come on, this is your crazy Aunt Cathy we are talking about! So, it was Monday during Beat-Army week and..."

Tully and I continued to walk past 8th Wing as another story began to unfold...

Academic Year, December

I was lying on my back looking up at the ceiling. I could feel the springs of the old lumpy mattress pressing into my back. My eyes had focused on one of the blue lights among the string of colored Christmas lights that wrapped around our room. I stared at it until it became blurry. I was having trouble believing that it was almost Christmas. I had never thought that the 49 days of Plebe Summer would ever end; it felt like I would be trapped in it forever. The days of white works, marching, and Mr. Ball were long gone. We were already four months into the Academic Year with exams around the corner. One thing that hadn't changed since Plebe Summer, however, was "Man in the Arena." Montgomery lived right next door to me, and he and Teddy Roosevelt's passage still haunted me every day.

The round halos around the individual lights, blended into a warm, yellow glow. The lights fell on me like a heavy blanket. Soon the corners of the room became fuzzy, and my head began to tingle and spin... within a few short breathes, I was asleep.

Just as I began to enter into the darkness of sleep, I heard the buzz of the overhead light and felt the pain of its brightness as it pierced through my eyelids. A jolt went through my body as the light turned on, and in response, I jumped out of bed. I looked over to see my roommate Lily, who looked as startled as I was. Amidst the shock and confusion, we both ran to our door, pushed it open, and looked out into the P-way.

After the fog of sleep cleared, it soon became obvious as to what was going on. Our upperclassmen were in the process of keeping the famous tradition of "Army-Navy Week" alive. One of the traditions during this week was the old "sleep deprivation trick," in which the lights in our rooms were turned on every half hour throughout the entire night.

As we peered out of our room, we saw a few of our upperclassmen laughing at us as they pranced back down the hallway. We also noticed that our room was one of the few rooms hit; the other plebes had avoided the attack by locking their doors.

As Lily and I made it back to our room, we talked it over and decided that a battle had begun, and we were not going to lock our doors and let the war take its course. I thought of the famous quote by Commodore Oliver Hazard Perry during the battle on Lake Erie in 1813, "We have met the enemy and they are ours." We had met the enemy and soon they would be ours... for we were willing and able to fight. Able in the sense that it was Army-Navy week, the week that led up to the big football game on Saturday. It was a week of Naval Academy pride, pep rallies, special meals, and traditions. It was also the only time in the year in which plebes could get away with retaliating against the upper-class harassment. The retaliations were not mandatory; you fought back only if you dared. Many plebes, unfortunately, did not dare for fear of the repercussions in the weeks to follow, thus the reason for the locked doors. However, Lily and I were not worried about the future, only about the present. We were being denied our sleep, a very precious commodity for a plebe, and someone was going to pay for it.

Lily and I shut the door to our room, and we began to carry out our plan.

"Good thing we had prepared for this, Lily," I said as we both opened our lockers. I dug around in the back of the top shelf until I found my water gun, which had been hidden in a sweatshirt.

"Yeah, but now I'm wishing that I got a bag of 100 instead of 50," Lily said as I turned around to see her holding a bag of balloons. Yesterday, on Sunday, both Lily and I had smuggled weapons up on deck by hiding them inside our laundry bags.

Lily began to fill up the balloons with water and soon she had a pile of grenades at the end of her bed. I filled my large Super Soaker gun and placed it against the headboard on my bed.

Next, we took Lily's alarm clock and Duck-Taped it to the floor about a foot away from the door. I laughed as I looked at Lily's unique alarm clock... a white Rock and Roll rooster, complete with guitar and dark sunglasses. We positioned the rooster so that when the door cracked open it would bang into the top of its head, which, if pushed, would set the alarm off. With our alarm system wired and our weapons at our sides, we were ready for battle. *Bring it on,* we thought as we dozed back to sleep, this time on top of our blankets and with our shoes on.

About half an hour later, a sound shattered through the early morning quiet…

«*Hey baby wake up, come and dance with me…,*" The rooster was singing! Our alarm had been set off; enemies were in our territory! I leaped out of bed grabbing my gun, and in one quick motion, I fired off rounds in the general direction of the door. Meanwhile, Lily was in the process of launching the grenades.

"Attack!" yelled Lily as a smattering of colors flew into the hallway. After we had cleared the doorway, we ran out into the hallway to continue the attack. Grenades flew through the air slapping against bodies and smacking the walls. I was shooting at anything that moved, and soon I had created a tidal wave of water that was moving rapidly through the hallway. By this time, our upperclass were not only drenched, but they were retreating.

I heard one yell out in a state of confusion, "Holy !@#$! They have a Super Soaker."

We heard yelling and the sound of wet shoes squeaking across the floor. We continued the onslaught until our ammo ran out. When the bombardment came to an abrupt halt, and the last grenade exploded, I looked around the battlefield. It was completely cleared of all enemies. With the hallway now secured, I turned to Lily and we slapped wet hands. "Mission Complete!" we said smiling at each other.

"Nice work, partner," I said.

"Why thank you! Maybe they'll realize now… NOT to mess with us," Lily said laughing.

We walked back through the battlefield, which was covered in puddles of water and pieces of brightly colored balloon shrapnel. The walls were still dripping, and many of the wooden doors had water stains. I walked by the upperclass rooms with newfound confidence, holding on to my gun with control and power. It felt good to be the one to cause the fear. I laughed as I thought about the look on the faces of our enemies; the same look we must have had when they had first attacked us.

When we got back to our room, we reset the alarm system and re-loaded our weapons. We both figured that the enemy would be back.

After everything was set in place, we laid back down to catch a few more minutes of sleep. Lily was out in no time; I, however, was wide-awake with a surge of adrenaline racing through my veins. I began to look around our room, trying to relax and slow my racing heart.

Our room felt warmer and more welcoming than usual. Not only did it feel like this because it was a safe haven from our upperclass that night, but at this particular time, it was decorated for Christmas. We had colored lights strung from corner to corner. We kept them on at night, a nightlight that lit up the entire room with soft pinks, yellows, greens, and blues. To my right, in the middle of the room, against the radiator, was a tree about a foot high, which Lily had put up and decorated. As I looked over my shoulder at the windows, I smiled at the fake snow, frosting the panes. The headboards of our beds were wrapped in Christmas paper, as was the front of our door, which led out into the P-way. It was nice to have a break from room inspections and to have a small amount of freedom, which allowed us to decorate for Christmas. My eyes focused back on the Christmas tree. As I stared at the shimmering tinsel, I began to think about Christmas break and how much I was looking forward to being able to take a rest, mentally and physically. Our room in this state of softness and peacefulness began to close in on me and soon, I began to drift back to sleep.

I dreamt that I was on board a submarine. I was standing in front of a panel of sonar watching the glowing green line of light, circle around like a hand on a clock. I could hear the familiar resonating sound as the line passed over objects on the screen. It was dark in the submarine and I felt suffocated in this cylinder of metal and chipped paint. Suddenly the stillness in this quiet fortress was shaken by the sound of a loud siren. Red lights began to flash violently around me.

"Torpedo off port bow!" was heard among sounds of panic and chaos.

"Dive, Dive, Dive!" faded away behind me as I began to frantically run. As I ran, I noticed water wrapping around my ankles. I continued to run through a maze of pipework and flashing red lights. The ice-cold ocean water continued to rise around me. I came to a closed hatch leading to another compartment onboard the ship. I turned the gray metal wheel to the left. I did not even have time to open the hatch door, *for suddenly a wall of angry water came exploding through...*

I opened my eyes, now awake from my dream, to find myself where I had left off in my dream… engulfed in a wall of water. I began to scream as cold water slammed into my body from all directions. I tried to sit up, but the force was too much to overcome. I was unable to comprehend what was going on. I yelled out for Lily but the water hitting my face made it impossible for me to speak and my screaming sounded like gurgling.

After the water subsided, I bolted out of bed and dried my eyes. I looked in front of me to see three of my upperclass standing in the hallway holding on to a hose that was pointing right at me. I looked over at Lily, who was standing in a puddle of water, drenched like me, with an expression of complete horror upon her face.

We both ran to the door with our weapons as our upperclass ran back down the hallway. We followed them around the corner to where the men's head[96] was and soon it all became clear to us; they had connected a hose to the sink in the head. Not only were our upperclassmen laughing, but I also heard them boasting about "how sweet revenge is" and "how no one should *ever* attempt to mess with *them*."

"Were you able to catch who was involved?" I asked Lily, as I clutched on to the corners of my shorts, wringing the water out.

"I saw Mr. Daniels, Mr. Shen, and Mr. Jackson," Lily replied angrily.

"Oh… they'll pay," I said shivering.

"If only they knew that this was just the beginning," she replied through her gritted teeth.

"*I have not yet begun to fight,*" I said quoting John Paul Jones.[97]

....

96 *Head:* Navy slang for the "bathroom."

97 In 1779 Jones would go down in history as one of the greatest naval commanders of the Revolutionary War. En route to raid British shipping, Jones' warship, Bon Homme Richard (named after Benjamin Franklin), came head to head with the more powerful English warship *HMS Serapis* off the North Sea. After three hours of relentless gun fire between the two vessels, Jones slammed *Bon Homme* into *Serapis,* strategically tying them together. Legend has it that when the British asked if Jones was ready to surrender, he famously responded: "I have not yet begun to fight!" After one of Jones' naval officers tossed a grenade onto causing severe damage, it was the British who ultimately surrendered. Jones' surprise victory against the better-equipped British naval ship had turned him into an international hero. "John Paul Jones," History.com, https://www.history.com/topics/american-revolution/john-paul-jones

We sloshed back through the hallway leaving a trail of wet footprints and cold shivers. When we stepped back into our room, we quickly began to dry off our computers. Our towels, which had been hanging, were soaked, so I opened up my closet and pulled out T-shirts. I was afraid that the computers had been damaged, but amazingly enough, they had continued to work after the attack.

We were cold and wet and had to be up and dressed in an hour, so at that point, Lily and I decided that it was useless to try to fall back asleep. The newspapers would be delivered soon, so we decided to get a jump-start on reading our three articles and memorizing our rates for the day. We also needed to plan for the rest of the week now that Army-Navy week was in full swing. We had four more days to raise hell and get away with it.

On the defensive end of it, we planned to keep our alarm set at all times, but we had no control over what was going to happen in our rooms while we were gone during the day. On the offensive end of it, we were well on our way to putting "Operation Shen" into effect. Mr. Shen was probably the weakest of our enemies, the most hated, and thus the first of our targets to destroy. I was already on his *hate list* from the successful *wildman* I had gotten him with.

After each meal that day, Lily and I both took extra food from King Hall, to bring back to our room. Midshipmen were allowed to have a small amount of food in their room; this included any of their food or extras from the Hall. Often, you would see midshipmen walking back to their rooms with loaves of bread, jars of peanut butter, fruit, or cartons of juice. The food Lily and I brought back, however, was not going to be used for a typical afternoon or midnight snack.

By the end of the day, we had collected quite a mixture of rancid milk, sticky oatmeal, and wilted salad. As the food spoiled, it soon became a mixture of brown and green slime… and to us, it became a unique form of ammo. We decided to set "Operation Shen" into effect that night before anyone would be able to smell our secret brewing.

That night we woke up at two o'clock. Holding my nose, I grabbed the bucket of ammo that had been hidden in our closet. I glanced over at Lily, quickly saying.

"Are you ready?"

"You bet," she said with an evil smirk spreading across her face. With our bucket in hand, we quietly tiptoed towards the back shaft. It was dark in the hallway and I could feel the cold hard floor through my cotton socks. We passed through the middle shaft, quietly moving past the sounds of sleep… the rumble of snoring, and the slow rhythm of deep breathing. Soon we were standing at the second door on the left in the back shaft. I looked up at the nameplate, which read, "Mr. Shen '95."

Without hesitation, Lily and I both took a deep breath, and then I whispered, "On the count of three… One… Two… Three!"

We charged through the door, disturbing the slumbering room. Whatever dreams had been floating in and out of that room were now shot down and replaced by a nightmare. It was pitch black in the room, but Lily and I knew where our target would be. We located the rack on the right side of the room, and then with one heave, we dumped the contents of the bucket. We threw the bucket down, ran out of the room, and then bolted down the hallway as fast as cotton socks on a slippery-waxed floor could take us.

"That was him on the right, wasn't it?" I asked Lily as we raced through the middle shaft.

"Yeah, I'm pretty sure, and I have a feeling that it will be confirmed soon," Lily replied as we rounded the corner into the front shaft.

As we slid into our room, we simultaneously plunged into our beds as if diving into a swimming pool. I pulled my blanket over me, tucking it under my chin. I was trying to calm myself down and hold my nervous breathing when suddenly I heard yelling. It was Mr. Shen, and as expected, he did not sound happy, "Ervin, Sinclair, I know it was you two!" I shut my eyes, pretending I was asleep. I could feel Shen standing outside of our door. I imagined him covered in a lumpy and slimy coating of King Hall leftovers.

His voice trembled with anger. "Both of you are in deep trouble! I don't care if this is Army-Navy week, that was uncalled for!" He then stormed off yelling profanities all the way back to his room.

Attacks from Lily and I continued to occur morning, day, and night, as did the upperclassmen's counterattacks. Lily and I would often wake up to our room smelling like a medicine cabinet and looking like a Pep Rally. Toilet paper would be hanging from the ceiling with graffiti such as "Class of 95" either smeared on our mirrors with soap or clinging to our walls with shaving cream. It was also common for us to wake up and find that it had snowed baby powder overnight upon our clean black uniforms. Lily and I were the only two plebes that were constantly and unmercifully attacked. We were proud of this fact, knowing that the upperclassmen were having fun with us and us with them. This was tradition, and we wanted to be a part of it. We did not want to lock our door and shy away from it.

Mr. Shen, however, did not take part. It took him the rest of Plebe Year to forgive us for what we had done to him that night. That next day after "Operation Shen", he had brought by a stack of his yearbooks, to show us that we had ruined them. (Apparently, they had been innocent bystanders during our attack.) We apologized and told him that only he had been our target in the operation. An apology, however, was not good enough, and he demanded that we pay for the ruined books. We refused his demands and brushed aside his weak threats.

At one point, Mr. Steinmann came by and told us not to worry about Mr. Shen. According to Steinmann, "Mr. Shen needs to learn a lesson. He is one of those who can dish it out, but they can't take it. He has no idea what this week is *really* all about."

I began to think of what Mr. Steinmann had said. I understood, and I agreed. I had realized what this week was really about. The purpose of "Army-Navy Week" was more than just a giant pep rally to get us pumped up for the big football game. More importantly, it was a way to bring the Academy together as a united force. Not only were we a united force against Army, but also we were a united force against the nations of the world. After "Operation Shen" I began to realize that many midshipmen had missed this whole idea.

Every corner each plebe turned while running in the hallways was accompanied with a "Go Navy, Beat Army Sir!" shouted at the top of their lungs. Every sports game ended with the singing of the song, "Blue and Gold," followed by a pounding of the chest while yelling "Beat Army Sir!" From the moment we had stepped onto the Yard as a plebe, we learned the importance of saying "Beat Army," and soon it became as commonplace as "Yes, Sir" and "No, Sir."

Was all of this "Beat Army" though, just motivation for our sports teams? Was it just to develop a competitive spirit among the midshipmen? Was it just a mandatory phrase to be yelled out by the plebes? As the year went on, I began to realize that there was much more to "Beating Army," and with each turn of a corner, I began to yell a little bit louder, with each pounding of my fist, I began to pound a little bit harder.

I soon understood that "Beating Army," was not just about winning a game, it goes deeper than that. It is a glue that bonds all midshipmen together. Because of it, we become this "united force," a brother and sisterhood, unlike any college fraternity or sorority. It is a bond that links every class together, from 1845 to the present. It is a bond that holds together one of the strongest militaries in the world. Army-Navy week was reinforcement, a reminder of this bond. All of the upperclass harassing and the plebe retaliations was a part of this bonding.

It bothered me that I had upperclassmen that did understand what this week was all about and that I had classmates who locked their doors to it.

To me, they not only missed the tradition and significance of "Army-Navy week," but more importantly, they missed out on what it truly means to "Beat Army."

CHAPTER 23:

THE BEST FIVE MINUTES

"BEAT ARMY!" Tully yelled as he jumped with excitement.

"That's right, Tul, and don't ever again say "Beat Navy" around here like you did back up in 8th Wing with Mr. Wyatt!"

Tully and I laughed as we walked towards the airplane that Tully wanted to visit again. Suddenly a shrill whistle pierced through the air. Tully and I both froze and looked towards the direction of the sound. I noticed movement on the football field across from us. The whistle blew again, and I was able to see a group of helmeted football players running across the field.

"Oh, my gosh," I said as I looked down at Tully. We both took off running, forgetting about the airplane. We ran across a street and over to the fenced-in field of artificial grass.

"Tully, I can't believe this—it's the Navy football team! Do you want to watch them practice for a little bit?" My question had already been answered, as I watched my nephew slowly push open the gate and step onto the sidelines. I followed him and motioned for him to move back out of the way of the practicing quarterbacks. We leaned up against the fence behind a row of un-helmeted players that were waiting to get into the scrimmage.

"Tully," I leaned over whispering in his ear, "This is 'Turf Field,' the football team's practice field, and it looks as if they are playing a practice game."

There was an empty row of stands to our left, a large field of real grass to our right, and the seawall now behind us.

"I can play football," Tully said as we watched the blue and gold jerseys dash back and forth across the field.

"Yes, you can!" I said as my eyes followed an incomplete pass into the end zone. The sounds of whistles, yelling coaches, and teammate chatter filled the air. Tully and I were so close to the action that the bone-crushing sounds of helmets hitting pads made us feel like *we* were right in the middle of it.

I looked down at Tully who was electrified with excitement. At home, Tully would often dress up in a small maroon and gold uniform. With the Redskins logo on his helmet and Darryl Green's numbers on his back, he would transform himself into a real football player. Tully and I held practices out on our yard as well as games, in which I played for Dallas, the ever-popular enemy team. He considered football to be the best sport of all sports, and I agreed with him.

"Did you know, Tully, that the best football game *ever* is when Navy plays Army?"

"Why?" Tully asked.

"Well, Army and Navy are very much alike, they are like brothers, so they really want to beat one another to prove who is the best!"

"Oh!" Tully replied as he kept his eyes focused on the players.

"I hope Navy beats Army this year!" I smiled.

"Me too!" Tully shouted as he jumped in the air with excitement.

We continued to watch the players upon the green turf, players practicing for that one important game. Little did they know that they were practicing for a game that would be their ultimate teacher. I began to think about the day in which Navy football had taught me something—something that would stay in my heart and in the hearts of all of those who wore blue, as well as in the hearts of all of those who wore gray...

Army Navy Football Game, December 3, 1994

I was marching through a tunnel. The tunnel was cold and dark but was a barrier against the wind that whipped and whined violently on the outside. I could see a small opening of light ahead of me; a light which was coming from the Arena. As I continued to march towards the light, I couldn't help but think of the *arena* I was so familiar with, "Man in the Arena." During any spare moments of time, I would practice reciting the passage in my head, with the fear that Montgomery was waiting around some corner ready to ask me, "Ervin! 'Man in the Arena'—*go!*"

I continued marching, marching to my own cadence, *"It is not the critic who counts, not the one who points out how the strong man stumbled or how the doer of deeds might have down them better. The credit belongs to the man who is actually in the Arena, whose face is marred with sweat and dust and blood, who errs and comes short, again and again, who know the great enthusiasms, the great devotions and spends himself in a worthy cause; who if he wins, knows the triumph of high achievement; and who, if fails, at least fails while daring greatly."*

The darkness that had surrounded and protected me was fading, fading like the cadence in my head and the voices surrounding me. All I could hear were the sounds of the footsteps I was enveloped in. I was having trouble keeping in step, in unison with the others; the excitement was clouding my concentration. My body trembled as I began to see light ahead of me; the light widened with each step I took. Then suddenly, as I took a deep breath, I stepped into the light. I continued marching, still struggling to stay in step. I tried concentrating on the person in front of me; this concentration only lasted for a few seconds, for I had to look up.

A sea of color was surrounding me. Rows upon rows of color reached up high into the sky. I felt so small, yet I knew everyone saw us. I noticed that the sound of our marching and the sound of my breathing suddenly became muffled. My ears began to tingle as a bellowing noise broke through the cold air. I tightened my hands inside of my leather gloves, and then I took another deep breath. The icy air stung as it rushed into my lungs. I looked up into the sky, a sky that was gray but looked as if a brush had covered it with a thin coat of milky white paint. The sun was covered but there seemed to be light coming from somewhere else. The winter air smelled crisp like ice and was blowing a fierce coldness. The cold, without luck, was trying to pierce through my O-coat[98]. The grass beneath me was soft and springy; it felt like carpet as I walked upon it. The sounds around me became more deafening; it was a mix of rumbles coming from all directions.

Suddenly, everything began to slow down. My body became light, and I began to feel detached from my surroundings. The sounds around

....

98   *O-Coat:* "Officer Coat" A long, heavy, wool black coat worn by midshipmen and Naval Officers.

me were getting louder, yet I was unable to hear them. I was still marching, yet I don't remember moving. I could no longer feel the cold or smell the air; it was as if I had left my body. It felt surreal and almost religious. Religious in the sense that I felt that I was in the presence of something very sacred. I was part of an overwhelming feeling of pride. A pride that was so sacred, so holy, and so pure. A pride that was around me, that had taught me, and that I had now become.

As I felt pride all around me, my chin lifted a little higher, my back got a little straighter, and my fists got a little tighter. *This was what it was all about*, I thought to myself, *not just pride in our team, but pride in ourselves, for who we were.* I looked out in front of me. We were now standing at attention and facing the *coats of gray*. Simultaneously, all 4,000 of us uncovered our heads, raised our covers to the crowd, and shouted, *"Beat Army!"*

I had shouted "Beat Army" hundreds of times prior to this point, but never did it feel as it did on that wintry day. I will never forget how I had felt during our "March-On"[99] in the opening ceremonies of the 95th Army-Navy Game. It had only lasted a few minutes, but its impact would last for a lifetime.

After the "March-On," the Brigade of Black left the field and walked back to the sections of seats reserved for the midshipmen. As I followed my company to our seats, I looked up into the crowd. The arena was filled; the arena being Veteran's Stadium, home of the Philadelphia Eagles. I walked past the end zone, noticing the turf lacking its typical Eagle green and gray. Today it was painted in Navy blue and gold with the opposite end zone in Army black and gold. It was neutral ground today; neutral for a rivalry that rivals any other in college football and any other sports competition in general.

I looked over to see our mascot Bill the Goat with horns painted blue and gold and wearing his traditional Navy cape draped across his back. Bill was attached to a leash, and he was standing complacent and very still. He did not seem to represent any feelings of strength and power,

....

99 *March-On:* As part of tradition, both Military Academies march on to the field during the opening ceremonies of a football game; march-ons are a demonstration of pride in the Academy, they are a display for the public, and they are a salute of good luck to the other team.

yet he did represent Navy. Bill has been a loyal mascot ever since his first appearance at the very first Army-Navy game. As I passed by Bill the Goat, I thought of that very first game and the beginning of the Army-Navy rivalry.

The story begins back in the summer of 1890. An army cadet by the name of Dennis Mahan Michie was on a leave of absence from the Military Academy (a.k.a. West Point). While on leave, he met a group of midshipmen from the Naval Academy (a.k.a. Annapolis). Amidst their conversations, the topic of football came up and in no time at all the mids had challenged Michie and the cadets to a game. The challenge was presented even though the midshipmen were at an advantage. The mids already had a football team for the past two years, and the cadets had no team at all.

Michie wanted to accept the challenge but he first needed permission. He knew that the Military Academy was not ever permitted to leave their post at West Point, so he presented the idea of the midshipmen coming to New York for the game. Also, according to West Point rules, the challenge would have to originate from the midshipmen, which Michie informed the Academy that it did. He intensified the challenge by presenting the fact that the pride of West Point was at stake, and as men of courage and honor, they could *not* turn down this challenge. Luckily, Michie's dad was a senior member of the faculty at the time and was easily persuaded with the idea. The Superintendent and Commandant both agreed to the game and gave Michie their support as well. With support, the midshipmens' challenge, and the terms of the game, the Academic board at West Point agreed to the game.

Although the midshipmens' challenge was now accepted, and the game was officially set in motion, Michie still faced several difficult tasks. Not only did he have to form a team, but he had to obtain equipment and uniforms, as well as raise money to pay for Navy's travel expenses. With only 271 cadets in the Corps and only three who had ever played football before (with Michie being one of the three), the pickings for a team were very slim. Michie was able to form a team and took on the added responsibilities of head coach, team manager, and trainer. With practices held on Saturdays (when the weather was too bad to drill or parade), and early morning runs around the campus,

Michie was determined to develop his team. To bring the mids to New York, all 271 cadets agreed to a 52-cent deduction from their cadet store account, which ended up covering half of Navy's expenses. The players also agreed to pay for their uniforms, which consisted of canvas jackets, white breeches, black socks, and black wool caps.

In no time at all, it was November 29—game day. The New York sky was gray and foreboding as a ferryboat appeared on the river surrounded in a mist of white. A group of eager midshipmen unloaded on to the banks of the Hudson and had their first glimpse of the dark, stone, gothic buildings lurking high on top of the hill. It felt as if they had stepped back in the 16th century, as they stood in the shadow of castle-like buildings. Soon they would be face to face with a group of knights eager to defend their castle and their honor.

With nervous anticipation, the mids began their climb up the hill toward the Parade field. On their way, they passed by a scrawny goat, who at the sight of the mids began to kick up its heels. The mids decided that this high-spirited goat would not only make a good mascot but that it would also bring good luck to their team. They took the goat with them as they continued up the hill to meet the cadets.

Two thousand people attended the game on that gray, wintry day. Navy won the toss and proceeded to dominate the game. Despite Navy's experience and advantage, Army played with admirable effort and fortitude. The midshipmen walked away victorious with a score of Navy 24, Army 0.

Despite the disappointment, Michie was determined to not give up on football at West Point, and soon he took on the challenge of preparing for the following year. He immediately searched for a coach, knowing that this was the prime importance for his inexperienced team. In the following year, Army had a coach, an experienced team, permission to leave West Point (for the first time), and most importantly, they had a strong sense of revenge and determination to avenge the pride of their school. The second time around, the battle would take place on the banks of the Severn, and this time Army would come out victorious with a score of Army 32, Navy 16.

True to these first two contests, the competition between Army and Navy has remained close. Over the past 131 years, the wins and losses between the two schools continue to sway back and forth. Neither team has dominated and as of now, Navy holds a narrow lead at 61-53-7. And true to that very first game, the game is much more than just a win or a loss.

And now here I was, a part of the game. As I looked around me, surrounded by my classmates, I knew that I was experiencing something that only a few ever have, and I was feeling something that could not be put into words.

The black O-coats that surrounded me filled at least five sections of seating. We were located in the lower tier to the left of the goal post on the southeast side of the stadium. As I looked across the field, I could see a blanket of gray covering the northeast corner of the stadium. There, only yards away, was the enemy. They were an enemy with equal strength in number, with equal athletic talent, with equal intelligence and ingenuity, and with equal pride and fortitude. They were an enemy that I respected; yet, they were an enemy that I wanted to beat.

I had wanted to beat them ever since I had heard their name breathed into the hot Annapolis air on July 1st. For the past five months, I had been focused on beating this enemy. The enemy's name was yelled by every plebe around every corner in the hall; it was worn on letter sweaters by the upperclassman; it was spoken in the locker rooms after each regular-season game; it was printed on banners spanning across Annapolis; it was sung at the ending of every Blue and Gold song, and it was etched forever in the hearts of every midshipman young and old.

Now, as I gazed upon the gray across from me, for the first time *"Beat Army"* became real. What was echoed in the halls of Bancroft had finally materialized right in front of me. I could hear the enemy, I could see them, and I could feel their presence. As I heard our band play, I knew we were ready for battle. Everyone in the stadium was ready, as I could feel its energy building. The bands were playing as loud and as hard as they could, the cheerleaders were raising team colors into the air, and mascots were being led around on the sidelines. A miniature battleship patrolled the waters on Navy's side, while a tank rumbled across Army's terrain. Camouflaged midshipmen and cadets manned separate cannons, while a knight in black armor rode by on horseback, his cape with the yellow letter "A" flapping in the wind. Camera operators, newspaper reporters, sideline officials, high-ranking military officers, and security filtered in and out among all the commotion down on the sidelines. Little did I know that this was only the beginning.

Suddenly, the stadium was filled with the crackling sound of the intercom system.

"Direct your attention…" buzzed a voice from speakers around us.

Immediately, I looked up to see a cargo plane circling high up in the sky.

"And there they go," echoed the voice with excitement.

Suddenly tiny black specs, like flies, fell from the plane. They were falling fast and in the direction of the stadium. Soon they became larger and color became visible, gold rectangular parachutes were circling in various directions above the stadium. I was following one coming down on the right when all of a sudden, I heard voices cheering and fingers pointing to the left. Suddenly from above the goal post, there was a parachute, guided by outstretched arms, rapidly descending. It skirted past us and circled inside the stadium, lining itself up for the runway. The runway was an orange "T"-shaped marking laid down at the west side of the field. The dangling silhouette of a man could be seen pulling down on lines attached to the parachute. The chute was gold with blue lettering that read "NAVY." The lines were pulled until his feet touched the ground on the marker, with accuracy and precision. As soon as he came to a stop, the chute collapsed and became limp and lifeless as it flopped upon the field. The man quickly pulled the chute, tugging at the many lines, and began bundling it together. He quickly moved out of the way, as another chute with "SEALS" printed in blue was blowing in from the right. With a similar, precise, and perfect form, another "Leap Frog"[100] had landed.

....

100   *Leap Frogs:* The U.S. Navy's Parachute Team. The team is made up of 15 Navy SEALs (Sea, Air, and Land commandos). Each member comes for a 3-year tour then returns to active duty in a SEAL team. The Leap Frogs began back in 1969, when the SEALs (a.k.a "Frogmen") volunteered to give performances at weekend air shows. In 1974, they were officially commissioned by the Chief of Naval Operations and were assigned with the mission to demonstrate Navy excellence throughout the United States. They support the Navy recruiting effort and they promoted the Naval Special Warfare community to the public. The Leap Frogs jump at 12,500 feet, accelerate at up to 180 mph., and are renowned for their complex formations and daring maneuvers. "Legends of the Sky," Navy *Leap Frogs*, https://www.navyleapfrogs.com/index.html

"Oh my gosh," was heard as I again looked up and saw two parachutes connected, one dangling below the other. The gold parachutes with "ARMY" printed in black, swooped down and inside the stadium, detaching from one another at the last possible minute. Not only did these formations take impeccable timing and accuracy, but they made it look so easy. The last one to land arrived with a special delivery: *the game ball.* The crowd went crazy as Leap Frogs and Golden Knights[101] went off to their respective sides shouting "Beat Army" to the Brigade of midshipmen, and "Beat Navy" to the Corps of Cadets.

A rumble from off in the distance soon muffled the rumble of the crowd. The crowd grew quiet as heads turned in various directions, scanning the sky for the cause of the sound. The rumble intensified, the ground shook, and the inside of my body began to vibrate. Heads were once again straining as they lifted upwards, held in position too afraid to look down in fear of missing something. Suddenly from the south side of the stadium, four F-14 Tomcats flew across so low that they barely cleared the top of the Stadium. With a shrill and sharp whine, they roared by in a diamond formation. They were so close to each other that they seemed connected at the wingtips. They left a buzz in our ears, and a shaking in our stomach as they headed off back into the gray sky.

Soon a familiar rhythmic sound of rotation and metal blades chopping through the wind could be heard. I looked up to see the bellies of five black Apache helicopters, with blades spinning and guns hanging off their spider-like legs. They passed overhead, and soon they became silhouettes cutting a straight path across the sky.

The crowd cheered, and the electricity continued to surge throughout the stadium. The opening ceremonies were not only a display of pomp and pageantry, (which the military is known for), but it was so much more. It was a demonstration of pride in the United States military and was a salute to those in uniform; it was motivation for others to join the military and was an inspiration to those who had the dream. Most importantly, it was a good luck wish, and a pat on the back to those who were wearing the football jerseys.

....

101 *Golden Knights:* The U.S. Army's Parachute Team. Their mission is similar to the Leap Frogs, but of course, they are not of the same high caliber, and could never equal the Leap Frogs, because this is *Army* we are talking about here!

Within a matter of minutes, the two teams emerged from opposite sides of the field. Like bulls that had been pinned in, the gates had finally been opened and the players all charged forward onto the field ready for the inevitable battle. Quickly they fell into ranks and stood along their respective sides of the field. Helmets were taken off as the American Flag appeared on the jumbotron. The Star-Spangled Banner was sung with respect and patriotism as teammates stood at attention.

I took a deep breath as the players placed their helmets back on and formed up into a huddle of cheers, shouts, and nervous anticipation. The Navy players knelt, as Coach Marshall led in prayer. Knowing Coach Marshall's strong faith, I can only imagine that he was thanking God for his team, for the players, and for their safety on and off the field. Later I had found out that he had thanked the seniors for their guidance and leadership. He had prayed for their safety as future officers that would be sent out to defend the country. He prayed that they would always hold their head up high, that they would always be proud of who they were and what they represented.

For the 10th straight year, Navy won the coin toss, and for the 10th straight time, Navy elected to kick off. I watched as the captains from the two teams shook hands, wishing each other luck. I couldn't help but think of Army's star, Dennis Mahan Michie, shaking hands with Worth Bagley, Navy's great quarterback, back in 1890. They were two players that would develop mutual respect for each other, despite their fierce competition.

A cannon boomed, timed perfectly with the foot of Navy's kicker contacting the football. The ball bulleted through the air, over a field of golden helmets, and landed into the arms of a white jersey. A swarm of navy-blue jerseys rushed to the other end of the field, as the ball was put into play. As I watched the game—the fumbles, the interceptions, the passes, the carries—I wondered who would end up *"triumphing in high achievement"* and *"who would fail while daring greatly."* I held my breath with each pass, with each carry, with each kick. I never once pulled my eyes away from the field; I did not want to miss one moment of this feeling. I will never forget the feeling of victory as Navy colors crossed into the end zone, and the feeling of defeat as Army's colors crossed on the opposite end. I will never forget the cheers of the crowd as they echoed deep within my body. I will never forget the rumble in the stands as vibrations shot straight up through my feet. I will never forget the sea of black and the rolling waves of blue and gold pom-poms hoisted into the air. I will never forget the pride as I recognized the familiar players, friends from my platoon at NAPS. I watched as safety Diego Manalo had one winning tackle after another—the start of his stellar career where Manalo would earn the second-most career tackles in USNA history.

As the game continued, the sky became grayer, and the air became colder. As I looked down upon the field, I noticed that the colors were not as bright, that they had dulled. The field indicated a battle, and the players indicated a war—a war in which you could still see the same amount of intensity and passion; a war that had not dulled but continued to rage on, despite the cold, the pain of injuries, the exhaustion, and the mental tiredness. Each minute was played as if it was the last, and each minute that went by, only fueled this intensity and passion. As I looked at the players, marked by the signs of war, *"their faces marred with sweat, and dust, and blood,"* I could only think of that first Army victory in 1891, where it was reported that,

> *Clarke scored for Army once again and the West Pointers led, 18-6. By this time the field was a bedlam—the players on both teams battered, bleeding, and groggy. Stockings were torn off, five noses were bleeding, one man's ear was split, two midshipmen were knocked unconscious, recovered, and along with Army's Lane Prince, managed to stagger and crawl along the edge of the game, until Timberlake's final touchdown put Army ahead 32-16 and the match was over.*[102]

I continued to watch the battle in front of me, never once wanting to miss a moment. As I continued to watch, the clock ticked away time. As the clock turned 0:00, the battle was over. The war had ended.

I stood in silence, in shock, as I stared at the scoreboard, disbelieving what I saw:

102 Gene Schorr, *The Army-Navy Game,* (Dodd, Mead 1967)

NAVY: 20
ARMY: 22

All movement had stopped among the brigade and was replaced by an eerie stillness. Complete stillness. All cheers among the sea of black had ceased replaced by silence. Complete silence. All faces were filled with disappointment, as despair swept through all of us as quick and as cold as the winter wind.

As the clock turned 0:00, and the final whistle was blown, a cannon exploded and a blanket of gray fell from the stands, covering the field and cloaking the heroes. The cadets were yelling, hugging one another, and jumping up and down. Some threw their hats; some fell to their knees in prayer. The celebration was quick and intense, like the cannon that had sounded. It did not last long, and it was not a spectacle. It paralleled Army's first victory in which it was said that Army went absolutely wild with joy. The cadets dashed out onto the field and carried off the victorious players, singing, dancing, shouting, as they marched off the field with a tired but happy Army squad.

Immediately after congratulating one another, the cadets moved towards the midshipmen. I watched as the two Team Captains shook hands and embraced. Immediately, I thought again of the first Army-Navy game.

The story has been told that at the end of the game, Army's Captain, Dennis Michie, shook hands with Navy's Captain, Worth Bagley, and said "Till we meet again." Bagley played two more years of football for Navy and Michie stayed on as Army's head coach for two more years. Although the two had vowed to meet again as a mark of friendship, this would never come to pass. In a sense, however, they did meet again out on the battlefield, for they both took part and were killed in action in the Spanish American War in 1898. Bagley was the first and only Naval officer to be killed during the war. He was killed aboard the USS Winslow. Captain Michie was killed during the battle of Santiago. He was shot by a bullet while leading a patrol along the San Juan River while attempting an assault on San Juan Hill.

As I watched the two teams intermingled, it was more than just handshakes that could be seen being passed around, the players embraced one another; they wept upon the shoulder of the other, and then walked arm over arm across the field. They knew that one day, they would be on the same team, fighting the same battle. They would meet again as Bagley and Michie did united under the same colors.

I continued to watch as the cadets and midshipmen stood together, side by side, with their helmet in one hand and their other hand placed over their heart. The cheers had been pacified, the sobbing was muffled, and then silence fell over all of Veteran's Stadium. The fans in their seats, the cadets and midshipmen on the field all stood in reverence as everyone turned to face the Brigade of midshipmen. The brigade was standing with their hands placed over their heart in complete stillness and silence. My hand was on my heart as I looked out to the faces which were looking back up at us. The Navy Band began to play the slow, familiar song, and as I looked out onto the field, I joined in singing the *Navy Blue and Gold*:

> *Now, college men from sea to sea,*
> *May sing of colors true,*
> *But who has better right than we*
> *To hoist a symbol hue?*
>
> *For Sailor men in battle fair,*
> *|Since fighting days of old,*
> *Have proved the sailor's right to wear*
> *The Navy Blue and Gold.*

As Army's Alma Mater was sung, and as I faced the blanket of gray, Blue and Gold tears streamed down my face, for I now understood—I understood *why this game is and will forever be the greatest of all games.* The greatest because this is a game played for the love of the sport and for the camaraderie. This is a game where the entire student body and faculty attend. This is a game where the players do not play for a national championship. This is a game where the team records and point spread do not matter. This is a game where none of the players are on a scholarship. This is a game where the stands are empty of NFL scouts. This is a game where General Macarthur announced the victor in the middle of a battle during the war in the Philippines. This is a game steeped in tradition and history. This is a game that began back in 1890 and is still played with the same amount of intensity, passion, and commitment. This is a game where team colors are not on jerseys alone, but they are hoisted on top of a ship mast, a conquered hill, or a captured fort.

This is a game that is the ultimate sibling rivalry. A rivalry where team members are bonded in a brotherhood, born in separate hospitals, WestPoint and Annapolis, but from the same mother, the United States military. They were taught the same core values of duty, honor, and country. They were woken up at the same hour and had to overcome the same degree of physical, mental, and academic struggles. They both had to learn how to follow and then learn how to lead. They developed their character based on discipline, responsibility, integrity, and honesty, an unwavering character both in and out of uniform. They were both prepared for their future job; a job they would both eventually share, the job of defending their country and ultimately giving their life for another.

Whether they *walked in the long grey line*[103] or among a brigade of black, they had walked a similar path, and as a midshipman or as a cadet, as a Michie or as a Bagley, they knew that those paths would eventually meet and that one day they would walk together side by side under a flag of red, white, and blue. At this moment, they may have been enemies on the football field, but they would forever be brothers on the battlefield.

In those last five minutes, when the alma maters were sung, when the helmets were taken off, when the enemies saw each other eye to eye, when they saw their brother, a brother that they would die for, that is when it truly becomes the "best five minutes in all of sports"[104]

....

103   The phrase "The Long Gray Line" is the continuum of all graduates and cadets of the United States Military Academy at West Point, New York.

104   John Feinstein, sportswriter and author of a book about the Army Navy Game titled "A Civil War," has called this game's dramatic closing moments: *"the best five minutes in all of sports each and every year."*

CHAPTER 24:
HONOR

"I WANT TO PLAY football," Tully said walking towards an opened
bag of footballs.

"Oh, we can't play now Tully, the mids are playing a game and we
wouldn't want to disturb them," I said guiding Tully back out through
the metal gate.

"I would like to take you to a Navy football game at the big stadium,"
I said hoping that one day he would get to experience the Army-Navy
game.

"Where Bill the Goat is?" Tully asked with excitement.

Yes!" I replied, "You will love it!" Tully and I walked on the sidewalk
alongside the field. I looked over to my left spotting the window of my
old room in the 8th Wing of Bancroft.

"Tully, come here I want to show you something." I led Tully across
the street and over to an enclosed tennis court at the base of 8th Wing.

"Remember the story about my bed being thrown out the window,
well this is the tennis court where it had landed and see that window
up there?" I pointed to the window, second from the top and second
from the right. "That is my old room, where you were up on deck a
few hours ago!"

"Oh," Tully said as we both stared at the green court. I bent down to
touch the sandpaper-like surface. As soon as my fingers made contact, I
felt a surge of fear race through my hands and into the rest of my body.
I could almost feel my palms burning again, the burn I had felt when I
had been dropped for push-ups on this sunbaked court: Montgomery's
"Grinder."

I looked up and noticed Tully following the white lines around the
perimeter of the court. I remember as a plebe, rushing over to one of the
white lines; they always seemed slightly cooler and made the burn a little

easier to tolerate. When I thought about it, being on the tennis court was not as bad as the alternative. We were often dropped for push-ups on the pavement. The burn on a tennis court is one thing, but nothing compared to flesh bubbling and blisters from asphalt. I can still hear the cry of my classmates next to me as our palms were sacrificed to the black pavement on those hot summer afternoons.

"Where is the Tennis net?" Tully asked as he walked over towards me.

"This court doesn't have a net, Tully," I said as I looked out across the court.

"Why?"

"Well, it is used for other things, not for tennis. Remember the story about the Ladder of Death, Mr. Ball, and the Grinder? Well this is the *Grinder.*"

Tully's interest suddenly changed as he noticed a police car driving by.

"Aunt Cathy," Tully said loudly, "There's a police car, let's go tell the policeman."

"Oh, not now Tul, when we go back down to the Annapolis docks we can talk to a policeman."

"We have to tell him about the locks," Tully continued with all seriousness.

"We will Tull, I just want to wait until we get downtown. I am so proud of you though, that you are being such a good citizen."

On our way into the Academy that morning, Tully had found a pile of combination locks underneath a bush outside of the Academy walls. All the locks had been cut, with what appeared to be by a bolt-cutter. Tully and I both had questioned what we had found. The only reasonable guess that I could come up with was that someone may have been stealing items that were locked up, like bicycles and such, and were disposing of the evidence under the bush.

What was even more surprising was Tully's response at the apparent crime scene. He immediately told me that he wanted to go tell the police and show them what he had found. Without me saying anything, he knew that he had witnessed something immoral, the act of stealing, and that it should be reported to that which is moral: the police. At the age of 4, my nephew was being an honorable person.

"Did you know Tully," I said bending down to hug him, "that you would make a great midshipman. You see the midshipmen have to follow what is called "*The Honor Concept.*" It says that midshipmen are good people *who do not lie, cheat or steal.* Not only do you know that stealing is wrong, but you are being brave by wanting to report it. That is called having *moral courage.*"

With the serious look still upon his face, Tully looked down at the ground shaking his head. "Those bad guys shouldn't have stolen. It's not nice."

Tully and I continued to talk about the locks, the bad guys, and moral courage as we walked back past 8th Wing. I couldn't help but think of the time when "The Honor Concept" was more than just a plastic blue card, carried in my uniform shirt pocket, the time when the words printed on the card became real…

Academic Year, February

I looked across at them pacing back and forth and for the first time they appeared different to me, they appeared real. For the first time since July 1, they appeared *human.* I could see the fear on their faces and the nervousness in their walk. I saw emotions that I never thought they had. Throughout the year, I had only seen them in the way in which they were supposed to be seen, as strong and unfaltering upperclassmen. They had been machines of perfection and masters of disguise. They kept a safe emotional distance from us and kept interactions on a professional level. Never once had I seen any one of them let down their guard.

As I stood across from them in the hallway, I felt like Dorothy who had just discovered the real Wizard of Oz. For the first time, it was becoming apparent to me that this all-powerful, omnipotent unit of upperclassmen *was just like me.*

I stood away from them, alone. I felt like I had pulled back the curtain and was now witnessing something I should not have been. I stood alone, with none of my classmates beside me.

I watched as my upperclassmen paced solemnly back and forth through the hall. Some were trying to keep their mind off the present situation by talking among themselves. A nervous laugh or a silent pause in conversation made it clear that the talk was superficial and was just a façade. I noticed others fidgeting with their uniform, and some just standing quietly with their eyes on me.

I watched as they each took turns entering through the closed wooden doors. I knew that in no time at all it would be my turn. I was so nervous that I could not focus. I had lost all train of thought, and my well thought-out speech was somehow non-existent. As if perfect timing, when I was least ready, my name was called. My knees grew week and I whispered a quick prayer.

As I approached the door, I told myself to not be afraid. I thought back to when I was in a similar situation at NAPS, the time when I went before Major Parrino and testified to the sexual harassment that had occurred in my English class. As before, I knew that all I had to do was, to tell the truth, and speak from my heart. I opened the door and once again putting my trust in God, praying that whatever would happen, it would happen for a reason.

I walked into a blue-carpeted room, trimmed with mahogany wood, and centered around a large rectangular table. Out of the corners of my eyes, I noticed large brown leather seats occupied by starched white uniforms. I suddenly felt my knees wobble again as I noticed the numerous gold stripes on a majority of the shoulder boards.

I looked to my left at the head of the table and directed my attention to the man with four gold stripes across his shoulder boards. "Midshipmen 4th Class Ervin reporting, Sir."

"You may take a seat, Miss Ervin," the Commandant[105] said pointing to an empty seat on my right. As I sat down, I became more nervous at the sight of a microphone positioned directly in front of me. I sat with my back rigidly straight and my sweaty hands clasped in my lap.

"Miss Ervin, whenever you're ready," the Commandant said smiling reassuringly.

....

105   *Commandant*: The Naval Academy Commandant is similar to the Dean of Students at a civilian university, and is responsible for the day-to-day conduct, military training and professional development of more than 4,400 midshipmen. " 98th US Naval Academy Commandant Announced," *USNA.edu*, https://www.usna.edu/NewsCenter/2021/01/89th_U.S._NAVAL_ACADEMY_COMMANDANT_ANNOUNCED.php

With a slight tremble in my voice, I began, "Sir, I am aware that 1st Class Kamau Imani is being charged with violating the midshipmen Honor Code; I understand that he has been accused of cheating on a Lab exam. I am also aware, that Mr. Evan's character is on trial, and I am here to testify on the character of 1st Class Kamau Imani." As I spoke, I could feel the presence of Mr. Imani. I dared not look around the table to find him, for I knew I had to keep my focus.

"I have had the privilege of knowing Mr. Imani over this past year. I have come to know him as a person who has many admirable qualities that I look up to, and that I will continue to look up to.

First, as my squad leader, he has always exercised good leadership. He is committed to his squad and has personally been committed to me. Earlier in the year, I had gone through what was called by many of my upperclassmen as a "perception problem." Mr. Imani was dedicated to helping me through this difficult time. He saw me for who I was, and not others' perceptions. He was always honest and fair with me; he approached situations positively; he always conducted himself in a professional manner. Not only did I learn to trust him, but also I looked to him as a guideline as to the type of leader I wanted to become.

Secondly, as a fellow volleyball player, I was able to witness these qualities in another arena. He was always committed to his team as well as to me. Often, he took me aside and helped me with various skills or difficulties I was having. As co-Captain on the men's volleyball team, he demonstrated strong leadership, honesty, hard work, and discipline."

I realized that my voice was still shaking. Not only was it the nerves, but also the release of built-up emotion that I had bottled inside. I quickly glanced over to Mr. Imani. His brown skin contrasted sharply against his Summer White uniform. His eyes were wide with a sense of sadness and tiredness. I noticed how thin and frail he looked. I pictured his tall and lanky body sliding across the volleyball floor. I was always amazed at how strong he was, yet how weak he looked. I continued as I looked back towards the Commandant, "As I said before, I am proud to know Mr. Imani. He is the type of leader that I hope to become one day."

After I finished speaking, I began to wonder what exactly I had said. The emotions, the nervousness, and probably my typical lack of sleep, made it hard for me to remember what exactly I had been saying. The only thing that was reassuring about my testimony was that I knew that I had spoken from my heart. Other than that, no comments were made when I had finished, except for "*Thank you, Miss Ervin,*" spoken by the Commandant.

As I walked back out in the hallway and past my remaining upper-classmen, I could feel my body collapse. I felt like a puppet whose strings had just been cut; my body folded becoming looser and looser as I walked down the hallway. I had felt so tense in the room among the senior officers and staff. I had worried for so long as to what I would say, and as to how everyone would react. I wanted to make things better for Mr. Imani. I wanted them to hear my story and conclude that Mr. Imani was not guilty of the crime.

That next day I received an email from Mr. Imani,

Date: Tue, 28 Feb 1995 11:04:59
From: Midn Kamau Imani m952345@usna
To: Midn Catherine Ervin m981938@usna
Subject: Thanks

"Hey, Cathy (I think I can call you that now),

Thanks for being there last night. I just want to tell you that even though my future seems bleak at this place, I believe in myself. There are a lot of problems with this honor system and they need correcting. Too late for me to correct, but not too late for you. If ya ever get to become an honor representative, become one and make a difference if not for me, but yourself. Don't worry about me, I'll graduate with a degree from somewhere else and will be playing volleyball at that school. No worry there. But the only worry I have in my mind is the kid who lied. He will have the trust of other peoples' lives in his hands, and I pray to God that nothing will happen if he turns to those means of deception again. All the credit I have is due to God. Only the mistakes have been mine. Print this out and save it, because one day our paths will cross again. If you ever want to hang out after I'm outta here and at

another school, just write to me. I think I'll pursue being
a math teacher. I've enjoyed knowing you and being your
squad leader. I hope that you really consider making the
honor concept a living thing so when you are a Firstie,
things will run the way they are supposed to.

And always remember to square yourself to the net when
ya set. All right.

See ya,
Kam

On Monday April 24th, after further investigation by the Brigade
Honor Staff and by the Academy, midshipmen 1st Class Kamau Imani
was found guilty of cheating. Not only was he denied graduation, which
at that point was only two months away, but he was struck with a blow
that only the strongest survive: his honor had been destroyed.

   Mr. Imani had told me the news himself. As I read his message on
e-mail, my throat tightened and tears filled my eyes,

   Date: Mon, 24 Apr 1995 21:32:01
   From: Midn Kamau Imani m952345@usna
   To: Midn Catherine Ervin m981938@usna
   Subject: Last e-mail message

   Well Cathy,

   I'll be leaving tomorrow or Wednesday. It looks like I just
   wanted to say thanks and give ya my address.

   See ya, Peace Out,
   Kam

   I stared at the cold, lifeless message on my computer screen in disbelief. I could not believe that it was finalized now, that the decision had
been made, and as far as I was concerned, it was the wrong decision.
Here was someone of good character being denied what he rightfully
earned. Mr. Imani had been in the *arena*, for four long years, his *face
had been marred with sweat, and dust, and blood; he had strived valiantly*

and had spent himself in a worthy cause; he deserved the *triumph of high achievement*, but instead he had *failed.* And to many he did not fail while daring greatly, he failed in a dishonorable way.

I became upset the more I thought about it. I even got to a point where I began to question Mr. Imani and myself. *Was it all true? Did he really cheat? Did he lie to me? Have I been standing up for someone I don't really know? Was I standing up for someone I made him out to be? Have I been blind to the truth?*

What if the cause *was* so worthy, that any means necessary were used to gain the *"triumph of high achievement?"* What if Mr. Imani' morals were compromised for this achievement?

Mr. Imani left that Wednesday and I have never seen him since. We kept in touch for about a year, writing letters back and forth. At that time, he had been going to school at a University in Providence Rhode Island where he was a graduate student in the computer-engineering field. In one of his letters, he had told me that he aspired to be a college professor and that he hoped he could reach his students as he had done with my squadmates and me in 34th Company.

I don't know if I will ever know the truth. All I do know is that I am grateful for everything Mr. Imani did for me. Mr. Imani taught me to believe in myself, whether it was on the volleyball court or in 34th Company. Day in and day out he had worked with me to improve my skills as a setter and to improve my performance as a plebe. Most importantly, Mr. Imani had motivated me to want to be the best I could be. I looked up to him and respected him because of his character and the set of values he taught and instilled in me. Whether or not he truly lived these values he taught is not up to me to determine, only he will ever know. What I do know is that I was determined to "make the honor concept a living thing" as Mr. Imani had told me to. As Shakespeare had once said,

> *Mine honor is my life; both grow in one;*
> *Take honor from me, and my life is done.*

CHAPTER 25:

THE CLUB

AS I WALKED with Tully, I continued to picture Mr. Imani. I could see him in the tall oak trees that lined the sidewalk, his tall body blocking an enemy hit at the volleyball net. I could see him in the gentle breeze that stirred the leaves, his calming and gentle instruction as I stood in front of him, moving me to work harder. I wondered where he was now and what he was doing. Did he miss the Academy? Had he restored honor to his life, or had it never been lost? In my heart and to this day, I believe that his honor had never been lost. He had faith in me as a Plebe, and I would always have faith in him—and his honor.

As I continued to think of Mr. Imani, Tully pulled me along wanting to see more of the Academy and hear more stories.

"What are they doing over there, Aunt Cathy?" Tully asked as we walked past 8th Wing. I looked down the road and noticed a company of midshipmen marching.

"That is one of the companies, Tully, from the practice parade that we had seen earlier. It looks as if they are still practicing!"

"Aunt Cathy, I know what company it is!"

"You do!" I replied with acted surprise.

"30th Company, Aunt Cathy—see? Do you see the flag? It has the number 30 on it!"

"Good job Tully, you are learning a lot today!"

Tully and I watched as the 30th Company guidon fluttered in the wind, guiding the midshipmen behind it.

"Hey, Tully, did I tell you that there are 30 companies here at the Academy, but that when I went here there were 36?"

"No."

"The Naval Academy is made up of 'companies.' Six companies form what is called a 'battalion.' When I went here, we had six battalions. And the six battalions form what is called a brigade.' We call the midshipmen, a 'Brigade of midshipmen.' The Brigade represents a Fleet out in the real Navy. A fleet is a group of ships that operates under one command."

"Now, Tully, here is a test for you: if you get this question right, I will give you a piggy-back ride, but if you get it wrong, you have to drop and do five push-ups!"

Tully looked up at me and smiled. "It will be like I am the plebe and you are Mr. Montgomery!"

"Um… sure… I just won't make you recite the 'Man in the Arena!'"

"What is that?"

"It is something I had to memorize for Mr. Montgomery, and I could never get it right. I was always in trouble because of it. Anyways, here is your question: what company was your Aunt Cathy in when she was here at the Academy?"

"34!" Tully yelled as he jumped with excitement.

"Correct, Tully, very good! I think that was too easy!"

As Tully nodded in agreement, he decided to drop and do the push-ups anyways. I joined him and then continued teaching him about *brigades and companies.*

"Tully, the company is the most important unit of the Brigade of midshipmen. My best memories of the Academy took place in my company. I ate, slept, marched, studied, and worked with them. We learned to trust one another and to rely on each other in difficult times. We were proud to be in 34th Company. *It was a privilege.*"

As I thought of 34th Company, I began to tell Tully another story, a story where my pride in 34th Company waved for everyone to see, like a company's guide-on. A story that showed how proud I was to be a part of "The Club."

Academic Year, March

I was face down with my hands clenched in the cold, damp grass. I could feel the March air creeping through my camouflage, a far change from the hot Plebe Summer days. Darkness was all around me—thick, black, and foreboding. My eyes still had not adjusted and so all the objects surrounding me seemed distorted and unfamiliar. My body felt numb, as I laid motionless, listening to the silence. I continued to concentrate on drawing every movement out of my body. I slowed my breathing down… in and out… until it was one steady rhythm. However, I could not control the racing of my heart. I could feel its beat in my fingertips, in my legs, and my head. It was beginning to penetrate the quietness that had shrouded me. I tried to ignore the pounding inside of me. I wanted to suppress these feelings of anticipation and nervousness so that I could focus on the task at hand. Eerie sounds began to shoot through the darkness causing every nerve inside my body to jump and my thumping heart to skip a beat. Suddenly, I heard the snapping of twigs. I looked behind me to see my roommate, Lily. I looked to my left and right as three other dark bodies were inching their way towards me. When we were all together, I quietly said, "Try to stick together, remember the most important thing is to never leave a man behind. Remember what Mr. Wyatt said, that if a Jimmy Leg[106] is after you, run, do not stop. We do not want to get caught. If we do get caught, we will use 'The Code of Conduct.'"

Everyone in the military abided by the Code of Conduct, and it was on the long and never-ending list of plebe rates to learn and memorize. I began to think of the different articles of the Code as we all took a brief rest under the cover of the bushes.

> **Article 3:** *If I am captured, I will continue to resist by all means available. I will make every effort to escape and aid others to escape. I will accept neither parole nor special favors from the enemy.*

> **Article 4:** *When questioned, should I become a prisoner of war, I am required to give name, rank, service number, and date of birth. I will evade answering further questions to the utmost of my ability. I will make no oral or written*

---

106 *Jimmy Legs:* In modern USNA contexts, a disallowed slang term referring to any or all of the NDW-NSA (The Naval District Washington-Naval Support Activity) Annapolis Police Department, who provide security for the grounds, and enforcement for some of the regulations, such as the one forbidding town visits over the wall (whether wall or chain-link fence) at night. "United States Naval Academy," Wikipedia.org, https://en.wikipedia.org/wiki/United_States_Naval_Academy

statements disloyal to my country and its allies or harmful to their cause.

I felt the grass between my fingers again, as I snapped back to my present situation. I looked to my left to see darkened bodies lying beside me. To my right was a huge gray house with blue and white-striped awnings. The yard was well kept, as I had noticed by the feel of precision-cut grass. There were orderly rows of bushes and flowers leading up to the front door. The house gave off a feeling of dignity and pride. Its power seemed to overcome everything around it, especially at night. I felt out of place like I didn't belong there—and actually, I didn't belong there. I was a plebe crawling around on sacred ground, the front lawn of the *Superintendent.*

The Superintendent, Admiral Charles B. Foster, was the man in command of the entire Academy. Not only did he rank as an Admiral and hold the prestigious title of "The 55th Superintendent of the United States Naval Academy," but he was well decorated from the many accomplishments in his Navy career. One of his greatest achievements (besides graduating from the Naval Academy in 1958) was that he was promoted to the rank of a "four-star"[107] upon his appointment as Commander of the Pacific Fleet (CINCPAC) from 1991–1994. Whether he was flying aircraft off the carrier USS Shangri-La, leading onboard nuclear submarines, or serving as a Naval Aide to the President, Admiral Foster excelled in all of his missions and exemplified leadership, dedication, and duty.

The mission I was taking part in seemed so trivial compared to the missions that Admiral Foster had accomplished. Only a few of the plebes decided to be a part of the mission; Sinclair (Lily), Miles, Shoots, Garner, and myself. The first part of the mission was to escape by *"hopping the wall."* The fifteen-foot-high gray stone wall surrounded the Academy grounds and separated two different worlds, the midshipmen's "Annapolis" and the city of Annapolis. This escape into the streets of downtown Annapolis would provide us with something which every plebe desires at one point, freedom. A moment to break free from the

---

107 *Four-star:* The rank of admiral (or full admiral, or four-star admiral) is the highest rank normally achievable in the U.S. Navy. (https://www.military-ranks.org/navy/admiral)

chains of upperclass slavery. For me, it was not only the chance for freedom, but it presented me with a challenge. When I had been questioned by the other plebes as to why I was partaking in this risky endeavor, I would reply with the same reply that the famous mountain climber, George Mallory, replied with when he was asked as to why he wanted to climb Mount Everest: *"Because it is there."* The wall was there and I was going to climb it.

"Hopping the wall" had more potential than the other means of escape on the Yard. The other way, which had been used for years, was the "Ho Chi Minah Trail."[108] I had never seen the trail, but I had understood it to be an underground system of pipes, which if followed, would lead you out of the Academy. I had also heard stories, though, of surveillance cameras placed in the entrance of the underground trail to prevent any midshipman's attempt at escape. Thus, "hopping the wall" seemed to be a safer attempt. There were some dangers, however. Not only did we have the Jimmy Legs, which could present a problem, but we also had the watchful and well-trained eyes of the Marine guards to worry about.

The five of us crawled out of the shadows of the bushes and out into the open. I reached out to clench two handfuls of cold, slippery grass, and then placed my elbows hard against the ground. Next, I lifted one knee, then the other, alternating back and forth while keeping my butt and head low to the ground. This form of combat maneuvering was called the "low-crawl." Within no time at all, we had made it across the highest-ranking lawn on the Yard.

"Okay, now from here we are going to go past the officer housing, we will bear right at the fork in the road, and then proceed to the section of wall behind the Chapel. We will regroup once everyone makes it to the wall. Stay low and stay alert, and don't forget about the Marine

----

108   *Ho Chi Minh Trail*: a military supply route running from North Vietnam through Laos and Cambodia to South Vietnam. The route sent weapons, manpower, ammunition and other supplies from communist-led North Vietnam to their supporters in South Vietnam during the Vietnam War. The trail was named after Ho Chi Minh, the president of North Vietnam. During the 1960s, the Ho Chi Minh Trail (actually a network of trails, footpaths and roadways) " moved several tons of supplies each day through rugged mountain ranges and dense jungle. "Ho Chi Minh Trail," *History,com*, https://www.history.com/this-day-in-history/u-s-jets-bomb-ho-chi-minh-trail

Corps guards. One by one, we began to low-crawl across the lawns of the officer housing. I grabbed my ponytail, tucking it back into my black-knit watch cap. I took a deep breath of the chilling, 2-AM air, and then with Lily at my heels, took off into the night's shadows. A simple five-minute stroll across a row of six houses becomes a difficult task when you are trying to escape. We zigzagged back and forth from one tree to another, crouched in and out of bushes, low-crawled through open and exposed areas of lawn. Soon we were crossing a street in a full sprint. We ducked for cover underneath the shadow of a parked car.

After catching our breath, we slowly made our way to the wall. Suddenly, I realized that I could no longer see any movement from my classmates in front of us. I automatically dropped to my stomach and pulled myself under the parked car. Lily followed suit, and within seconds, we were face down in silence. I lifted my eyes to see a small beam of white light bouncing back and forth alongside the ground to the right of us. The light was getting brighter and closer followed by slow and heavy footsteps. I watched the light continue to bounce along, shining on the droplets of dew, and creating a sparkling glaze upon the pavement. I saw a pair of black shoes pass by, and my eyes followed them upwards until it became evident that we were in the presence of a *Jimmy Leg*. My heart began to pound so hard that I thought it was going to beat its way out of my chest and then blow our cover. Lily and I dared not breathe. Now I understood why I had lost sight of my squadmates, for they were hiding as well.

Five minutes later, the squish of the patent leather shoes faded into the distance, and the Jimmy Leg was soon out of sight. I began to hear the rustle of leaves and the crackle of branches as two dark figures were moving towards the wall. Lily and I slowly crawled out from our blanket of safety and continued in the same direction. Soon the five of us were rejoined in a huddle.

"Sorry guys," Miles calmly whispered. "That Jimmy Leg, I think, had spotted me for a brief moment when I rounded the corner here. He then stopped his car and as you-all know, took a look around."

"Stay low guys," whispered Shoots, "One of the Marines just stepped out from the post." We looked down the road to see the silhouette of a rigid body pacing back and forth across Gate 3's entrance. Now and then a small flutter of orange light lingered in front of him, as he stopped to puff on his cigarette. We waited patiently for ten minutes until the guard returned into the shadows of his post.

"Let's move," said Lily as she approached the wall. We helped each other by lifting and pulling until all five of us were up and over the wall. It was a surreal feeling as we turned our backs to the wall and fled into the shadows of freedom. We quickly made our way down the cobbled side streets of Annapolis, past Colonial row houses and sleeping flowerbeds. A half-hour had passed and unfortunately, our mission came to an abrupt halt.

We had suddenly found ourselves standing in the shadow of a tall man. I looked at his silver badge, a cat's eye in the dark, shining as it reflected the headlights from his squad car. His walkie-talkie came to life as it began to crackle and buzz with static. A few voices broke in and out of the noise, but they were ignored.

The outline of his starched uniform, his deep voice, and the silent whirl of red and blue lights was my wake-up call in a dream that had been going so well. I wanted to turn the alarm off, but it kept ringing.

"All of you better turn around right now and get back on Base before I change my mind."

"Yes Sir!" "Right away sir!" I answered as I stood shivering in the cool darkness. The eight months of discipline and training were evident in my quick and submissive reply.

"I would take you all in, but I don't feel like dealing with this tonight. What I *will* do is just inform your *Officer of the Watch* that you have been caught off Base and disturbing the peace." The police officer paused and flipped back the cover on his citation pad.

"What Company are you in?"

"34th Company, Sir," I replied proudly.

With a sigh of impatience, the officer quickly scribbled a few marks upon his citation pad. He then motioned us with his black nightstick to leave, as if brushing away a swarm of annoying flies.

"Go on back now, and you better hope that I never catch you out here again. Is that understood?"

"Sir, Yes Sir!" the five of us replied in unison.

With our heads down and our spirits crushed, we turned around and headed back to the Academy. Just twenty minutes earlier, we had been crawling around the front lawns of these houses, zigzagging in and out of the bushes from one property to the next. Unfortunately, a few of my squadmates did not understand the importance of being "stealth," especially when you are sneaking around on private property, in the middle of the night, with a face painted black, and dressed in dark clothing. (At times like this, I had noticed that common sense did not register in a mind that was built for other things, things such as calculus or electrical engineering.)

Anyways, the peace we were trampling through had been disturbed. Our squadron of non-stealth planes had been picked up on radar. A frightened woman in a pink bathrobe and curlers had spotted us. Within a matter of seconds, she had frantically turned on every single light in and around her house. At that point, we were like escaped convicts being exposed by the beams of the prison searchlights. The police were called and in no time at all, we were turned around and heading back to the Academy with an incomplete mission.

"Wait a minute," I said, as I looked up at the other four dark bodies slowly moving ahead of me. "We can't give up now, we didn't complete the mission! We stopped and circled into a relaxed huddle. I looked into the four sets of eyes; the white popping out from the black faces, faces that had blended into the darkness around us.

"We made it over the wall, though, we escaped didn't we?" Shoots quietly said.

"Right! That is my point," I replied. "Our first attempt to hop the wall earlier in the year, when we were with Mr. Wyatt, had been a failure. But we came back, we tried again, and tonight we succeeded. We still have time, so why don't we turn around and give it another shot."

"I'm finished," Garner said tiredly. "I just want to get some sleep."

"Yeah man, I can hear my rack calling me," Shoots said as his shoulders drooped with exhaustion, "If we head back to the Yard now, we will still have a good three hours to sleep!"

I was disappointed by the lack of motivation.

"I'm staying," I said confidently, pulling my black watch-cap further down on my head.

"So am I," Lily said as her tiny body shivered inside her baggy uniform.

"I want to finish this too," Miles said as he crossed his arms.

"Good luck then," Shoots muttered as he and Garner turned around and continued walking. Soon they faded into the blackness of the Annapolis streets and then they were gone.

"Well, it will be easier now with fewer tag-alongs," Lily said with a laugh. I noticed that Lily still had the white bundle of cloth tucked inside of her camouflaged blouse. I reached inside my pocket to make sure that I still had the handful of twine. I felt the tangled mess of it, and I tucked it further down.

After the cop drove away and the terrified woman was back in her house, the three of us positioned ourselves in a row of bushes along the sidewalk that ran past our target, St. John's College.[109] Our sights were locked on the lawn, that spread across the front part of the campus. In the center of the lawn was a large oak tree. Its knobby branches stretched more outwards than upward, creating an umbrella effect. The trunk was twisted and gray with age. Its thick roots were bulging out of the soft lawn and spanning out in all directions. Not only was this tree a landmark on the campus of this liberal arts college, but also it was *a historical symbol of Maryland.*

"The Liberty Tree," was the largest known Tulip Poplar in America, standing 100 feet tall, at an age of 460 years old. History rested in the shade of its sprawling 60-foot branches, for it was here that a group of Colonial rebels secretly met before and during the Revolutionary War to plot their activities and forge the fires of liberty. The idea of liberty embodied in a living tree, first came about in 1765 when the Sons of Liberty from Boston, voiced their opposition to the Stamp Act under the cover of a large elm. Throughout the twelve colonies, these *Liberty Trees*, became symbols of strength, which had taken root in a young Nation, and symbols of resistance, growing strong and standing firm against arbitrary rule. Like the one preserved on the campus of St. Johns they were a symbol of pride in our country and a memorial to those who helped to define the meaning of "liberty."

....

109   *St. John's College:* A co-educational, four-year liberal arts college known for its distinctive "great books" curriculum. *St. John's College,* http://www.stjohnscollege.edu)\

Lily, Miles, and I laid in the bushes as we stared up at the majestic-looking tree, its fame momentarily casting a spell upon us. The shadows from its crooked branches stretched like witches' fingers upon the ground. We waited for fifteen minutes, calculating the right time to attack. When it looked safe to go, we bolted out of the bushes and sprinted across the lawn, making beelines straight for the tree. I quickly pulled out the twine from my pocket and began to untangle it. Lily unfurled the bundle of white cloth, while Miles helped to spread it out upon the ground.

We looked up scanning the canopy of the tree for any branches that would be in reach for us to climb. We needed at least two good branches to hang the sheet from. To our dismay, however, the branches were more than twenty-five feet above our heads. Not only were the branches too high, but also the tree-trunk was too wide. (The trunk had a 40-foot circumference to be exact.)

I spread my arms out around the tree as if hugging it; Lily did the same on the opposite side. Our hands were not even close to each other. Our idea of shimming up the tree like monkeys was out of the question. We even tried standing on shoulders, but we needed more than two sets of shoulders to reach the branches.

Lily, Miles, and I began to panic. Our only real concern had been hopping the wall; we didn't think that we were going to have any problems with the rest of the mission. We just figured, *how hard could it be to hang a sheet on a tree?* The smart thing to do would have been to have a Recon mission beforehand, in which scouts could have been sent out to collect valuable information to help execute our plan; valuable information such as knowing that there were unreachable branches on the tree. What made matters even worse was that we didn't even have a back-up plan.

I looked over to see the skinny, lanky figure of Miles circling the tree like an anxious squirrel.

"Well, what the heck are we gonna to do now", he said in his slow southern drawl. Miles was from a small farm town in North Carolina. He came from a world of tractors and pick-up trucks; a true-blooded country boy from the heartland of America. He was often at the heart of plebe jokes because of his southern walk and talk, but when it came down to it, Miles was a great person. Not only was I glad that he was part of the mission, but also that he was part of 34th Company.

I looked at the white sheet upon the ground as my mind raced for an answer. I suddenly began to hear faint voices in the distance. I looked up and turned to my right, facing the south side of the campus. I noticed movement on the steps of a brick building. The voices became louder, as I noticed three people quickly walking toward us.

"Hey man, what are you doing?" one voice said. Lily, Miles, and I said nothing as we waited for the voices to get closer.

"Dude, this is our tree man! What are you doing to it?" another voice said.

I was now able to see whom the voices belonged to. Standing in front of us were three longhaired guys with tie-dyed t-shirts, baggy shorts, and sandals. It was obvious that we were face to face with three "Johnnies": students of the college. By appearance, these three fit the midshipman's stereotype of a "Johnny": artsy, peace-loving hippies that spent their time sipping coffee, reading Shakespeare, and smoking pot.

As Lily, Miles, and I stood dressed in our get-up of camouflage and black paint, I am sure that we were reinforcing their stereotype of a midshipman: immature jocks, who played with guns, and pretended to be soldiers.

"Go back to the Academy, man, we don't want you here," said one of the Johnnies.

"We'll be out of here in a minute. We just have a banner here to hang-up," I said calmly. Our dilemma was now getting complicated thanks to the Johnnies. *What were they doing up at 3 AM anyhow?"* It then occurred to me that this was a "normal" college and that there were no "Taps" here in which lights had to be out. Besides, there was probably not the same amount of stress here, and thus a good night's sleep was not a high priority.

As I continued to tie the twine to the ends of the banner, I noticed one of the Johnnies walking away.

"I'm getting security. This is way un-cool," he said slowly.

"Do you know the importance of this tree, how beautiful it is?" Another Johnny said as he smiled lovingly at the tree.

"Yeah, its importance is that it's in a *prime* location to hang our banner!" Lily said as I looked at her and laughed.

Undaunted by the Johnnies, Lily, Miles, and I re-grouped to discuss a new plan. We knew that one thing was for sure, we wouldn't be able to just wrap the banner around the tree. If we did, the tree-hugging Johnnies would wait for us to leave and just rip the banner down.

As we stood by our banner discussing Plan B, *the non-existent back-up plan*, a beam of light bounced along the ground off in the distance. A flashlight was quickly approaching us with a security guard attached to the other end of it. The over-weight guard, dressed a in white untucked top and black pants approached the three of us as the Johnnies continued to stand next to their tree. "Leave the grounds immediately or else I'll call the cops," the guard said as he tugged on his pants that were hanging below his round belly.

In unison we replied, "Yes Sir!" Lily rolled the sheet back up, tucked it back into her shirt, and the three of us began to walk away. I turned around and looked back at the three Johnnies who were now sitting underneath the precious tree that they had defended.

"Go ahead and have your tree," I quietly whispered, "You can't have our determination."

Within a few minutes, we had snuck back into the bushes and we were now patiently waiting to make another attempt.

"*I will find a way, or make one*," Miles whispered, quoting words attributed to Robert E. Perry.[110] I looked down at my watch and pressed a button. "3:45" was momentarily displayed by the fluorescent green Indiglo light. Time was running away from us and it was moving fast.

"Well we better find a way soon," I said as I breathed a wisp of condensation into the frigid air.

"I checked my watch, guys, and it is already—"

I was unable to finish my sentence when Lily's fragile voice interrupted, "*The bell tower*."

....

110   *Robert E. Perry:* U.S. Arctic explorer usually credited with leading the first expedition to reach the North Pole (1909). Peary entered the U.S. Navy in 1881 and pursued a naval career until his retirement, with leaves of absence granted for Arctic exploration. "Robert Perry," *Britannica*, https://www.britannica.com/biography/Robert-Edwin-Peary

Miles and I turned our heads quietly avoiding the branches. We looked over to the left where Lily was looking.

"The bell-tower," she repeated as if in a trance. There to the left of the Liberty Tree was a large building of brick, with a bell tower rising out of the center of the roof.

Miles and I didn't even need to question it; we were both on the same page as Lily. The far-right corner of the building would be a perfect spot to hang the banner from. Not only that, but it was accessible by way of the bell-tower. We would be able to get onto the roof by climbing through the bell-tower, where we could then hang our banner.

Without hesitation, the three of us crawled out of the bushes, and after a few ducks, dashes, and jumps we were standing in the shadows of the back of the building. Miles and I began checking the windows, hoping one would be unlocked in which we could crawl through.

"Umm… guys… this may be easiest."

I turned around to see Lily holding a door open.

"What? This is too easy," I said as Lily laughed.

The door led into a small dark room. In the center of the room was the start of a spiral staircase. Lily led the climb up as quietly as heavy combat boots on metal steps could take us. We continued to wind and twist our way higher and higher into the shadows of the tower. As we reached the last step of the staircase, we pulled ourselves up into a small circular room. We had to move around on our hands and knees, for the ceiling was very low. The room, with its beautifully arched windows, circled a large iron bell that was hanging in the middle.

"Hey, ya'll think this is the bell tower?" Miles cackled. I looked over at him and laughed as I looked at the bell, hanging six inches from my head. The three of us moved around the room like thieves, checking for any unlocked windows.

"Quick! *Duck down!*" Lily said as her head lowered below the windowsill. The three of us crouched lower onto our stomachs.

"What is it?" I asked turning to Lily.

"I saw some movement down below us, and I'm just afraid that we could be spotted," Lily replied quietly.

"I don't know wach-ya mean. How could anyone spot us in a room full of windows?" Miles said laughing at another one of his bad jokes.

"Well, pa'tner," I said imitating Miles, "You're quite the comedian tonight!"

The three of us laughed quietly as we waited for whoever was down below, to leave. When we felt it was safe, we slowly got back up on our knees and peered over the edges of the windowsills. We did a 360-degree scan of the area, and soon we had determined that it looked safe to move on with the plan. I pushed open a window on the side of the bell tower that faced the front of the campus; to the left was the corner of the roof, from which we would hang the banner from.

"Okay," I said as I began to place a leg through the opened window, "I will tie one corner of the banner on the left side here, someone else has to tie the other end down."

"I'll do it," Lily replied, pulling out the banner from her camouflage jacket.

"Great, cuz I sure as heck wasn't gonna do it. I'd end up break'n my neck or sump'n," Miles said as he smiled his crooked-tooth smile.

"You can keep a lookout for us, Miles," I said as I placed both feet onto the black shingles. "Let us know if you see any movement at all." I looked back at Lily. "Let's get this done quick, Roomie!"

"I'm right behind you," Lily said as she handed me a handful of twine attached to the left side of the banner. I could feel my feet sliding from underneath of me, unable to grip the smooth shingles. I decided to sit on my butt and slowly inch my way down with my feet out in front of me. I crab-walked my way over towards the left corner of the roof. I stopped and looked down around me. I had been calm up to this point, but when I realized what I was actually doing, I began to panic. *One slip*, I thought, *and that's all it will take for me to go sliding off this roof.* The drop looked painful, a forty-footer. I carefully turned my head to the right to find Lily. I saw her slowly inching her way down as I had been doing.

"It is extremely slippery, Lily," I whispered. Ironically, as soon as I whispered this, Lily's feet suddenly slipped out from underneath her. I watched as her body began to slide down the roof as if in slow motion.

"Lily!" I screamed in a whisper. I was too far away from her to help. I watched her frail body slide as her tiny arms and legs frantically grasped to hold on. Black shingles were crumbling as she struggled to stop herself. I had noticed that she had let go of the banner. I held on tightly to my end as I watched the other end slowly rolling off the edge. The image of Lily rolling off the edge flashed through my mind. I looked over to see my roommate on the edge of the roof, on her back with one leg dangling over the edge. Somehow, she had managed to stop herself.

"Lily," I said desperately, "Are you okay?"

"I'm fine. You're right Cath, it is a little slippery up here," Lily replied quivering.

"How were you able to stop yourself? I thought for sure—"

I was unable to finish my sentence before Miles cut in. "Quiet y'all… there is movement to the right of us." I looked down to see a couple walking hand and hand past the bell tower. Lily and I lowered our heads and said nothing. After they had passed, Miles continued, "Holy jump'n jack-rabbit Sinclair, I thought you had bought the farm. Are ya okay?"

"I'm fine," Lily replied. "Luckily I was able to find some traction on a few of the shingles which helped to stop my slide." She suddenly paused and frantically looked around.

"I dropped the banner didn't I," she said turning to me.

"Your end is just hanging off the edge to the left of you," I replied, "I have the other end here." I held up my hand wrapped in the twine that was tied to the corner of the sheet. Lily inched her way down closer to the banner; her leg was still dangling over the edge. I was afraid that the weight of her combat boot would pull her over.

"Lily, please be careful, I don't feel like scraping you off of the ground tonight," I said as I watched her slowly reach over the edge.

"I just have to pull up this end here… I've got it," she said as her hand re-emerged above the edge holding on to the twine. We both quickly tied the rope onto the wooden trim that hung below the tile. After we finished, we crab-walked backwards up the slanted roof. Miles moved out of the way so we could climb back through the window.

"So what kind of knot did ya'll use to tie the banner," Miles asked as we crouched back down into the circular room.

"I don't know, Miles? Geez! We just tied it alright," Lily, said aggravated.

Miles' mouth widened into his toothy grin, "Are ya'll sure it wasn't a *slip*knot?" Miles began laughing uncontrollably.

I glanced over at Lily, and I couldn't help but laugh as well. Soon all three of us were on our stomachs laughing as quietly as we could.

"Hey, how about we get out of here" I said pushing myself up from the ground.

"Yeah, we don't want to upset the Johnnies," Lily said, moving towards the staircase.

"After all," Miles added, "We don't want to hurt their *beautiful bell.*" Miles reached out for the bell pretending to hug it. We continued to laugh, as we spiraled back down the tower. I cracked the door open and slowly peered outside checking for any Johnnies. The coast was clear, except for the sounds of voices coming from within the dorms near us.

I stepped outside and with my back against the brick, I sidestepped to the left. I slowly peeked around the corner. It was all clear. I looked to my right and motioned to Lily and Miles with a pointed finger, indicating for them to follow. We all crouched as low as we possibly could while trying to stay on our feet.

As I started to cut to my left towards the direction of the road, I spotted movement up ahead. I placed a fist up over my head, indicating for Lily and Miles to stop moving and crouch down.

Great, I thought, *I can see two Johnnies heading straight for us, but I don't think they've seen us.* I quickly looked to my right where a row of thick bushes bordered a small building. I motioned with my finger to the bushes and began to low crawl into them. Lily and Miles followed.

The three of us laid in silence as we watched two pairs of brown sandals scuffle by us. I closed my eyes, enjoying the smell of whatever flowering bushes we were lying in. After the Johnnies were at a safe distance away from us, I motioned for Lily and Miles to crawl through the bushes to the other side.

I emerged from the bushes in the shadows of a brick building that looked like all the others on campus, only smaller. As the other two crawled over next to me, Lily whispered, "Ya know, I was thinking that maybe we need to take some kind of *souvenir* back to the Company to prove that we were here."

"What about the banner, though, that proves that we were here," Miles said retying his boots.

"Not everyone may get a chance to see the banner," Lily answered.

"I see what you mean Lily," I said turning to her. "I think it's a good idea. In fact, I think I see a great souvenir already," I pointed to a metal sign that was hanging off of two wooden posts in front of the building. Lily read the sign aloud

"*St. John's Library*"

"Arr you crazy," Miles replied, "It's a little big and we ain't got a ten-gallon cowboy hat to hid it und'r!"

"It's perfect," Lily laughed, "Big enough to put on display for our company and tells exactly where we have all been tonight!"

"Exactly!" I said. "It's perfect, now let's go grab it—*quick!*"

The three of us crawled across the sidewalk that led up to the main door of the library.

"Miles, you're on look-out again," I said as Lily and I approached the sign. We quickly unhooked the sign. Lily insisted that she could carry the sign; she had gotten used to keeping things tucked inside her BDU blouse. The two-foot by two-foot sign could only be partially hidden, and it was awkward to carry, but she was somehow able to manage it.

The three of us, now high from adrenaline, ran, low-crawled, and tiptoed back to the Academy. It was around 0500 hours when I opened the door to the 8th Wing staircase; we had made excellent time.

"Hey guys," Lily said walking away from the staircase "I say we should use the elevator!" I looked over at Lily and smiled, she didn't even need to ask me.

"Sure, why the heck not? We'll probably get in trouble anyhow, with that sign an everythin," Miles sighed exhaustedly.

As we rode up to the 3rd Deck, Lily turned to us and said, "I tell ya, it sure feels nice riding this. I can't stand running those stairs every day. Those firsties have it easy."

"They're all just weak!" I said smiling.

We all gave each other a high five as the elevator stopped with a slight bounce, and the door opened.

Miles took off his black watch-cap and scratched his dirty blond head, "Well ya'll, I'm hitt'n the hay."

"Good night Miles," Lily said affectionately.

"And thanks," I whispered, "I don't know what we would have done without you."

Miles smiled, yawned, and soon he had disappeared into the black hallway. I turned to my roommate who was still holding on to our souvenir. "I am so proud of ourselves, that I just want to go show this to someone right now," I said looking at the sign.

"So why don't we?" Lily smirked.

"Okay, but who?" I replied.

We both looked away for a fleeting moment and then simultaneously said, "Steinmann!"

We both knew that he would be the proudest of us, and more importantly, he would not mind being woken up by us at this hour.

Lily and I immediately ran to Steinmann's room. We quietly pushed the door open and snuck inside. It was too dark to tell which bed was Steinmann's, the one on the left or the one on the right. I moved over towards the left one, and as I bent over to get a closer look, a strong hand suddenly grabbed my neck. At the same time, I felt a flat piece of cold metal against my throat.

"Sir, it's me, Ervin," I choked as I tried to pull free from the hold. I quickly repeated, "Sir, it's *Ervin!*" as I gasped for air.

"Ervin? What in the hell are you doing?" The familiar voice confirmed that I had chosen the right bed.

"Sir, I can't breath," I said gasping, unable to move.

Mr. Steinmann released his grip on my neck and then jumped up out of bed.

"What is going on here?" Steinmann asked placing his knife back under the pillow.

"You sleep with a knife, Sir?" Lily whispered moving over closer to us.

"Sinclair's here too," Steinmann lowered his voice even deeper, "What is going on ladies?"

"Sir," I said rubbing my sore neck, "We came to show you something."

"Did it have to be at 5 in the morning?"

"Yes," replied Lily as she pulled out the sign from beneath her jacket. She brought it closer for Mr. Steinmann to see.

Steinmann glanced at the sign that was now illuminated from the moonlight streaming through his window. Steinmann glanced back up at us. "You didn't?" He said questioning.

"Yes, we did Sir?" I replied proudly.

"Did you two go alone?"

"No, I said turning to Lily, "We had four other plebes, but all but one abandoned the mission after the cops came. Miles stayed with us."

"*Cops*?" Steinmann barked, "Should I be hearing this?"

"Yes Sir," I said hesitating.

"So… let me get this straight," Steinmann said crossing his arms, "You, Sinclair, and Miles hopped the wall, and stole this Saint John's sign alone, without the accompaniment of an upperclassman?"

"Yes Sir!"

"Did anyone put you up to this?"

"No Sir, it was done out of motivation."

"And the reason for our mission will be revealed tomorrow," Lily chimed in.

"Well, nice job you two, but maybe next time you can wait to tell me at a more decent hour."

"Yes Sir," I said as I noticed the Steinmann smile stretching across his face.

"Now go on, get out of here before I get in trouble for having two females in my room with the door closed." He said crawling back into bed.

Lily opened the door as we quietly slid out. Before closing the door behind me, I turned around and poked my head back into the room. "Oh and Sir, don't worry about me ever waking you up again, I don't think I want to *risk my life* again to do it," I said laughing. I pulled my head back out of the room and closed the door.

It was already 0530 by the time Lily and had gotten back to our room. Luckily, it was Saturday, and we knew that at some point we would be able to catch up on the sleep we had missed.

Before we knew it we were standing, half asleep, in the middle of our P-way at morning meal formation. Mr. Montgomery was pacing back in forth in front of the company.

"Who is responsible for this?" he asked pointing to the sign that Lily and I had left on the ledge of the chalkboard. (A strategic location, I thought, since the whole company would be able to see it.)

I stuck my fist out in front of me, as did Lily and Miles, indicating that it was us.

"Well, we got a call from St. John's this morning—they were pretty upset about the missing sign, and it needs to be returned immediately. Is that understood ladies?"

"Yes Sir," Lily and I said proudly.

"Oh, Ervin just for shits and giggles—why don't you recite 'Man in the Arena' for us all?"

I hesitated, as I was not ready for this, once again:

> Sir, It is not the critic who counts, not the one who points
> out how the strong man stumbled or how the doer of deeds
> might have done them better. The credit belongs to the
> man who is actually in the arena, whose face is marred
> with sweat and dust and blood, who errs and comes short,
> again and again, who know the great enthusiasms, the great
> devotions and spends himself in a worthy cause; who if he
> wins, knows the triumph of high achievement; and who, if
> fails, at least fails while daring greatly... so that...

Suddenly, I stopped.

My mind went blank, once again, as it always did. *Why does he always do this to me?* I thought as I stared with a defeated look upon my face. *Why can't Montgomery ask me about the menu for morning meal or to recite the 5th Law of the Navy?* I was mad that Montgomery was more worried about this one passage and was not even slightly impressed with my heroic mission at St. John's last night.

As I stood there feeling stupid and small, Montgomery stood in front of me and said, "Maybe you should think about spending more time in your rack at night memorizing 'Man in the Arena,' rather than making night-time visits to St. Johns."

"Yes, Sir," I said even more upset. He had no right to be mad at me, I thought. Wait until he sees the banner we had hung; the banner that we had hung for him and the Navy Croquet Team. I may not know "Man in the Arena," but I sure as hell know about pride in my upperclassmen, team support, and loyalty to 34th Company.

I tried to relax as I stood at attention waiting to be dismissed for our weekend liberty. I was tired and was hoping to get some rest, but I had to immediately report to King Hall for breakfast with my volleyball team. We had an all-day tournament today. Unfortunately, I would be missing the big croquet match between the midshipmen and the Johnnies. This matchup was unique in the sense that croquet was the only game played between the two neighboring colleges; it was a younger Academy tradition, one which had started back in 1982.

The story of the first croquet match varies, but basically, a midshipman who was at a party with some Johnnies bragged and said that the Naval Academy could beat the Johnnies at *anything*. A sharp-witted Johnnie challenged the midshipmen to a game of croquet. The midshipman accepted the challenge and soon found himself in a predicament. Not only did he have no clue as to how to play the game, but the Academy didn't even have a croquet team. The Mid ended up persuading his company, *34th Company*, to help him form a team, and to this day 34th Company has supplied players ever since. The midshipmen lost that first game to the Johnnies, and throughout the years, the Mids have only won seven out of the thirty-seven games played.

This famous croquet match, called the "Annapolis Cup"[111], is an all-day event, one in which the front lawn of St. John's is transformed into an old-fashioned social gathering. Picnic blankets are spread with baskets of food under the shade of oak trees. Women in summer dresses watch from underneath the cover of their parasols. Women in summer dresses watch from underneath the shade of their parasols. Old-time music is played, and champagne is toasted as the players stand in dignified concentration among one another.

As I thought about the match, I began to imagine my upperclassmen standing on the green lawn, dressed in white pants and cardigans with blue and gold bowties, sipping champagne, and swinging wooden mallets. Suddenly, I imagined them looking up and spotting a banner hanging from the bell tower. They would recognize the large

....

111 *Annapolis Cup:* History: according to legend, the rivalry began in 1982 when the commandant of the U.S. Naval Academy was speaking with St. John's freshman Kevin Heyburn and remarked that the Midshipmen could beat the Johnnies in any sport. "What about croquet?" was the Johnnie's retort. He later proposed the match to a group of Midshipmen in the interest of fostering better relations between the schools. With the 2019 victory, St. John's has won the Annapolis Cup 30 out of 37 matches. "Croquet Facts Sheet," *St. John's College*, https://www.sjc.edu/annapolis/events/croquet/facts

black clover painted in the center, the same clover that is the "club" in a deck of playing cards. They would know that it was the symbol for their Company, "Club 34." They would smile knowing that the banner was from their plebes. They would feel pride—pride in their plebes, pride in themselves, and pride in the "Club." They would feel what I had felt that night when the banner had been hung.

Unfortunately, I was unable to see the croquet match because of my volleyball tournament. That evening though, I had run into Miles as I was leaving the Academy. He was in the 8th Wing parking lot, as I was, waiting to be picked up by his Sponsor Family for the weekend.

"Hey, did you go to the match? I asked him.

"Yeah," he replied, "and you will never guess what happened," he said, lowering his head in disappointment.

"What, did we lose the match—*again*?"

"Well, yeah, but even worse, Cath, the *banner*..." He paused.

"What, are we in trouble?"

"No, our croquet team didn't even get to see it. Nobody did, for the darn wind had blown it up, and it was all flipped over on top of the roof"

"What!?" I said in shock.

"It was barely visible; all you could see was a bit of white. I was the only one that noticed it, obviously 'cuz I knew about it. I pointed it out to the upperclassmen; I think they only believed me that something was up there because of what had happened this morning with the sign."

Miles lowered his head again. "All that work for nothing."

As I left the Academy that night, I asked my parents if they could drive by St. Johns. They asked why and I told them that I just needed to see something. We drove past the front of the campus. I looked out across the empty lawn imagining the picnic blankets, parasols, wire wickets, music, and champagne.

"What is it?" my mom asked turning around to look at me.

"Do you see anything up on the roof of the bell tower?" I asked as my father slowed the car down.

"Nooo," they both said after a long pause.

"Yeah, I don't see anything either," I said. "But there is something up there."

I proceeded to tell the story to my parents, the shortened version, of course, in which I left out any mention of cops and near-death experiences.

As we drove away, I thought about the last thing that Miles had said to me that night, "All that work for nothing." I had first been upset also about what had happened, but then I realized that it *wasn't* for nothing.

The Club was more than just a banner; it was the friendships that had developed, whether on the croquet team or whether on a dark night hiding inside a bell tower; it was the pride—pride in being a part of the "Club."

A banner had been blown away that day, but the
message had not—and that was all that mattered.

CHAPTER 26:
LIBERTY

AS I FINISHED my story to Tully, I smiled as I thought of 34th Company, the Club, and how I will always be proud to have been a part of it. In fact, to this day, when I drive by St. John's campus, I often catch myself glancing up at the bell tower, somehow still hoping to see a sheet of white waving in the wind.

"Can we go back to Grandma's now?" Tully asked.

"Yes, and Grandma will be so happy to see you! She has missed you all day."

Tully smiled as thoughts of Grandma wrapped around him as warm as the golden sun setting in the distance. As I held on tightly to my little angel, I thought of how comforting the thought of "Grandma" or "Grandma's house" was to him. Tully had been raised by our family, mostly by my mother. In order for Tully's mother, Sarah, to go back to school and to work, my father and mother had decided to take her and Tully into our home. Tully had been with us since the day he was born and most of his waking hours were spent in the gentle care of my mother. Every member of my family developed a special bond with Tully but the strongest of the bonds was that which was between Tully and Grandma. For Tully, Grandma was home.

As we walked quietly down the sidewalk, I gently rubbed Tully's back. I could understand how Tully felt, for the thought of this home brought comfort to me as well. This home that now Tully is a part of, was the home that I had grown up in.

Our home was a modest end-unit townhouse. It's red brick was flanked by two towering pines, and pinned with wood shutters. The small patio off the side was surrounded by a fence covered in ivy. The ivy had taken over, climbing and entangling every inch of space, until it transformed our patio into an English garden.

Home had changed over the years. The ivy was pulling the fence down, the shudders were fading, and the pines were balding. New neighbors lived in the tiny cul-de-sac and the row of baby pines across the street was now full grown. The woods behind the cul-de-sac had been cut down and replaced with apartments, and the streets were empty of children riding bicycles.

There were familiar smells as you stepped in through the front door. Warm banana bread baking in the oven, smoke from dad's famous grilled steaks sizzling on a charcoal fire, clean towels folded on the couch after a hot tumble in the dryer, a vanilla candle lit on the dining room table. There were familiar sounds: the heavy refrigerator door rattling shut, the hum of the air conditioner outback, the cries of the spoiled cats, and Beethoven floating in the background.

With Tully now in the house, there were new sights and sounds. The English patio had been taken over by an American force of toy soldiers, tanks, and aircraft. Toys covered every spare inch inside the house, aircraft carriers sat in the sea of carpet, as dogfights rumbled through the kitchen. Small plastic orange work cones set up perimeters of detour, creating obstacle courses on the floor space. Couches were transformed into fire trucks, pirate ships, Army forts, and helicopters, with precise placement of cushions, bedsheets, and a child's imagination. Sounds of squad cars during a getaway chase, the shrill of missiles and artillery, and the laughter and squeals of pure delight filled the silence in each room.

To both Tully and I, home was more than the familiar sights, sounds, and smells. Home was a feeling. It was where you felt comfortable, where you could let down your guard and feel free to be you, it was where you felt safe and protected, it was where you felt like you belonged, and most importantly it was where you felt loved. We were blessed to have a home that was all of these, a home that my parents had built based on unconditional love and support to everyone who came to live under their roof.

"Tully, did you know that when I was a plebe, Grandma, Grandpa, Pop[112], and Uncle Lindsay were my *sponsor family*?"[113]

"No," Tully replied as I continued to carry him past 1st Wing.

"Well, as a plebe, you are given a sponsor family to help you out, and my sponsor family was *my own family!*"

Sponsor families were a "home away from home." Not only did they provide a caring family to support you, to help pull you through during the tough times and cheer you along during your accomplishments, but more importantly it was a place to eat, sleep, and unwind from the daily struggles of 4th class life. Because my family lived only fifteen minutes from the Academy, I was one of the lucky few whose sponsor family was their own actual family. Besides taking me in, my family agreed to sponsor three of my close friends from the Prep School.

"They also sponsored my friends, Kala, Abby, and Meghan. They would pick us up on the weekend and we would go home and eat and sleep and have fun. It was called liberty."

"I like home." Tully replied with a yawn.

"So do I, and I think we better start heading back so we can get you there. You have had a long day!"

As I walked with Tully towards the Chapel, thoughts of home drifted by like the spring breeze, lifting my spirits and awakening my soul. I wanted to tell Tully a story, but he had already heard the story, for he had been there…

Academic Year, April

From Parents Weekend on, Abby, Kala, Meghan, and I were granted liberty. There were three types of liberty: yard, town, and weekend

....

112 *Pop:* The name Tully calls his Father, my brother Paul.

113 *Sponsors:* Sponsors have historically provided necessary friendship, understanding and encouragement to Fourth Class midshipmen as they meet the challenges associated with a demanding Plebe Year. Sponsors provide a "home away from home" for midshipmen." "USNA Sponsor Program," *USNA.edu*, https://www.usna.edu/Sponsor/index.php

liberty.[114] Weekend liberty was the best for we were able to go home. We came home to my house; a house full of love, laughter, and support. My family was always there for us. Their hugs washed away our tears and healed our plebe pains, their food saved us from plebe starvation, and their words filled our weakened minds with strength and encouragement. They were an anchor to a ship of plebes who would sail in every weekend, battered from rough seas and unforgiving squalls. They kept us grounded. They reminded us of who we were and kept us focused on our goal and the importance of our endeavor, making it through our stormy Plebe Year.

My parents treated Abby, Kala, and Meghan as if they were their daughters, and adopted stray plebes that followed us home on occasion. Most of our weekends were spent sleeping, eating, and watching TV—valuable commodities which each plebe was lacking.

According to the Naval Academy Sponsor Program,

> *Fourth Class midshipmen are expected to act as mature adults and future Naval and Marine Corps officers at all times. Only the highest standards of personal behavior, etiquette and accountability are acceptable. Fourth Class midshipmen are aware of the regulations to which they are subject and should not place a Sponsor in any pressured situations regarding midshipmen rules. Fourth Class midshipmen are also encouraged to keep Sponsors involved in Naval Academy activities and to express their appreciation for a sponsor's generosity.*

This was never the case, however, for our weekend liberty was a time for us to enjoy our freedom to rebel against being a plebe. Our *"highest standards of personal behavior and etiquette"* was never thought of,

---

114   *Liberty:* Liberty where midshipmen are authorized to participate in activities within the Yard. Plebes have Yard liberty from 0530 until 2000. Town Liberty: Liberty where midshipmen can leave the Yard on Saturday from 1200 to 2200, and Sunday for religious services only from 0800 to 1300. Plebes shall go no further than 22 miles from the chapel dome during town liberty. Weekend Liberty: Liberty where plebes may depart on Saturday not earlier than 12:00 noon or last military obligation and must return Sunday by first military obligation and no later than 1700. USNA Sponsor Program," *USNA.edu*, https://www.usna.edu/Sponsor/index.php

especially during the weekend when we had a family food fight, where mom's home-cooked meal became ammunition and the dining room turned into a war zone. I will never forget our cats licking the cheese-cake off the walls.

We never *"acted as mature adults"* in fact, when two stray plebes from California came to our house, they experienced their first snowfall and ran barefoot in the white powder, shouting and playing as if they were children.

We were all *"aware of the regulations to which we were subject"* but we choose to ignore them like the one night, where the girls and I ventured out to a local Blockbuster dressed in unreg[115] civilian clothes. We spotted two upperclassmen and had to low crawl out of the store in order to escape.

We did, however, *"express our appreciation for a sponsor's generosity,"* by helping out around the house, like washing dishes. The girls and I had gotten into a bad habit of cursing and we lived up to having a *sailor's mouth*. The constant verbal abuse we received from our upperclassmen rubbed off on us, and to my mom's dismay, we brought our new vocabulary home with us. My mom started a new rule in the Sponsor House, *that if anyone was caught using their sailor mouth, they would be punished with dish duty*. I, of all the plebes, spent the most time in the Galley.[116]

Our Sponsor family consisted of my father, my mother, and my two brothers. My father was born in Texas and grew up as an Air force brat. My grandfather was a doctor for the Force and moved the family wherever the winds of the military would take them. From the beaches of the Philippines to the hills of England, my father's childhood was like a "Denis the Menace" movie. The cute blond-haired and blue-eyed boy spent his days launching bottle rockets, sneaking off base, and crawling in and out of Pubs at the ripe age of 15. My grandfather was adamant about my father following his bootsteps into the military, and

....

115 *Unreg:* Abbreviation for "un-regulation" which means, "not allowed." Usually, if you are a plebe, everything is "unreg."

116 *Galley:* The galley is the compartment of a ship, submarine, train or aircraft where food is cooked and prepared. It can also refer to a land-based kitchen on a naval base." "Galley," *Wikipedia*, http://en.wikipedia.org/wiki/Galley_%28kitchen%29

to his disappointment, my father followed his heart and choose another path. He decided on a career as a Golf Course Architect, a profession my grandfather believed would not be secure enough and provide him with any success. My father worked hard holding on to his dream and soon had his own business. For the past 25 years, he has established himself as one of the top designers on the East Coast with a repertoire of award-winning courses. My father exemplified what he passed on to me, that in life, "love is all that matters" and in business "love what you do." His family always came first, and his love was endless. His work was never "work" for him; it was his passion. I grew up wrapped in his arms of unconditional love and his example of following whatever dream was in your heart.

My mom grew up in Medford, Wisconsin. With three older brothers and one younger, she captured the attention of a quiet, gentle farmer. Her father favored his little girl of brown curls and blue eyes. A country girl at heart, Mary loved the open land, her pet pigs, and the simple Midwest life. At the age of 6, her father died from a heart attack and left Mary with a broken heart and sudden change. The financial instability led my grandmother to place her children in an orphanage where she could earn money and be close to the children. The orphanage was a new world for Mary, one that was hardened and strict, much differ-ent from what she had known. Beds were made with hospital corners, rooms were cleaned with a white glove, halls were patrolled by strict matrons, and haircuts were all the same. Now as I listen to her child-hood stories, I realize that in a way she had had a Plebe Year as well, and in a way, I feel as if I was connected to her in the past. My mother was a straight-A student, graduated with a teaching degree, and grew into a woman of strength, beauty, and faith. She met my father in 1968 in Geneva Illinois and they have been blessed with 50 years of marriage. My mother defines what it means to truly be a mother. She takes care of all of us physically, mentally, and spiritually. Her gentle touch healed us, her words comforted us, and her prayers protected us. She has been the glue that has held our family together during the storms and she has been the strength that has lifted us after our falls. What is even more special is that not only is she my mother, but she is my dearest girlfriend; I often call her "Mary" instead of "mom." We act as if we are childhood friends, two young girls picking flowers from a church's garden, or watching "chick flicks" at a slumber party; two teenagers shopping at the mall and checking out the cute boys; two 30-somethings sharing our troubles and concerns over a cup of coffee or afternoon tea. Mary is the best girlfriend I have ever had, and the mother that I hope to be.

I am fortunate to not only consider my parents my best friends but my two brothers as well. This, however, has not always been the case. The three of us have had our share of spats, fights, and all-out wars. There was a time when my parents thought they would never see the day when we would get along. But that day did come, and throughout the years we have grown closer and closer, until Lindsay and Paul are now more than just my blood.

My oldest brother, Lindsay, is a compassionate person who has been my travel buddy, my friend, and my teacher. With a mountain-man brown beard and long hair pulled into a ponytail, he looks as if he grew up in the woods of Montana rather than the suburbs of Crofton. His gentle spirit and quietness make those around him feel relaxed and comfortable, and his intelligence shines through when you ask him to explain Quantum Physics or Nuclear mechanics. He taught Kala, Abby, and me the complex world of Calculus, spending his time assisting in our unforgiving plebe-homework. But more importantly, Lindsay continues to teach me about humility, perseverance, discipline, and his love for God. He openly shares about his struggle with alcohol addiction, his recovery, and his present battle with mental illness. He went through a dark period and overcame it and with perseverance and discipline which has changed his life. As his life changed, his love for God was rekindled with a flame that burns so pure and true that those that meet him feel his goodness and closeness to God. He is also a talented musician and composer who continues to amaze me with the unwritten language that pours from his heart.

My younger brother, Paul, is a wonderful person as well. With blond hair, blue eyes, and a 6'1" muscular frame, Paul has the look of the all-American guy. The tattoos that cover his arms and neck pay homage to our Viking heritage. With his size and war paint, he intimidates at first glance, but if he is given a chance, you will uncover a person full of compassion and love who will win your heart over. He is my other half. We were playmates and inseparable at a young age. We spent our waking hours together, building forts in the woods, catching frogs, and jumping out of trees. Our friendship developed in the arms of Mother Nature and our bond grew stronger as we developed a love for adventure and adrenaline rushes as well. We differed in that, by the time we were older, Paul's adventures became illegal, and he began feeding his need for a rush by getting involved in drugs at a very early age. He was an aggressive child, a leader, and one who had a "no fear" mentality. His roller coaster ride with drug abuse took him in and out of rehabs, jail, and hospitals. Each time he felt pain, I could feel his pain like a sword piercing my heart. It has been a difficult road to recovery, but it has made us stronger—stronger as individual people, and stronger as brother and sister. Paul has taught me that you can never give up on a person; that unconditional love means just that: no conditions. He is the one I think about when I see a pink sunset, or a night sky full of stars. He will take time to enjoy watching a cloud float by or to feel an autumn breeze. Paul's greatest achievement is being the father of Tully. By bringing Tully into our lives, our family has been blessed in a very special way.

The definition of a sponsor is "a person or agency that undertakes certain responsibilities in connection with some other person or some group or activity, as in being a proponent, endorser, advisor, underwriter, surety, etc."

My family undertook the responsibility of caring for my friends and me. They were our support and our sanctuary. They were a shoulder to cry on, an ear to listen, and open arms that held us up. They were the truest definition of what it meant to be a sponsor. For the majority of the plebes, a Sponsor's house was a place to go to eat, sleep, and have freedom. My home was not just a place, it was a people.[117] I was blessed for I had so much more than just liberty. I had people who would love me no matter what, who raised me, and who gave me the freedom to be me. I had my family, and "Life without liberty is like a body without spirit."[118]

....

117   "My home is not just a place, it is a people." Lois McMaster Bujold, *"Barrayar,"* (Spectrum Literary Agency, Inc., 1991)

118   Quote from Kahil Gibran: Lebanese American philosophical essayist, novelist, poet, and artist. "Kahil Gibran," *Britannica*, https://www.britannica.com/biography/Khalil-Gibran

My mom and best girlfriend

My dad and the first man I loved

My brother Lindsay

My brother Paul

My husband Greg

CHAPTER 27:

MT. HERNDON

AS THOUGHTS OF FAMILY wrapped around me like the gold of the setting sun, I bent down and hugged the newest addition to our family. "Tully, before we leave the Academy, there is one last thing I want to show you. Look over there." I pointed my hand towards Blake Road, the small road that wrapped around the front of the Chapel. "Do you see that?" On a patch of well-groomed grass off the starboard side of the road rose a monument of gray granite. Tully nodded his head yes. It was guarded by tall oaks, whose branches seemed to bow reverently. Although dwarfed by these guards and the Chapel dome hovering a few feet away, it stood the tallest. Well, at least to me it did. It may have been a monument, but to those who had been forged in the Academy fires, and weathered by the waters of the Severn—to those, it was a mountain.

Tully raced ahead and was soon circling the base of the 21-foot obelisk. It resembled the National Monument in Washington, D.C., with a 4-sided rectangular stone column that narrowed towards the top. As I looked at the pyramidal top, its summit, I could almost see a flicker of gold beckoning me closer.

"Tully, this is Herndon. It is a monument that was named after Commander William Lewis Herndon,"[119] I said as I reverently moved toward my mountain.

"What is it?" Tully asked as he tried climbing onto the ledge of the base.

....

119 *Commander William Lewis Herndon:* The monument was a tribute to him after his loss in the Pacific Mail Steamer "Central America" during a hurricane off Georgia on September 12, 1857. Herndon had followed the long time custom of the sea that a ship's captain is the last person to depart his ship in peril. Commander William Lewis Herndon possessed the qualities of discipline, teamwork and courage. These are the attributes necessary to fulfill the Herndon tradition. The monument was erected in its current location on June 16, 1860 and has never been moved even though the Academy was completely rebuilt between 1899 and 1908. "History and Traditions of Herndon Monument Climb," *USNA.edu*, https://www.usna.edu/PAO/faq_pages/herndon.php

"It is the most important monument at the Academy if you are a plebe," I replied lifting him onto the base.

"Why?"

"Well, plebes have to climb to the top of this and if they make it, they are no longer plebes!"

"Really!" Tully tilted his head up, as he wrapped his arms around the polished stone.

"Yes! Would you like me to tell you about *my* Herndon climb? Or are you too tired?"

"I'm not tired, Aunt Cathy, I want to hear—please!" Tully sat down on the mountain's base as I placed my hand upon the smooth granite surface, connecting to my memory. The coolness of the stone seeped its way into my warm hands, as my story seeped from deep within my memory.

"Now before I begin, there is one thing I have to tell you."

"What, Aunt Cathy?"

"That this is a story about teamwork, courage, discipline, and determination. It is everything that Plebe Year is all about.

"Okay, okay—just tell the story!" Tully demanded as his dangling legs kicked in anticipation.

> It was a warm spring day in May: birds were chirping, boats were sailing, the sun was shining. Then all of a sudden, BOOM—a loud cannon was fired. Was the Academy being attacked by an enemy ship?

I paused to enhance the excitement. Tully's eyes were wide as he hung on to the ledge and my every word.

> "No, but Herndon was about to be attacked, suddenly there were hundreds of plebes flooding out of Bancroft and racing towards this here monument, like a swarm of bees to a soda can, or better yet, they were like a pack of wolves ready to attack, wild and crazy, tearing of their shirts, yelling, .screaming, hungry for a kill—and so Tully, this is where my story begins..."

End of Plebe Year, May 13, 1995

Finally, the day had arrived. It arrived in full May splendor with blue skies, golden sunlight, and fresh spring air. Triumphant birds announced the day's arrival, as electricity buzzed among the flowers and trees. The yard was alive with sponsor families, friends, tourists, TV crews, and newspaper journalists who had all gathered to witness this day of days. The countdown was finished; today was finally here.

I was staring up at the white structure as the smell of wet grass, sweat and dirt sent my stomach into somersaults. Greased bodies pressed from all directions as shouts and screams rang in my ears. I looked up at Herndon and thought of something that Mr. Montgomery had once said: "Every inch of the Yard has a story to tell, and every 34th Company plebe should and will know these stories."

I had learned that the obelisk, the structure Herndon resembled, first came into existence in Egypt in the year 2465 BCE. Born out of ancient sands, obelisks were erected in pairs at the entrances to temples. They were carved from a single piece of stone, usually red granite from the Aswān quarries. All four sides of the stone were decorated with hieroglyphs, pictured dedications to their gods or to their rulers.

I smiled at the similarity of the ancient obelisks to ours. I looked up at the once gray stone structure that was now covered in a thick coat of white greasy lard. The youngsters, our second-year upperclassmen, had etched writings on all four sides of the monument:

"*Class of 97*"

"*Do you rate this?*"

"*This is not a Tomahawk*"

and my personal favorite,

"*Caution: Slippery when greased.*"

I smiled at the youngsters' dedications to us; we may not have been gods, (the firsties yes—or so they thought they were), but we *were* being honored.

Pulling my gaze from Herndon's hieroglyphics, I looked around for my parents, my safe harbor throughout the year. I was bobbing up and down in an ocean of plebes, unable to locate them. The old me would have panicked; a ship once afraid to be away from the port. However, I was a newly built ship, confidant when alone at sea, capable without a harbor.

All one thousand of my classmates swarmed about the base of the monument dressed in pep gear shorts and t-shirts. Many of the shirts had been either ripped off or defaced with motivational writing. Wild with adrenaline, our disciplined plebe behavior had been ripped off, as our t-shirts had been. We were an unstoppable force in the middle of an attack. We were attacking Herndon, attempting to climb to its summit, to claim the prize.

The tradition of "Herndon" or the "Plebe Recognition Ceremony" involves the entire class of plebes working as a team. The seemingly simple task of climbing to the top of the monument and replacing a plebe cover (aka: hat) with an upperclassman's cover, is anything but. Over two hundred pounds of lard is applied to a two-story monument with no handholds, crevices, or slope. In mountain climbing terms, it would be given The Yosemite Decimal System rating of a "Class 6" which is "a climb devoid of hand and footholds and can only be climbed with aid." Our mountain was devoid of anything except lard, and the only climbing aid we had was each other.

Once Herndon is conquered, Plebe Year is officially over; a stripe is added to the empty black shoulder boards of the plebes, branding them as "youngsters," or "3rd class." As I stared up, from the sea of plebes, I thought of the Egyptian obelisks again. Their pyramidal tops were covered with electrum, an alloy of gold and silver. The top of our obelisk would soon contain gold as well, the gold anchor of an officer's cover.

As plebes, we had been counting down Herndon since July 1st, I-day. It became part of our daily lives, a mantra-like "Go Navy, Beat Army, Sir" that was echoed throughout the halls. "331 days until Herndon, Sir. 330 days until Herndon, Sir." The Class of 98, however, had a special relationship with Herndon early on. A relationship that went beyond the simple daily countdown.

During Plebe Summer, we had a talent show, and in one of the skits, some plebes did a spoof on Bob Dylan's song "Knock'n on Heaven's Door," in which they sang it as "Knock'n on *Herndon's* Door." Like a barrage of grenades, our detailers exploded with anger and like a wildfire, word spread quickly to the entire Brigade. The Class of '98 required an attitude adjustment and increased punishment. Each one of us was tainted by this poor choice for a skit, we were marked with a scarlet letter: the letter H. Every upperclassman made sure that each one of us understood that we were nowhere close to knocking on Herndon's door, *and that we might never be.*

Like the ancient obelisks, the summit of Herndon pointed to the afterlife. Life after Plebe Year would be like heaven. Our pain and suffering would come to an end and a new life would begin. As I stared up at Herndon, I could not believe that we were finally here. We had made it and we *were* now knock'n on its door.

I could not help but think of Montgomery, who had made Herndon so important to us. He made it more than just a "plebe recognition ceremony," or "a tradition." More than a countdown of numbers to remember, more than the end of Plebe Year, and more than a history lesson. He wanted Herndon to mean something to each of us, and to each one of us, it did.

During the first 20 minutes of our climb, the planned attack had been put into effect. We would first form a circle of the strongest football players along the base of Herndon. Next, a second and third tier with strong but lighter individuals would build upon the first. We would then have a tall lightweight climb up the ladder of bodies to reach the top. The rest of the plebes would push against and support the base. As I joined the mob pushing at the base, I thought of Iwo-Jima.[120] (More history, thanks to Montgomery.)

....

120   *The Battle of Iwo Jima* was an epic military campaign between U.S. Marines and the Imperial Army of Japan in early 1945. Located 750 miles off the coast of Japan, the island of Iwo Jima had three airfields that could serve as a staging facility for a potential invasion of mainland Japan. American forces invaded the island on February 19, 1945, and the ensuing Battle of Iwo Jima lasted for five weeks. In some of the bloodiest fighting of World War II, it's believed that all but 200 or so of the 21,000 Japanese forces on the island were killed, as were almost 7,000 Marines. The American's captured the island on March 26, 1945, despite the questioning of its strategic value. Iwo will forever be remembered by Joe Rosenthal's famous photo of the Marines raising the American flag on Mount Suribach. "Iwo Jima," *History.com*, https://www.history.com/topics/world-war-ii/battle-of-iwo-jima)

Even though historians described the US attack against the Japanese, as "throwing human flesh against reinforced concrete." Herndon could never be compared to this famous battle in the Pacific. Yes, we were literally throwing flesh against stone, but Herndon could never be compared to Mt. Suribachi. Nor could plebes be compared to the Marines of the "28th Regiment 5th Marines." What made me think of a comparison with this famous battle was the human spirit.

As I pushed in Herndon's shadows, I could picture the famous image of Iwo, the men pushing the flag up on to the mountain's summit. Their human spirit, the desire to continue to fight, to never stop climbing until the mountain was conquered, and the Japs defeated—that spirit is in all of us. Some may never have a chance to test it. Others may but opt to keep it buried inside. And then there are others, like those Marines on Iwo, whose spirit inspired the world, whose spirit pushed others to climb mountains.

The plan to conquer our mountain was going as planned and by the 22-minute mark, Mike Palazzo, a wiry but strong Napster, was on the third tier, and his six-foot-long body was closing in on the top. Everyone held their breaths as Palazzo attempted to grab hold of the prize. Racing through our minds was shock and hysteria; we were about to make Academy history! No class of plebes had ever reached the top under the 30-minute mark! (Well, except for the Class of 1969 who holds the record at 90 seconds, but who had cheated by wrapping chicken wire around the monument!)

Within an inch from grasping the prize, we all watched wide-eyed as Palazzo's bony body swayed as the second tier slipped from the wobbling weight above them. We watched as Palazzo's hands desperately clawed to hold on, but within a matter of seconds, he slipped. Like a tower of dominos, the tiers collapsed, and the pyramid of greased bodies fell to the ground.

The cheers were silenced and the crowds around us stood in disbelief. Besides the midshipmen and officers looking on, Herndon was surrounded by parents, locals, and tourists who had all gathered to witness this unique rite of passage. Pictures were being taken, videos were being recorded, and local reporters waited anxiously by their vans with notepads in hand. After Palazzo s fall, EMTs exited their parked ambulances to check on potential injuries.

Suddenly the silence of the crowd was shattered as *"98!",* was yelled out among the plebes.

Spurred on by the battle cry of those two magic numbers, the plebes regrouped with shouts of determination. Within a matter of minutes, a second attempt was made to summit the mountain of lard. Another wobble, another slip, and within a matter of minutes, another failure.

Suddenly a voice shouted out next to me, "Send Ervin up!" I looked around to see a few of my company mates moving towards me.

"Send Ervin up!" was shouted again as butterflies flocked into my stomach.

I smiled and said, "Let's do this!" I grabbed ahold of a sweaty football player at the base of the monument and said, "Send me up!" He gave me an encouraging nod as I stepped into his interlocking fingers.

As I felt my classmates lift me, I was overwhelmed with pride. I was proud of the fact that my company never once made me feel any less. Being a woman had its own set of challenges at the Academy, but I was never looked down upon. I was an equal, and I was often looked up to by my classmates. I had heard stories of women being pulled down off of Herndon, but I never witnessed anything like that.

I stepped onto a slippery ladder of heads, shoulders, and hands, putting faith into my balance and strength. In no time at all, I was mashed up against a plebe on the second tier. Lard covered his face, but I could tell he was motioning me to use him. As I climbed up his back, I soon became noticed—no amount of lard could hide my blond hair. Shouts rang out from below.

"Yeah, Ervin! GO, Girl!" I could hear the voice of Lily, my roommate, and others from 34th Company. These voices were my ropes of encouragement; ropes that had supported me throughout the year. Unlike the belay ropes used in climbing, these ropes would be tied to me forever.

I had one knee up on the shoulder of the 2nd tier plebe and began lifting myself as he helped. The lard and sweat ran down my face stinging my eyes, testing my discipline. I did not waiver, I had been tested before. I had spent hours standing at attention with sweat pouring down my face, unable to move to wipe my eyes. There were also countless times when I had to straight-arm hold a 10-pound rifle while reciting "Man in the Arena." I had held on before, and I would hold on now.

I pulled myself up to the third tier, my hands grasping lard, my feet slipping on shoulders of lard. The sturdy human ladder now wavered like wet noodles beneath me. A slight tremor below caused my foot to slide, and suddenly I found myself falling from the tower. . I was disappointed in myself, but I had felt failure before. I had fallen many times as a plebe and I knew that I would get back up.

I landed in a cushion of bodies. I stood up, wiped the lard from my eyes, and pushed myself back into the middle of the pack.

I continued to push through the pain as pressure from hundreds of bodies threatened to collapse my lungs. I continued to push through the smell like sweat, body odor, wet grass and lard that threatened to suffocate me.

I remember watching tennis shoes thrown up in an attempt to knock the cover off, and unsuccessfully they just stuck to the lard like flies on fly tape. T-shirts were ripped off and used as towels in an effort to scrape the lard off. With each new pyramid of greased bodies, came new hope, and with each fall, came new respect for our upperclassman's difficult challenge. Never once, did any plebe doubt we would reach the top. However, the end had seemed so close early on, and now it seemed even farther away.

The hours seemed like days, and after four hours, the level of intensity had changed. Exhaustion had set in, from both the plebes and the crowd. Pyramids toppled quicker, and the shouts of encouragement burned off into the afternoon heat.

We were periodically doused with water from a hose to prevent any overheating. With each slip, with each fall... a large sigh echoed from the restless crowd, a crowd that began to wonder if this group of plebes could do it. As batteries in video cameras ran out, as the shouts from parents quieted, and as children turned away with lost interest, the fire continued to burn inside of each of the plebes. We had not come all this way—*we had been through 331 days as a plebe*—we would not fail. *We would not give up the ship.* We would get to the top!

As I continued to sweat, and support, and cheer, I pushed back a strand of my hair, cleared away the lard out of my eyes, and looked up, another tower of bodies was slowly rising. On top of the tower was a confident plebe, who stayed steady despite his wobbling support. Within a matter of minutes, his hands were inches from the cover. The crowd was brought back to life, as clapping and cheering jolted around the monument. We watched, as if in slow motion, as the two hands grabbed a hold of the cover.

The tower collapsed with the excitement, but the plebe hung on to the hat, dangling against the monument. The hat did not budge, and therefore, neither did the plebe who was now alone hanging from the top of the monument. In a display of sheer strength, the plebe pulled himself up and onto the top of the monument, as if the hat had been his pull up bar. He was now sitting on top of the monument straddling the hat. I was proud as I notice that our hero sitting on the top was Dan Sanders, a Napster and a Navy Seal.

Everyone continued to cheer because we had made it to the top, but soon the cheers became whispers and quizzical looks replaced the elated smiles. The mountain was summited, however, the prize was still being held, prisoner. Sanders could not remove the Dixie Cup. His chiseled muscles strained with each pull as we all strained for an understanding. The cover was obviously attached somehow, it had not just been "placed" up at the top.

Sanders continued to struggle and as the lard was pushed aside, it became evident as to how the mountain had a grip on the prize, the cover had been attached with layers of packaging tape.

Suddenly, a quick-thinking plebe from below asked an officer in the crowd to borrow his cover. The plebe proceeded to take off the gold anchor that was pinned in the center. He then threw the pin up into the outstretched hands of our hero.

Without a backing, the gold pin had a sharp point, which was then used to scrape through the tape and the embedded twin. Thirty more minutes passed as Sanders sawed his way through the tape.

Finally, the moment we had all been waiting for happened, as a triumphant arm was raised in the air. Clasped in a greasy hand was the cover, freed from the jaws of the mountain, and we… the Class of 98, were freed from the hands of our upperclassman. Plebe Year was officially and finally over! It may have taken 4 hours (4 hours, five minutes and 17 seconds, to be exact), setting an Academy record, but victory is glorious no matter the details.

It was as if the floodgates had been opened, and the raging waters of freedom poured out. I was swept away in a sea of emotion as I hugged my family and my classmates. We cried, we laughed, and we cheered with endless joy. As I left with my classmates, I turned around and looked at Herndon. The monument was stained with tennis shoes and t-shirts, the once beautiful green lawn had been stripped bare and reduced to a pile of mud. Worn and tired bodies walked among the chaos. It looked as if a battle had taken place, and it had—a battle that had been overcome by each and every plebe.

As I looked at the stone monument, I began to think of all that it symbolized to me and the other plebes.

Herndon symbolized the struggles that we went through at the Academy and that we will continue to go through in the military and our life. We will slip, we will fall, but we will have the discipline and determination to get back up—and to succeed.

It symbolized the fact that we need one another, we need teamwork, to accomplish a task. Every single one of the plebes cheered, climbed, or supported.

Like the ring of football players around the base, it symbolized the fact that the Academy provides us with a strong foundation. It provides us with values, academics, and military training, which we will take with us out into the fleet to build upon.

Like the writings etched in the lard, it symbolized the opposition that we will meet along the way, voices of doubt, words of negativity, words we need to ignore so we can stay focus and believe in who we are.

It symbolized courage, for it takes courage to be a plebe at the United States Naval Academy.

I will never forget that final walk back to Bancroft. Arm and arm, we sloshed back to the hall leaving a trail of lard behind us. We were glowing with pride (and greasy lard) as we walked slowly up the steps onto our deck, tasting the sweetness of upper-class privileges. How strange it felt to *not* be a plebe, to walk and *not* have to "chop," to look around in the hallways and *not* have to "have eyes in the boat", to be asked a question and *not* have to answer with only five responses. To finally *not* have to recite "Man in the Arena."

Not only did we climb Herndon that day, not only did we officially finish our Plebe Year, but also, we climbed to the height of ourselves and we summited a mountain that symbolically represented Plebe Year.

I thought of Montgomery and my constant recitation of "Man in the Arena." We had been "stained with sweat, and dust, and blood," we "knew the triumph of high achievement" and we "failed while daring greatly," but our place would never be with the "cold and timid souls who knew neither victory nor defeat."

> *As Montgomery had wanted, Herndon was important to me, and I was proud to have fought in the Arena—and as I was proud to stand on Herndon's summit.*

From Mount Herndon to Mount Everest

CHAPTER 28:
TANGO

"AUNT CATHY, did *you* climb Herndon?" Tully asked as he continued trying to climb the stone monument.

"Yes, I did! I climbed it with the class of '98. I didn't get to the top, but I helped somebody else get to the top. It took us a very long time, but we did it and we were so proud!" I looked up and smiled, grateful for what the simple stone monument had taught me. I grabbed Tully's hand.

"We should get going now, it's getting late, okay?" I quickly snapped to a position of attention.

"Tully, would you like to learn how to *march*, just like the midshipmen?" I had noticed that Tully was getting tired and I needed some motivation to keep him going.

"Yes!"

"Then follow behind me, stepping with the same foot that I step with, okay?"

"Okay," Tully said quickly moving in behind me.

"When I say 'Forward March' we will begin with our left leg," I stuck my left leg out, "This is your left…" I then stuck my right leg out, "… and this is your right."

Tully hadn't perfected his left from his right yet, so this, I thought, could end up being a perfect teaching opportunity.

"Are you ready?" I asked glancing at Tully over my shoulder.

"Yes!" Tully eagerly replied.

"For-ward march!" As I took the first step I begin to sing,

Left… left… left-right-left
Left… left… left-right-left
Left-right-lol-li-pop…
Let-me-hear-your-left-foot-drop

Um, I-like-it
Um, one-more-time
Um, slow-it-down
Now... STOP!

As I said, "Stop" I came to a halt, and immediately Tully ran into the back of me. He laughed with delight as he stood with his head buried in the back of my t-shirt. I turned around and laughed with him. "Did you like that? Isn't that a fun song to march to?"

"Yes," Tully replied, "Can we do it again—do the lollipop song?"

"Definitely, we call these songs, cadence," I said standing back at the position of attention.

"Wait!" Tully said as he pulled at my T-shirt. I turned around to see Tully looking down at his two feet, "Is this one my left or my right?" Tully was pointing to his left foot.

"That is your left, and that is the foot that we start with when we march!"

Tully and I continued our march down past the Chapel and the officer housing. Tully had instantly taken a liking to the song and hadn't requested a different tune. The lollipop song was one of the few in my cadence repertoire that had a "G" rating, and therefore was a much better choice than the others that had been passed down from my upperclassmen such as "Walking in a Sniper's Wonderland."

As we continued to march, I was momentarily transformed back to midshipmen 4th Class Ervin. It felt as if my body was cloaked in the starched white works. I could almost feel the weight of a ten-pound rifle propped up against my right shoulder and could hear the sound of 100 footsteps stepping to a simple one-word cadence. In no time at all, I soon found myself singing,

Ro... me... o,
Ro... me-o!

Romeo was the name of my company, "R Company," during Plebe Summer. There were twenty different companies, each with a designated letter of the military alphabet ranging from "A" to "T." From Alpha to

Tango Company, unique and creative cadences, chants, and artwork were developed. Not only did it distinguish one company from the other, but also it joined a random mix of plebes in camaraderie, and it instilled a sense of pride. Whether it was Company H singing, "Living it up at the Hotel California" or Company P shouting, "Who's your Papa?"—company marches, competitions, and gatherings came to life. Color, enthusiasm, and even *fun* could be found in a simple letter.

As I continued to march, I began to think about "Tango Company." Tango Company was unlike the other companies; it did not have a clever cadence or a catchy phrase. Tango Company was an exception; it was colorless, and void of any enthusiasm or fun. It was a company absent of pride and was one that was looked down upon. *It was often not spoken of, not unless you had been to Tango company, and few would ever return to talk about it...*

Limbo, May 15, 1995

It was May 15, 1995, two days after climbing Herndon. I was sitting at a desk, alone in a room; a room in an area designated "Tango Company." This was the first time in 331 days that I had been without my classmates of 34th Company. The morning sun was dancing through the window blinds. Lines of light stretched across my body as I laid my sore arms on the desk and rested my head upon them. For the past two days, I had taken part in the extraction of old mattresses out of the 4th Wing to make room for new ones. I had carried heavy, spring-loaded mattresses up and down flights of stairs; mattresses that sagged with old age no longer caring to stand up at attention. I didn't mind their heaviness but rather how cumbersome they were; they twisted and folded and slipped from my hands. It was a job for those who were on *restriction*, or for someone like me.

I turned my head towards the window and bathed my face in the light. The warmth of the sun's touch calmed me, but it could not erase the darkness I was feeling inside. I rested in the sun's warmth for a moment longer and then I opened my eyes.

TANGO IS THE LIMBO BETWEEN
WHAT MIGHT HAVE BEEN AND WHAT WILL BE.

A piece of corkboard, with these words scribbled upon it in black ink, was hanging on a cinderblock wall in room 5020. I stared at the simple yet profound phrase and reread it repeatedly. It seemed as if those words had been put there just for me. They seemed to have read my heart and in one short breath, they spoke what I had been feeling over the past five days.

I lifted my head and stretched my arms out in front of me. I slowly got up out of the chair, walked over to where my bed was and stood in front of a full-length mirror. As I looked into the mirror, I saw a new person staring back at me, no longer that stranger I had seen on I-day. Her eyes were a bolder blue and pierced through the mirror with strength and fearlessness. She was dressed in a stiff white uniform. She stood straight and appeared taller, with pride and discipline. Her thick blond hair was braided back tightly against her head. A black lacquered nametag was pinned above her left shirt pocket. It was engraved with yellow lettering that read, "ERVIN 98."

I know who you are. I thought to myself as I stared at the reflection. It was in my weakest moments, that I had found my greatest strengths. I found that I could endure. I found that I could be what the Academy wanted me to be. I had found that in order to change, I had to fight myself, not my upperclassmen. I had to fight my own shortcomings, my doubts, and my fears. My faith in myself strengthened and within time, I developed a pride in who I was becoming. I had always been proud that I was at the Academy; proud that I played on the varsity volleyball team, but now I was proud of the fact that I had become the plebe that my upperclassmen had wanted me to be. The marks of different perceptions had finally been erased, and a new mark had been left behind, *the mark of a warrior, one who fought through a battle, and conquered herself.*

I turned away from the mirror, away from the person whom I was proud of. I grabbed a handful of rope on top of a large laundry bag, and with one quick pull, I cinched the bag, closing it. I heaved the bulging bag over my right shoulder. It was the bag I had been issued on I-day. It was a bag that after 331 days had been filled with so much more than just running shoes and shampoo.

I was given armor—armor, which has enabled me to stand tall; armor which has given me the confidence to continue to hold my head up high and to always believe in who I am. A sword of courage and a shield of integrity were given to me to fight for duty and honor. I was given a flag of Stars and Stripes, a pride that I will forever wave. I was knighted with leadership and was given an army of responsibility. I was skilled in the areas of military combat, history, etiquette, and professional knowledge. I was given an education unparallel to any other four-year institution. I was given friends who fought beside me with true loyalty, camaraderie, and self-sacrifice. I was given upperclassman who taught me more than they will ever know.

I picked up a white sheet of paper off the desk and took one last walk around the room. I glanced around corners, down at the floor, under the desk, making sure that I wasn't leaving anything behind. I pulled the blinds halfway up the window, to their proper "half-mast" position, turned off the lights in the room, and then pushed back the wooden door. I took one last glance and decided that the room was in *proper order*. I left room 5020 in Tango Company and headed down the hallway with a full laundry bag and with my resignation papers.

I had been carrying around the weight of my decision for the past three weeks. My shoulders and my heart ached. I had spent those weeks in Tango Company[121] waiting to obtain the official release from the Academy. I had been in a state of *limbo* as I awaited the actions of my decision. I was still in that limbo, the limbo between "what might have been" at the Naval Academy and the "what will be" once released into the civilian world. It is like a bedtime story I would read to Tully. It was too long to finish in one night, so I would close the book, kiss Tully goodnight, and leave him wondering, sleeplessly in his bed. Tully had not learned how to read yet; therefore I, the storyteller, was his key to the unknown. The storybook is like our life, and God is the storyteller, only he knows how the story ends.

My family had known of my decision to resign early on. They had supported me with unconditional love and continued to emphasize that it was my decision and that all they wanted was for me to be happy.

....

121 *Tango Company*: A specific company where midshipmen were placed during their resignation process. It was located in the 5th Wing of Bancroft Hall among the restrictees. Restrictees are midshipmen who had broken rules and were placed on a period of restriction in which certain privileges were taken away.

They had also agreed with me, that I should finish my Plebe Year, and not make the decision while going through the toughest year at the Academy.

To others, my resignation came as a shock and a disappointment. I remember hearing responses from classmates such as: "No... not *Ervin*. She loved it here!" or "Ervin? She was going to be the first woman to be a Navy Seal."

From the outside, I appeared happy, extremely motivated, and content with where I was. Little did anyone know what was lying deep within my heart. Despite how I felt, I never once gave less than 100%. I was giving my all while knowing that I could not stay at the Academy.

One of my best friends turned away from me, and some of my upper-classmen began to avoid me when they had heard of my decision. The lack of understanding placed me in a constant state of turmoil. They made me feel guilty like I had done something wrong. I remember how evident this became especially when I had been approached by my roommate, Lily, a few days after we had climbed Herndon.

Lily had asked me if I had received "the letter" from Mr. Montgomery. Apparently, he had written a letter in which he thanked the 34th Company plebes for the challenging year and wished everyone good luck and godspeed. I, however, had not received such a letter. At first, I was a little hurt by the fact, but then as I thought about it, it was what I would have expected him to do. *Why should he write to me? What should he thank me for? For the headache I caused him? Or for the desecration of "Man in the Arena?" Why should he wish me good luck and Godspeed? I was leaving the Academy.*

I yearned for approval and understanding, yet I knew that this was *my* decision. This decision was based on what my heart was telling me to do. It was not based on what others wanted, or on what others had hoped for. It was a decision based on the fact that my reasons for being here were reasons that were not true to who I was. Day in and day out, I put on the uniform and I gave my whole self into what it stood for, but each time that I stopped and looked into the mirror, I felt as if I were looking at a *stranger*, and I knew that I was not being true to myself. I was torn between a childhood dream I had held and the reality of it now no longer being my dream. And it was no longer my dream, no matter how much I tried to deny it. I had wanted this for so long, but I finally came to grips with the fact that dreams can change, as you change.

The change had occurred when I began volunteering as a Catholic Sunday School teacher. Every weekend, I taught religious education to children of the officers on base. I will never forget the first time I stood in front of a classroom of children, I felt something click in my spirit... I felt my truest self; the person who God had made me to be. I did not hear the voice of God, I felt it. As I looked at myself in the mirror, I no longer saw an officer staring back at me. I saw a teacher.

I remained in Tango Company, even after I had left the Academy. It took me about a year until I was free from the weight of my decision when I was finally able to realize that it was *okay* to have not graduated from the Academy. I was able to deal with the questions, *"So why did you quit?"* or *"You went to the Academy but didn't graduate?"* The questions that always made me feel like I had failed.

Eventually, I would free myself from Tango for good. As time continued to pass, I realized that I was actually "triumphing in high achievement" for the "what will be" was happening, and it was what I wanted; it was where my heart had told me to go, and I dared to follow it...

CHAPTER 29:

IN THE ARENA

AS TULLY AND I continued to march, I thought about how I was now able to come back to the Academy without the feelings of guilt, that I had felt while waiting in Tango. Instead, I walked around with secret pride, knowing that the Naval Academy was *my* Academy and that I would always be a part of it. Although, I had been battling with the feeling of *fear* and anxiety all day, wondering where it was coming from. It now occurred to me that the Academy had such a profound impact on me; I had experienced things that I never had before, and that I couldn't help but relive those feelings. They would stay with me always, and I realized that it was a good thing, not a bad thing, for it meant that the Academy *had truly left a mark on my heart and soul.*

"Aunt Cathy, I'm tired—can we stop marching?" I looked back to see my little plebe dragging his tired legs out of step.

"Okay," I replied as I reached down to carry him. I picked him up and kissed him on the forehead. We walked past the Chapel, down and around past the Superintendent's house, and followed the sidewalk that led to the Main Gate. We passed tennis courts on our left, and Officer housing on our right. The houses, like officers, were all dressed alike. They were fully clad in gray stone with blue and white-stripped awnings. The lawns were well-groomed and the bushes were trimmed short. Nameplates, like ribbons pinned on a chest, were the only things that distinguished one house from the other. The houses stood at attention as we walked quietly by. The sun was beginning to dim and the last of its rays were lying softly upon the sidewalks.

As we continued to walk, I could feel the spring in my step, and the straightness of my back. My head was lifted high as I walked with control and discipline while holding Tully in my arms. I crossed King George Street, and onto the sidewalk that led to the Main Gate. As I walked with my head held high, I thought of myself as a plebe again, and out loud I said,

> "*It is not the critic who counts, not the one who points out how the strong man stumbled or how the doer of deeds might have done them better. The credit belongs to the man who is actually in the arena, whose face is marred with sweat and dust and blood; who strives valiantly, who errs comes short again and again, who knows the great enthusiasms, the great devotions, and spends himself in a worthy cause; who if he wins, knows the triumph of high achievement; and who, if fails, at least fails while daring greatly, so that his place shall never be with those cold and timid souls who know neither victory nor defeat.*"

As I finished the passage, I looked around and laughed.

Isn't this great, I thought—*I can finally recite it perfectly and Mr. Montgomery or anyone from 34th Company is nowhere to be found!*

If only I had realized back when I was a plebe, that if I had tried to *understand* the words, instead of just memorizing them, that maybe, just maybe, I would have been able to do it. That, however, was what I had to learn, and I have learned ever since.

"Hey, Tully," I whispered, "would you like to attend the Naval Academy one day?"

Tully lifted his head from my shoulder and looked at me.

"Yes… I like the Academy, Aunt Cathy!"

"I know Tul, so do I. You would make a great midshipman."

As I glanced to my right, I smiled at the Marine who was standing rigidly at attention inside his small booth. As we moved closer, I noticed that it was the same Marine from before. Suddenly, he turned and snapped a salute towards Tully.

"He saluted me, Aunt Cathy!" Tully said as he quickly lifted his arm to return the salute.

"Well he knows, Tully, that one day you are going to make a fine officer.

I squeezed the small boy in my arms as we walked past the Marine. The afternoon sun was setting, and the gray wall attached to the main gate was reflecting the pink, orange, and purple colors that had painted the sky. A soft breeze blew through my hair and the moist air left salt-water kisses upon my face and upon the angel that I held in my arms.

As I approached the gate, I stopped and stared at the huge gold emblem that shined like the setting sun, I began to think of that first day when I had passed through the gate, of all the days that had followed, and of the day that was upon me now. As I held on tightly to my nephew, I turned around and looked back at the United States Naval Academy.

"What are you looking at Aunt Cathy?" Tully asked noticing that I had stopped.

"I am looking at the *Arena*, Tully."

Tully turned his head and looked back at the Academy. "I don't see it," Tully replied confused, not quite sure what he was looking for.

"We were just in it, Tully—we were *in the Arena*."

EPILOGUE

Crofton, Maryland: June

I had received Montgomery's letter weeks after Lily and the rest of 34th had received theirs. I was at home packing for a summer in the woods of Virginia, where I would be working as a counselor at a wilderness adventure camp. I was looking forward to a real summer, free from being a plebe, when the letter came and reminded me of what I would never be able to forget.

At first, I didn't want to open the letter, because I already knew what it was about. Also, I had spent a whole year being tormented by this man, why would I want to continue this abuse via mail? However, there was a small part of me that was glad that I had received it; I didn't want to be left out. After leaving the Academy, I felt like an outsider and part of me still wanted to belong to "The Club." For me the letter symbolized that I still belonged, so I decided to open it, hoping to find what all my other classmates found.

What I found, however, was not the xerox-copied letter that Lily and the rest of my classmates had received, but rather a three-page handwritten letter. I wondered, *why is Montgomery writing to me personally? Is he really that upset with me? What did I do now?* As I began to read the letter my eyes filled with tears, and my body went numb with shock.

> *Cathy,*
>
> *"I talked to you briefly last May about you leaving Annapolis, but I want to make sure you understand my feelings. First off, let me say that I am probably more proud of you than anybody else that I had the honor of training last summer. You always had the guts to stick it out-and there was an inner spark in you—I like to call it "spunk"— that few possess. And when the Ac year hit and you were*

*going through a "perception problem," you just stuck it out
and did your job. That says a lot about you.*

*It took a lot of guts for you to leave Annapolis. It takes a lot
more courage to leave than it does to stay—I mean that. You
came to the decision that it was not for you—but you stuck
it out the whole Plebe Year. You climbed Herndon. You made
it through Plebe Year at the Naval Academy—something few
can say. And you should be proud of yourself for that.*

*To be honest, I was shocked when Lt. Sampson told me
you were resigning—I didn't want you to—that right
there should tell you how much I think of you. I had never
believed women should be at the Academy. You have
changed my mind about that. I felt you had listened more
than anyone and would really make a hell of an officer. It's
hard for me to put into words. I know that I had an impact
on a lot of you during those 28 days and during the Ac year.
As time went on, I could see that I was affecting some more
than others. Some just saw the screaming and yelling and
didn't really get what I was trying to* teach. *Then there were
those who "kinda got it." And then there were a few who I*
knew *really got it. Looking back, I honestly can say that I
think you got more of it than anyone.*

*"Never forget what you learned at Annapolis—and never
forget that it will always be a part of you."*

After I finished reading, I cried all the tears that I had kept inside.
I cried for the pain I had felt when holding my 10-pound rifle, I cried
for the sleepless nights huddled in my shower, I cried for the humilia-
tion with "Man in the Arena," I cried for overcoming my "perception
problem," and I cried for climbing Herndon. I cried for the fact that
Montgomery had changed me. I cried because as the letter had said, I
had changed him.

I cried because I had *actually been in the arena*, my face had been
marred with sweat and dust and blood of Plebe Year. I worked hard,
tried my best. I knew the importance of what I was doing and I *devoted*

myself to the worthy cause. I won a battle whether inside of Bancroft, or inside of me, and I *triumphed in that achievement.* I experienced failure, but I had *dared greatly* and had taken the risks. I am proud to say that I am *not a cold and timid soul,* for because of *this arena,* I know *victory and I know defeat.*

As I cried, my mother came into the room. When she saw that I had Montgomery's letter in my hands, she said, "Oh no, Cathy, what has he done to you now."

I wiped my eyes and looked up from the letter and replied,

"He gave me 'Man in the Arena' mom. He really gave it to me."

• • •

Stepping into the next arena: adventures and teaching in New Zealand

Stepping into the next arena: starting an outdoor adventure business

Stepping into the next arena: to the base camp of Everest

My Captain and anchor of my soul

ACKNOWLEDGMENTS

I would like to thank: Hellgate Press and Harley Patrick for believing in my story and for their dedication to our military.

The United States Naval Academy, for you will always be a part of me. I do not look back disheartened at what I have left behind, but instead, I am grateful for all that was given to me.

My nephew, Tully, who inspired this story.

My Dad, Mom, Lindsay & Paul, for your unconditional love and support and for always believing in me and my story.

My husband Greg, for being my steady rock and safe harbor along this journey.

My classmates, upperclassmen, and all our military for your sacrifice and service to our country. Lily, for your faith, tipped over boats, and for being the best roommate ever. Abby, for your contagious joy and your example of never giving up on a dream. Kala, for your friendship that never left my side and for your example of strength and courage. Mr. Wyatt, for always believing in me, never giving up on me, and for seeing the real Ervin. Mr. Steinmann, for your sense of humor, unwaver-ing discipline, and positive leadership. Sarah, for taking me under your wing as your volleyball sister. Mr. Imani, for having faith in my and keeping me square to the net. Senior Chief Flora, for being my truest example of a woman in the military and for being my "Navy mom." Mr. Montgomery, who forced me to memorize "Man in the Arena," but more importantly, for showing me how to live it.

To Jesus, who is my anchor and my captain. I hold fast to you during the sunshine and the storms, and I will trust you when my ship is lost at sea. I will continue to follow you into whatever arena I step into, and I will continue to honor you all the days of my life.

May he one day be "In the Arena," and may You always watch over him.

Dear God,

I ask you to bless my nephew. Give him the courage to explore new worlds, and to overcome the fears behind closed doors. May he pay attention to the details yet find fun along the way. May he feel a sense of belonging to a family, yet may he stay true to himself as an individual. Give him the wisdom to never leave a man behind and to thank those that have gone before him. May he always feel your protection and come to you if his soul needs repair. May his pain be temporary and his pride permanent with a fighting spirit that endures. May he guard the precious gift of life and let his light shine for others to see. May he feel the power of a team, and the strain of carrying the weight. May he always act with honor and have the moral courage to fix what is wrong. May he have the courage to follow his heart—to be a simple man or to be a hero. May he always have a home where he knows how much he is loved. May he climb his own Herndon and scale many mountains. May he never be a cold and timid soul. May he know victory and defeat. *May he one day be "In the Arena" and may You always watch over him.*

*"Throw off your bowlines. Sail away from the safe harbor.
Explore. Dream. Discover." —Mark Twain*

ABOUT THE AUTHOR

CATHY MAZIARZ is a teacher and outdoor adventurer who has filled young minds with her stories that educate and inspire. From climbing to the Base Camp of Everest to teaching on a Navajo Indian Reservation, from bungee jumping in New Zealand to starting her own adventure business, Cathy is always looking to explore, dream, and discover!

The Naval Academy was her very first adventure and inspired her to live her life *In the Arena.*

Cathy lives with her husband, Greg, and dog, Chessie, on a farm in Virginia, where she and her imagination are free to run wild, and where her stories have now found their way to paper. She hopes to share her adventures with you and to inspire *you to live your life In the Arena!*

To learn more, visit Cathy's website at www.truenorthadventure.net.

www.hellgatepress.com

Made in the USA
Middletown, DE
22 November 2021

52635368R00192